BULLET AND SHELL

THE
CIVIL WAR
AS THE
SOLDIER SAW IT

BRINGING UP A BATTERY.

BULLET AND SHELL

THE CIVIL WAR AS THE SOLDIER SAW IT

by
George F. Williams

Illustrated
from sketches of the actual scenes
by
Edwin Forbes

SMITHMARK

This edition published in 2000 by SMITHMARK Publishers, a division of U.S. Media Holdings, Inc., 115 West 18th Street, New York, NY 10011.

SMITHMARK books are available for bulk purchase for sales promotion and premium use. For details write or call the manager of special sales, SMITHMARK Publishers, 115 West 18th Street, New York, NY 10011.

Published by special arrangement with Platinum Press

ISBN: 0-7651-1768-1

Printed in the United States of America

10 9 8 7 6 5 4 3 2 1

Library of Congress Cataloging-in-Publication Data is available.

TO

MY OLD COMRADES

WHO CARRIED THE SWORD AND MUSKET

IN THE FEDERAL ARMIES

DURING THE AMERICAN CIVIL WAR

This Book

IS FRATERNALLY DEDICATED.

BULLET AND SHELL

THE
CIVIL WAR
AS THE
SOLDIER SAW IT

PREFACE.

THE time has come when a story of the American Civil War may be written without prejudice or passion. The memories of that gigantic struggle have mellowed, the bitterness of sectional feeling has died away; and men now view with clearer and calmer minds the issues which led to the conflict, and the motives governing its prosecution. The author of the following pages aims to present a faithful picture of scenes in camp and field, which, under the guise of fiction, will afford the new generation some idea of the tremendous contest waged on this continent during the memorable years of 1861–65. To the veteran my book may be the means of recalling many pleasant reminiscences of the days when he carried the sword or the musket. In order to preserve the unity of the narrative, I have taken an author's license in carrying the same regiment through the several campaigns from Big Bethel to Appomattox Hollow. My old comrades of the Army of the Potomac will find, however, that in this only have I departed from the actual course of events.   G. F. W.

CONTENTS.

CHAPTER   PAGE

I. BEGINNING OF THE QUARREL 11

II. TAKING SIDES 22

III. DEFINING POSITIONS 32

IV. A TRUCE 38

V. THE HAND ON THE HILT 44

VI. DRAWING THE BLADE 52

VII. THROWING AWAY THE SCABBARD 64

VIII. BANDAGE AND LINT 77

IX. A SAVAGE BOUT 90

X. AGAIN IN HARNESS 106

XI. A FEINT 123

XII. FOREST STRATEGY 137

XIII. A NIGHT OF TERROR 147

XIV. BEATEN DOWN 157

XV. A PAUSE 175

XVI. MOVING TOWARDS BATTLE 187

XVII. A NIGHT MARCH 196

XVIII. CHARGE AND COUNTER-CHARGE 203

XIX. A MIDNIGHT ADVENTURE 218

XX. A WONDERFUL CHARGE 225

XXI. FACE TO FACE 243

XXII. LOST AMONG THE DEAD 254

XXIII. MOVING IN PURSUIT 263

XXIV. AN ADVENTURE ON THE ROAD 272

XXV. FENCING FOR AN OPENING 286

XXVI. THE SCOUT'S STORY 298

XXVII. A CHANGE IN FORTUNE 323

CHAPTER		PAGE
XXVIII.	CROSSING THE LINE	338
XXIX.	THE ACCOUNTS BALANCED	351
XXX.	RUNNING THE GAUNTLET	360
XXXI.	TO THE RESCUE	366
XXXII.	IN FRESH TOILS	373
XXXIII.	BY MINE AND SAP	383
XXXIV.	IN FORT AND FIELD	391
XXXV.	THE CORRESPONDENT'S STORY	400
XXXVI.	DEATH OF A SPY	411
XXXVII.	A LAST EFFORT	418
XXXVIII.	BEGINNING OF THE END	426
XXXIX.	SMASHING THE TRAP	435
XL.	LAYING DOWN THE SWORD	444
	THE END	453

ILLUSTRATIONS.

PAGE

BRINGING UP A BATTERY . . . . *Frontispiece*

FRIENDLY FISHERMEN 12

THE END OF ARGUMENT 20

THE MARSHALL HOMESTEAD 23

FORT SUMTER BOMBARDED 46

"STOP FIRING, YOU FOOLS, TILL YOU GET THE WORD!" . . . 58

THE RETREAT FROM THE FIELD 61

IN THE TRENCHES 67

BESIEGING YORKTOWN 71

THE DEAD SERGEANT'S YELL 74

REPORTING TO THE SURGEON 78

"WE CAN'T SELL TO SOLDIERS" 81

A SURGICAL OPERATION FRUSTRATED 85

CAPTURING A GUN, — GAINES'S MILL 93

THE IRISH BRIGADE TO THE RESCUE 95

THE GUNBOATS IN THE JAMES RIVER 101

GENERAL VIEW OF CAMPS, WARRENTON JUNCTION . . . 112

PONTOON-LAYING — FREDERICKSBURG 117

REVIEW BY PRESIDENT LINCOLN — FALMOUTH, OPPOSITE FREDERICKS-
BURG 125

THE MARCH TO CHANCELLORSVILLE 131

CROSSING ELY'S FORD, RAPIDAN RIVER 135

PASSING THE SLEEPING CORPS 145

THE ROUT OF THE ELEVENTH CORPS, CHANCELLORSVILLE . . 151

ARTILLERY GOING INTO ACTION 159

BRINGING OFF THE WOUNDED 166

RETREAT ACROSS THE RAPPAHANNOCK, — UNITED-STATES FORD . 169

RETURN TO THE ABANDONED CAMPS AT FALMOUTH . . . 174

PAGE

The Confederate Spy 181

The Confederate Grave under the Roses 193

General Sickles wounded 209

The Dying Adjutant 213

Bucktails going into the Devil's Glen 216

A Council of War on Little Round Top 233

The Final Charge at Gettysburg 239

Relieving the Wounded 242

"Going for" the Rebel Sharpshooters 246

"Good-by, Tom" 252

Lost on the Battle-field 258

"A Drink of Water, for God's Sake!" 259

"Dey's all done góne, Sah!" 270

The Winter Camp 287

Arrest of the Spy 293

The Chase 305

Before the Confederate General 308

March of the Confederate Army into Pennsylvania . . 312

Crossing the Rapidan 325

Passing Grant and Meade 329

In the Wilderness 336

General Lee and the Prisoner 340

Among the Wounded, — Confederate Hospital . . . 346

Revisiting the Wilderness Battle-field 357

At the Warrenton Hotel 362

Under Guard 377

Going to Camp under Fire 389

Foraging on the Enemy 396

Going to the Rear with Dispatches 406

General Custer and the Spy 415

The Confederates capture Fort Steadman 421

Taken Prisoner again 433

Cavalry in Pursuit 445

The Flag of Truce 448

Lee's Shattered Army 452

Bullet and Shell.

CHAPTER I.

BEGINNING OF THE QUARREL.

"Between green fields and wooded heights,
The river stretched at ease."

IME, Summer. The year, 1860. Scene, the Valley of the Shenandoah, West Virginia.

On a sudden bend of the river which lends its musical name to the beautiful valley, two young men are sitting in an old, weather-beaten, rudely fashioned punt, idly fishing. Though it is now long past the hour of noon, and the sun has already begun its downward course, the air is still warm and oppressive, even in the shadows thrown upon the rippling stream by the huge trees overhanging its banks. The curve of the river, where our fishermen have anchored their clumsy boat, is caused by the intrusive presence of a spur from the massive range of the Blue-Ridge Mountains, which form the eastern boundary of the valley. Indeed, so abrupt and sharp is the turn of the current just there, that the river seems to be completely hemmed in by the dense foliage creeping down

11

to the water's edge on every side. Behind the occupants of the boat the mountain spur towers in lofty grandeur, its rugged sides clothed to the very summit with dark masses of oak and pine, while half way up its jutting face a broad seam of almost naked rock stands out in most threatening fashion, as though about to fall that instant into the shallow water below.

Beyond the fringe of trees on the opposite bank, in the shade of which the boat swings to its primitive anchor, wide fields of golden wheat can be discerned; and as the breeze sets the grain in waving motion it also brings to the ears of these young men the loud and careless laughter of the gangs of negro field-hands, busily engaged in harvesting. An air of perfect peace

FRIENDLY FISHERMEN.

and plenty reigns over the romantic valley; and the entire scene is one of rare loveliness, combining as it does the bold mountain outline, the picturesque and winding river, the fertile fields, and the signs and tokens of successful husbandry.

"Well, Frank," exclaimed one of the young fishermen, as he impatiently jerked his line out of the water to rebait the hook, "I still contend the South is right."

"And I insist that she is entirely in the wrong."

"How can you do that consistently? We have a perfect right to claim that slavery must not be molested."

"Who wants to molest it?"

" The abolitionists, — Garrison, Phillips, and the rest of that crew."

" Every Northern man is not an abolitionist. Why confound a few enthusiasts, who are more or less fanatical in their ideas, with the great bulk of fair-minded men in the free States?"

" I don't. But you can not deny that the sentiment in favor of abolishing slavery is gaining ground in the North. Why, you yourself are at heart almost an abolitionist;" and the speaker laughed disdainfully as he spoke.

" Perhaps so. I scarcely know, myself."

" To take away our slaves would be an act of tyranny. The South would not submit to such oppression."

" Tyranny and oppression? Those are hard words, Tom."

" They are the only ones I can use."

" How do you make that out?"

" Why, when the people of the North try to force us to give up our slaves, they act tyrannically and oppressively."

" We don't ask you to give up your slaves. We only say you shall not take them into the Territories, and so create new slave States. You seek to extend slavery. We want to keep it within its present bounds. There is no tyranny in that."

" Isn't there? Why shouldn't we take our slaves into the Territories?"

" Because slavery is really a curse to the country, Tom."

" That is a bitter phrase, Frank."

" Not more so than your talk of oppression and tyranny."

" But the new Territories belong as much to the South as to the North."

" Granted! yet why should you seek to import slaves into them?"

" To till the soil, of course, and so enrich the nation."

" Do you mean to tell me, Tom, that you consider the Southern slaves a source of national wealth?"

" Certainly I do. What else are they? The millions upon

millions of dollars invested in our slaves represent so much property, just as your farmers' horses and cattle do."

" Good Lord, Tom! you don't compare the slaves to horses or cattle?"

" Yes, I do."

" Yet you would go to war to retain them?"

" Why not? Wouldn't the farmers in the free States think twice before giving up their live stock?"

" The cases are not parallel at all."

" Oh, of course not! You Northerners will never admit any thing."

" I can not admit that, because slave labor is really expensive to the South."

" How so?"

" It's very simple. Your slaves are naturally indolent. They need constant supervision to keep them at their tasks, and even then don't half work. Then, again, you can not discharge a slave as you would an incompetent or worthless workman."

" We can sell him."

" Yes; and that is what makes slavery a curse. This constant barter in human flesh is horrible."

" Slavery has flourished since the beginning of the world."

" So has heathenism. Is that any reason why we should go back to worshiping idols?"

" Oh! if you are going to drag religion into the discussion, I am done."

" I don't want to drag it in. Look at the Roman empire: slavery was one of the elements of its ruin."

" That was partly because the slaves were pampered, and rose against their masters."

" And you expect that your slaves will never rise against you?"

" Now, see here, Frank: I've heard enough of that sort of thing. No doubt the North would rejoice to see the blacks revolt."

" There you are wrong again. But the time must come when the negroes will strike for their freedom."

" You talk like a regular border-ruffian, Frank. Why don't you go out there, and wear big boots, a red shirt, and a brace of revolvers?

" Well, I do sympathize with those border men in their efforts to keep the soil of Kansas free from the taint of slavery."

" Oh, confound you and your taint!" exclaimed Tom angrily. " But there's no use arguing any more about it. When we men of the South and the North once get to talking politics, we invariably lose our tempers."

" Speak for yourself, Tom, please," replied his companion in a quieter tone. " I am sure I have not lost my temper, even though I do not agree with you."

" But you Yankees never will give in, no matter how convincing the argument may be."

" Why do you call me a Yankee, as though it were a reproach? If it comes to that, Tom, you're as much a Yankee as I am."

" Ha, ha! No, you don't, master Frank," retorted the first speaker in a merrier tone: " you can't call me a Yankee, even though I did matriculate under the elms of dear old Yale. No, sir: I'm a true Southerner, born and bred, and, I'll admit, at times a hot-tempered one too, while you are as cold as the granite hills of your native State."

" Oh! I can be hot-tempered enough on occasion," replied the other. " I simply object to being called a Yankee in a reproachful sense, that is all."

" All right, Frank: I won't do it again. Hullo! by Jove! that was a bite in earnest," ejaculated Tom, pulling up his line again, and looking ruefully at his despoiled hook.

While these young men continue their pleasant pastime, and patch up their brief political quarrel as best they may, let us learn more about them.

Tom Marshall prides himself on being the descendant of an

old Virginia family, and as such a true son of the sunny South. Though still on the threshold of manhood, he is full of that passionate love for his section so noticeable among men of his age and class. Like all young Southerners at the time, Tom had already taken a deep interest in the political issues of the day; and, though he failed to understand their entire scope and import, he at all times expressed the wildest devotion to the South in general and his native State in particular. It is not my purpose here to discuss the question whether Tom was right or wrong; for that matter seems to have been settled long, long ago, and in a way that we all now deplore and strive to forget. I merely mention the fact to explain much that is to come, and as an indication of the young man's character. Tall and sinewy, Tom Marshall is handsome in feature, and a gentleman by instinct as well as by breeding. Unlike most men of Southern birth, Tom had finished his education within the walls of a Northern college, — Yale, — as the reader has already learned from his own lips. But, despite his contact and association with young men of the North, he had left college as intensely sectional in political sentiment as when he first entered. Indeed, he expressed himself as more eager than before to devote his energies to the interests of his beloved South, showing how strong and abiding are the lessons learned in boyhood.

Tom's companion need now only be described as a stripling of twenty, fair complexioned, quite tall for his years, and possessing a tolerable share of good-humor. He, too, is a Yale man, though not yet entirely released from study; and he was born in a pretty little village in New Hampshire. Tom and Frank had become warm friends in college; and the latter is now spending a part of his vacation with the Marshalls, whose plantation forms a prominent landmark in the valley. In fact, Frank Wilmot is your humble servant; and, as I shall have frequent occasion hereafter to speak of myself, the less said now about me the better.

A native of the North, and taught to view the course of public events from a widely different standpoint from that occupied by Tom Marshall, it was not surprising that I differed with him. True, neither of us knew much about the real merits of the grave questions we were discussing; but we thought we did, being therefore honest in our dispute, unwise and useless as it was.

Already had the two great sections of the country become arrayed against each other in thought and word; and men on both sides of the geographical line were anxiously looking forward to the approaching presidential election, for all felt that with it would come a momentous crisis in the nation's history. For years had the struggle been going on, until it had now reached a stage when some decisive action might be looked for. The result none could forecast, so cloudy and uncertain had the political horizon become. It was quite natural, therefore, that Tom and I should thus drift into a discussion; for, boys though we were, we considered ourselves men, like many a young fool before us.

Tom had proved himself a stanch friend in more ways than one. Indeed, much of the success I had achieved at Yale was due to his aid and counsel. Our friendship had been begun by his espousal of my side of a petty quarrel, simply because he deemed the odds against me. From that hour we had been like brothers; and I had now spent several happy weeks with him, enjoying the picturesque scenery for which his native valley is deservedly famous.

Tom quietly re-baited his hook, and we continued to fish in silence. The sunshine left us, the shadows of the trees grew longer, the air became cooler, and a deep silence fell upon the scene. Even the mountain above our heads seemed softer and less rugged in its massive outlines, now that it no longer stood in the fierce glare of the noonday sun. But despite the delicious beauty of the landscape, and the rapidity with which we were now pulling up the unwary fish, both Tom and I felt ill at ease.

Having fidgeted on his seat for several minutes, Tom at length broke the silence, exclaiming, —

"Oh, hang it, Frank! I can't stand this sort of thing any longer. Why should we quarrel? I'm sorry we have such conflicting ideas about these matters."

"I'm as sorry as yourself, Tom. We have been so like brothers ever since we first met, it seems hard to have a difference at this late day."

"Well, it can't be helped now, I suppose. But, Frank, you may depend on one thing: if the South does strike for liberty, I am with and for her, to the death if necessary."

"Liberty! You seem to think the South has none."

"Think! I know it! Don't you want to rob us of our slaves?"

"Gradual emancipation would not be robbery."

"And·when the slaves were free you would give them the right to vote, I suppose."

"In time possibly."

"By Heaven, Frank! you go too far. As if we Southerners would permit a nigger to vote! Better to secede at once."

"Secede! What! Leave the Union?"

"Yes, break away for ever."

"But you have no right to secede."

"Haven't we? Every State is a sovereign to herself. If she is dissatisfied she can withdraw from the confederation, and govern her own affairs."

"I deny it. States are sovereigns on local questions only. They can not sever the tie which binds them together."

"You forget we are talking of the whole South, not one solitary State. If we secede we shall go out in a body."

"And you really believe that?"

"Believe it! I know it. It's our only policy."

"But the free States will not allow you to secede."

"How are you going to stop us? The Southern people have plenty of sympathizers in the North. Your politicians are divided."

"Politicians do not rule this country."

"They have a good deal to say, at all events;" and Tom laughed sarcastically.

"Mere talk does not affect the destinies of a nation. Once let the people understand that the supremacy of the general government is in peril, and the political wire-pullers will be swept away like chaff before the wind."

"You are growing eloquent, Frank."

"Perhaps I am. But suppose we let you go peaceably. The South couldn't take any of the disputed territory with her."

"We could at least fight for it."

"That is just what might be expected: first secede, and then go to war for more territory. It would be far better for the North to fight first, and so keep you in the Union."

"Yes, and give us an abolitionist for President. We want no Frémonts or Lincolns to rule us."

"The President is not a ruler."

"Well, Frank, all I can say is, that the South will never tolerate a President who is opposed to her interests."

"I guess the South will have to take the President selected by the people."

"Will she? You wait and see. If that Hoosier rail-splitter is elected, there will be war, sure: that is, if the North really will fight." Here Tom again laughed in a sneering way that made me angry.

"Do you think us all cowards, then?" I asked hotly.

"Oh! I won't say that," replied Tom indolently. "But I don't suppose the 'horny-handed sons of toil,' as they call themselves, will be very ready."

"And why not? Look at Mexico. Didn't our regiments fight gallantly at Cerro Gordo, and Chapultepec, and Buena Vista? During the Revolution, were the men of New England inferior to those of Virginia or South Carolina?"

"But in the Revolution they fought against tyranny, just as we will if the North persists in its present course."

"Armed secession will be rebellion."

"You are very amusing, Frank. That was what King George and his Parliament called it when the colonies drew the sword. But when the colonies were victorious, our rebel forefathers became patriots."

"And you would give up your heritage to the blessings won by the Revolution?"

"Yes. If we are to lose our rights as sovereign States, there is no other course open to us."

"Say no more," I replied. "It is quite certain we can never agree upon any of these political questions."

THE END OF ARGUMENT.

"So it seems, more's the pity," said Tom gloomily.

"It's a pity indeed; but you see, old fellow, we have been taught to view these things so differently, we can not help being in antagonism, however unwillingly. Still I feel, Tom, that, though we may hereafter be separated by political sentiment, we shall never be real enemies."

"Of course not. If war does come, there will be but few personal hatreds involved. It will be purely a struggle for principle."

"Well, well, let us drop it now," said I. "My heart revolts at the thought of war. They say it will be a civil one, but I suspect there will be precious little civility about it."

"You don't suppose we Southerners fancy war to be a

pleasant pastime, do you?" exclaimed Tom contemptuously. "There will not be much fun about it, I imagine, for either side, but plenty of hard knocks."

"There, there! Let's put an end to this useless argument. I am sick of it." As I spoke I jumped to my feet, and began pulling up the stone which had anchored our boat in the stream.

"You're right," replied Tom as he took the oars, and rowed in toward the river-bank. "It's useless talking now. Let us hope, that, after all, there will be no need of any fighting."

"Amen to that, with all my heart!" I exclaimed, leaping ashore.

CHAPTER II.

TAKING SIDES.

> "Beware
> Of entrance to a quarrel; but being in,
> Bear it that the opposer may beware of thee."

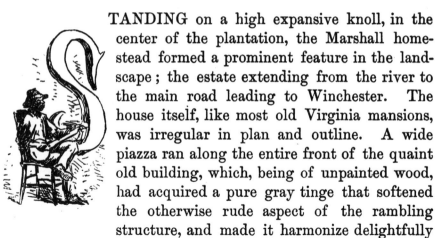

TANDING on a high expansive knoll, in the center of the plantation, the Marshall homestead formed a prominent feature in the landscape; the estate extending from the river to the main road leading to Winchester. The house itself, like most old Virginia mansions, was irregular in plan and outline. A wide piazza ran along the entire front of the quaint old building, which, being of unpainted wood, had acquired a pure gray tinge that softened the otherwise rude aspect of the rambling structure, and made it harmonize delightfully with the foliage of the giant walnut-trees which dotted the lawn and shaded the road.

The doors and windows in the old house appeared to have been pierced at random, as though each successive generation had striven to increase their number, regardless of the lack of symmetry which was the result. This impression was, however, dispelled on gaining the interior, for then it was seen that each had its proper use; though the new-comer found himself nonplused by the confused arrangement of the various rooms and passages, for they were a perfect labyrinth.

That the house was of great age, was shown by a bit of bare

THE MARSHALL HOMESTEAD.

log wall visible through the broken plaster at the back of the wide hall. In fact, the mansion had gradually grown from rude beginnings to its present dimensions, as the ancestors of the Marshalls increased in wealth and importance. It had always been a house famous for generous hospitality in the olden days, when the Marshalls had served their king in colonial times, or taken an active part in the subsequent revolt against him. Indeed, Tom usually grew eloquent whenever he related any of the romantic traditions clinging to the history of the family. The old spirit of hospitality still reigned in the mansion, and guests were entertained with a heartiness that was delightful for its simplicity.

Down in a hollow behind the house stood the immense barns; while beyond these were the negro-quarters, now vocal with the sound of many voices, as the field-laborers came trooping homeward. Round the homestead itself numerous house-servants flitted to and fro, getting into each other's way with that facility so peculiar to the negro race.

I had often experienced a warm sense of delight in these picturesque details of a happy and peaceful home; but in my present mood I found no pleasure in the familiar picture, as Tom and I walked silently up the road, after leaving the narrow path that led from the river through the standing wheat in the fields.

"There's that fellow Ned Charlton!" exclaimed Tom, looking back, and listening to the sharp clatter of a horse's hoofs on the macadamized highway. "I wish he would not come here so often."

"Don't you like him?"

"Like him! What! a braggart like that? You should know me better, Frank, than to ask such a question," replied Tom in a surprised tone of voice.

"He claims to be a gentleman, I believe."

"Claims! yes; and that's as near as he will ever get," retorted Tom with a sneer on his lips.

"Bin fishing, gentlemen?" exclaimed the new-comer, as he suddenly reined up beside us. "Had a good time?"

"Yes: we've been on the river," replied Tom indifferently; "but it was too hot for comfortable fishing."

"So I should jedge; but I dunno much 'bout fishing, myself. I'm fonder of a good horse than lines and fish-hooks;" and the speaker laughed in a disdainful way, as he glanced at our angling-tackle.

"If you call riding a horse to death on a broiling summer's day being fond of him," I remarked, "you show it pretty thoroughly. Why, the poor brute is in a perfect foam."

"He's got good blood in him, sir, and as such is fit to be a gentleman's horse," replied Charlton angrily.

"Oh! you need not show your own temper, sir, to prove your horse's pedigree. The animal is a good one, I admit: so much the more reason why he should be well treated."

"Mr. Wilmot is quite right about the beast," said Tom. "And you're over-fond of picking a quarrel, Charlton. It don't speak well for your own breeding. But get off your horse: I see my sister coming."

Charlton obeyed the hint, but as he leaped from his saddle he and I exchanged menacing glances. Ever since we first met, an involuntary spirit of antagonism had sprung between us. Half-educated, and insolent in his ignorance, Charlton had invariably displayed an arrogance towards me that was insufferable; and this, perhaps, had something to do with my unasked criticism on his riding. Overbearing in his manner, and an arrant boaster, he presented a type of character which contrasted strangely with the innate courtliness and modesty of Tom Marshall; yet it was of a class by no means rare in the South at the time. Constantly proclaiming himself to be a gentleman, Charlton betrayed his true character by every word and act. I had, therefore, no reason to admire the fellow. His presence just now was distasteful to both Tom and myself;

for we had been strangely moved by our political discussion, and were in no mood to tolerate him.

"What's the matter here?" demanded a musical voice. "You look as if you had all been quarreling."

"Oh! it's nothing, Kate," replied Tom hurriedly. "Frank and I have been talking politics: that's all."

"Politics! so you have caught that fever too, have you? It seems to be a perfect epidemic just now;" and the girl laughed ironically as she turned to accompany us homeward.

"There has been no quarrel, Miss Marshall," said I somewhat stiffly. "Tom and I could not agree just now; because, you know, we come from different sections. He belongs to the South, I to the North. It's only natural for us to hold diverse opinions on the issues of the day."

"I s'pose, sir, you think we Southern gentlemen must submit to the dictates of the Northern mudsills," exclaimed Charlton scornfully.

"I've no desire to discuss the question with you," I replied testily. "And I object to your sneers at the people of the Northern States. There are as many gentlemen there as here, a fact you might discover if you were a judge in such matters."

"Jedge, sir! What do you mean? Do you dare?"

"Dare! Dare what?"

"You don't mean to say, Mr. Wilmot," interrupted Tom's sister, "that you think the South is wrong in asserting her rights of sovereignty? Do you really mean that?" and as she spoke the girl stood still, her dark eyes wide open in unaffected wonder.

"Ha, ha!" laughed Tom. "That's right, Kate: give it to him.—I say, Frank, that was a shot you didn't expect."

"I beg your pardon, Miss Marshall: I scarcely know what to say."

"Give me a plain answer to my question, if you please. Do you think us Southern people wrong, or not?" persisted the wayward beauty, a big frown passing over her brow like a cloud.

"Well, if you mean an assertion of rights on certain issues, and an appeal to arms in their support, such as Tom talks about, I do certainly think them in the wrong. But, really, these are questions I do not care to discuss with a lady."

"Let me tell you, Mr. Wilmot," retorted the defiant girl, tossing her head imperiously as she spoke, — "let me tell you, sir, that we women of the South are heart and hand with our brothers and fathers on this question, as you men of the North may perhaps find out to your cost one of these days."

"Oh! come now, Kate," said her brother good-naturedly, but at the same time giving his sister an admiring look for her words, "you're altogether too hard on poor Wilmot. You must remember that he has a right to his own opinions: besides, he does not wish any further discussion; do you, Frank?"

"The whole subject is distasteful to me. First I am involved in a wretched dispute with my dearest friend, and now I find his sister apparently my bitterest enemy. Upon my word, I now begin to believe there will be a war."

And, as I uttered the last words, I bowed ceremoniously to the haughty girl beside me.

"There seems no help for it," said Tom sadly. "The sooner the struggle comes, the better it will be for us all. This suspense and dread of the future is the hardest to bear. But here we are at the house: so clear up that frowning face of yours, Kate. It won't do to let the governor see how we have been badgering his guest," and Tom again laughed as he unfastened the gate opening on the lawn, and his sister passed in.

"For my part, I hope there will be a war," remarked Charlton, "if it's only for a chance to teach you Yankees a lesson."

"If lessons are the order of the day," I replied hotly, "a few in politeness would do you no harm, my fine gentleman."

"What do you mean? Do you wish to insult me?"

"Take it as you will. I'm quite indifferent as to that."

"Oh, here! this won't do," exclaimed Tom impatiently. "You forget we are on the lawn, and the governor may hear you. No more of this folly, or I shall quarrel with you both in earnest. You must be on your good behavior here, gentlemen."

Charlton and I nodded in silence, and followed Tom towards the piazza where his father was quietly smoking his corn-cob pipe.

"Ah, boys! been fishing again, I see," said Mr. Marshall as we came within hearing. "I should think you would have tired of the sport by this time. If you keep at it much longer you will not leave a single fish in the river for the darkies."

"Not much fear of that, sir," replied Tom, as he threw down his pole and string of fish. "That Pomp and Cæsar of ours would find bites for their bait if we fished till Christmas. Let them alone for that."

"You're right, Tom. Those two boys know a great deal more about the ways of the river than they do of work in the fields, confound them!—Pomp, you black rascal, you know you do," and Mr. Marshall pretended to kick at a grinning negro boy who was squatting on the steps at his feet.

"He! he! 'Spect we does, Marse John. Dat's a fac'," said Pomp, as he rolled down the steps in a convulsion of laughter. "But, Marse John, sumbodder's got to fish de ribber besides young Marse Frank and young Marse Tom, dar, or de fish dey done run away wid de ribber, dare git to be so many ob 'em."

"Get out, you young rascal," cried the old gentleman. "See that you and Cæsar are out in the field, down by the willows, in the morning with the rest of the gang, or I'll give you something you won't forget in a hurry."

"Dat all right, Marse John: I'll be down dar in de field for shuah, 'less Missy Kate she done sen' me to de Ferry for dem books o' her'n, an' I 'spect she will," responded Pomp, grinning as if he intended splitting his face from ear to ear in the effort.

"You should have gone for them to-day, Pomp," remarked Kate. "I told you to go this morning."

"Couldn't go way down to de Ferry when de missy she tole me to take Marse Tom him lunshon! Couldn't do de two t'ings at de wunst, nohow," muttered the negro as he scratched his woolly pate confusedly.

"That's always the way with those two boys, Mr. Wilmot," said Mr. Marshall, knocking the ashes from his exhausted pipe. "They're more bother to me than all the rest of my hands."

"I'm afraid, sir, it's partly your own fault," I replied. "You never insist on their tasks being performed promptly; and the boys, as you call them, have studied your nature so well, they know just how far they can impose upon your good-humor."

"Quite true; but it can not be helped now, for I'm too old to change, and they're young yet."

"True Virginny ways, sah," began Charlton in his usual swaggering manner. "We gentlemen of the South are always kind to our niggahs."

"Not always, Mr. Charlton," replied Mr. Marshall. "I wish they were."

"Oh! if the niggahs do get a taste of the lash now and then, they generally deserve it. It's the only way to keep them in order."

"Indeed! It's a wonder you don't get a little of it once in a while: you need it," I said, glad of an excuse to annoy him.

"Me, sir! me flogged!" he gasped. "Why, I'm a gentleman, sir."

"So you are always saying. You seldom say any thing else," I retorted wickedly.

"Gentlemen! I'm surprised to hear you speak thus. One would almost think that you had been quarreling," said Mr. Marshall.

"Oh! it's only sectional feeling, as Frank calls it, sir," replied Tom, laughing in evident sympathy with me in my thrusts at Charlton.

"Indeed! So you young people have been discussing politics? I'm sorry to know it, for that is a dangerous topic in times like these. But I had forgotten: here's a letter for you, Mr. Wilmot. One of the boys brought it over from Winchester;" and the old gentleman handed me an envelope that had lain unnoticed on the railing.

"Read it after supper, Frank," said Tom, leading the way up the broad steps. "Here comes mother, and there goes the gong. Come, or the butter-cakes will spoil, and I'm so hungry!"

CHAPTER III.

DEFINING POSITIONS.

"Policy wills some seeming cause be had,
    To make that good which justice knows for bad."

AVE you forgotten, my dear boy, that the time for your going back to college is drawing near, and that we have not yet seen you? I am a little jealous of your Virginian friends, they are keeping my son so long from me. Come home soon, dear Frank, there's a good boy . . . "

Thus wrote my mother in the letter I had received; and as I sat at my window, and watched the evening shadows gather in the valley, my thoughts went back to the dear old village, and the loved ones waiting there for me. My mother was right: I had indeed overstaid the limits of my visit to Tom and his family. As I sat thinking over the events of the day, a strange feeling of unrest filled my heart. This hateful sectional antagonism seemed, all at once, to have rudely separated Tom and me.

Realizing the fact with grief and surprise, I resolved to obey my mother's summons, and leave, perchance for ever, the scenes marked by so much past pleasure and present pain.

For a moment I hesitated, and then, obeying a sudden impulse, rushed down-stairs to the piazza, where I hurriedly announced my intention of leaving on the morrow.

Tom was loud in his protests and disapproval of my decision.

"Why, you forget, Frank," he exclaimed, "we were to go

to Winchester to-morrow, and the next day to Martinsburg. Surely a few days more will make no difference."

"I *must* go, Tom. You know I have remained with you longer than I at first intended. Now my mother calls me home, and I shall obey. She has been very patient at my long absence."

"I can sympathize with your mother, Mr. Wilmot," said Mrs. Marshall. "I have been so happy in having my son and his friend with me, that I forgot there were other mothers in the world besides myself."

"But, mother," persisted Tom, "why should he run off so suddenly? — It's not like you, Frank."

"I am loth to go, Tom," said I; "for I have been very happy here. But I owe some attention to my mother."

"Your words are good and honest, Mr. Wilmot; and they prove you are as good a son as my Tom," remarked Mrs. Marshall, gazing fondly at her boy lolling on the railing, his handsome face disfigured by a look of discontent.

"Oh! since you take Frank's part, mother, I shall say no more. Your word has always been law in this house."

"I am sorry you are going away so suddenly, Mr. Wilmot," said Mr. Marshall, leading me away from the group. "Tom has been telling his mother and me of the foolish, unwise argument on the river, and also of Kate's saucy attack upon you. I trust, sir, these idle words among you young people have had no influence towards this determination to leave us."

"I must confess, sir, they have; though my mother's call is the strongest motive. I deeply regret these political differences, but it seems impossible for Tom and me to reconcile them."

"Ah! Frank, you are too young, and so is Tom, to clearly understand the troubles and dangers which threaten us. I am not as fierce, perhaps, as some of my neighbors, in asserting what they term the rights of the South; for I can see, what many do not, that if these claims are persisted in we shall eventually be placed in belligerent opposition to the government. If the ball of contention is once set rolling, God only knows where or when it will stop."

"Let us hope, sir, that it will not come to that pass," I replied.

"I am sorry I can not indulge in such a hope," said the old gentleman sadly. "The current of events is too strong, and the passion of political strife already too bitter, to permit my entertaining it. When you go home, Mr. Wilmot, please remember, that, though we men of the South may go into a war with the Northern States, many of us will do so with sad and heavy hearts; though honestly determined to do our best to win in the struggle, once it is fairly begun."

"I prefer not to think of it at all," I exclaimed impetuously. "It seems like a hideous dream, this possibility of a war."

"Hideous indeed. But it is far from being a dream: the dread reality will soon be upon us, I fear."

"And do you too believe a war is coming?"

"I see that there is great danger of one."

"But why?"

"Because the temper of the Southern people, just now, is such, they will not submit to see Lincoln made president. I know you will say that he can not be elected unless the Democrats, North and South, persist, as they threaten, in dividing their strength on rival candidates; but the division of that party is mainly due to the growing antagonism between the two sections of the country."

"How?"

"The Democrats of the North and the South can no longer agree on great national questions. And as neither side will give way, a hopeless division is the natural result."

"And because they can not agree on a candidate for the presidency, we are to have civil war? That seems strange."

"Not at all. If the new party — the Republicans — elect

their candidate by a plurality vote, as they must, he will not be the choice of a majority of the whole people. Therefore the Southern States will ask for permission to withdraw, and form their own government."

" That seems to me very childish. Because the South can not have its own way all the time, it refuses to be bound by the laws and precedents it helped to make and adopt."

" Very true. I grant you, it will only be a pretext. But the Southern leaders are reckless and desperate, and will eagerly avail themselves of that excuse for want of a better one."

" One would scarcely suppose from your words, Mr. Marshall, that you were a Southerner."

" I presume not. I speak thus candidly to you, Mr. Wilmot, because I know I can trust you. I'm an old man now, and love my country and my State too well not to see the dangers that threaten us. One of my brothers fought under Taylor in Mexico, and fell at Palo Alto; while an uncle of mine participated in the last war with Great Britain. I should regret to see my son compelled to fight against the flag they both served under."

" Compelled?"

" Yes, compelled. Tom is a son of the South, and a Virginian. If his State secedes, as seems very probable, he must obey her sovereignty, and take up arms in her defense. There is no help for it."

" That question of State rights was one of the very things Tom and I could not agree upon."

" Of course not. It is one of the vital issues of the day. Upon it hinges the integrity or the dissolution of the Union. Men everywhere are divided upon it. Even here in Virginia we are not all of one mind in regard to it."

" Tom says the South is afraid the North will attempt to abolish slavery."

" Wiser and older men than he believe the same thing; and with good reason, I fear."

"Just because the North will not consent to see slavery extended into the new Territories?"

"Precisely. Don't you see that that very denial as to the Territories is the entering wedge towards complete abolition?"

"But is slavery worth a war?"

"Ah! Frank, there you touch on the very marrow of the entire question. The prosperity of the South rests on her slaves. What would we be without them?"

"The free States are prosperous with free labor."

"Yes. But we need the negroes: if they were once free we should be without laborers."

"If freed, the negro would have to work for his own support and that of his family, just as the white man does in the North."

"You forget they have always been slaves, consequently shiftless. Set them free, and they will not know how to accommodate themselves to the new state of affairs. They are not accustomed to take care of themselves."

"So much the worse for the system which made them so."

"Quite right. I am not defending the system, though I am a slaveholder. But we have the slaves: why deprive us of our only resource? why not let well enough alone?"

Before I could reply, Tom approached us.

"What are you two talking so earnestly about?" he asked.

"We are discussing politics, Tom," replied his father, "just as you and Mr. Wilmot did this afternoon. He tells me your dispute is one of his reasons for leaving us."

"Indeed!" exclaimed Tom. "Why, Frank, I did not think you so easily angered. *We* had no quarrel, though you and Charlton came precious near having one."

"I am not angry, Tom; but I feel that we are no longer the same warm, fast friends we were before we fell into that hateful argument."

"Nonsense! We do not agree, it is true, on certain questions, owing to our different education ; but we are not enemies quite yet, I take it."

"No, thank God ! we can never be that. Still, Tom, I wish to go away now, because I feel that I shall be exposed to mis-apprehension if I stay."

"He is right, Tom," said Mr. Marshall. "Once the ques-tion of politics is touched upon in critical times like these, it is sure to lead to grave misunderstandings. I would fain see you and your friend part amicably while you may. He belongs to one section of this unhappy country, you to another. You can not agree, so it is better that you part until happier and quieter times come to us."

"Indeed, sir, I shall always consider Tom a true friend," said I.

"Just my feeling," exclaimed Tom, clasping my hand.

"That's right, my boys. Whatever happens hereafter, keep your boyhood friendship green in your hearts. It will be a pleasant memory to you both as you grow older."

"I promise you, sir, I shall do so," said I.

"And so do I," cried Tom heartily. "But come, governor, let's go in : the dew is beginning to fall.

CHAPTER IV.

A TRUCE.

"Nature I'll court in her sequestered haunts,
By mountain, streamlet, grove, or cell."

A S the sun rose bright and clear the following morning, it found me already up, busily engaged in preparations for my journey. I had often thought of a pedestrian trip to Washington, crossing the Blue Ridge into the Loudon Valley, thence through Aldie Gap to Centreville, a route described by Tom as exceedingly beautiful and interesting. I accordingly decided to go home that way, feeling that the tramp over the mountains would do me good. On making this announcement over night, Mr. Marshall decided to send the boy Pompey to Harper's Ferry with my baggage, while I was to shoulder my knapsack and trudge through the Gaps.

Tom was to accompany me as far as the foot of the range: so after a hearty breakfast, and a kind farewell to his parents, we set out together.

As he and I swung off at a rapid pace, on entering the road to the mountain-gap, we found the morning air deliciously cool and fragrant. The warm rays of the rising sun had already set the heavy mists in motion on the mountains; though they still clung to the peaks and lingered in the notches, thus concealing much of the bold grandeur of the range with which I had become so familiar during my sojourn in the valley. The foot-hills and outlying spurs were rapidly revealing themselves as the banks of fleecy vapor rolled upward: while down on the table-land stray drifts were lying, pencil-like, in the meadows; but even these were beginning to move as the sun grew stronger.

The wide stretches of ripening grain were again in the hands of the negro harvesters; and as we trudged along the wide road, their careless voices could be heard above the sharp swish of their cradles, cutting down the heavily laden wheat-stalks, and we caught sight of many bits of warm bright color as the laborers moved steadily forward at their tasks. The birds, too, were singing their joyful welcome to the coming day. The melodious whistle of the robin, standing on the stone fence by the roadside, was answered by the mocking cry of the saucy cat-bird as he swung like an acrobat on a slender bough over our heads; while farther on I could see the scarlet coat of the Virginia red-bird, flitting like a flame from bush to bush in search of food. The swallows were busily skimming over the fields, catching the unwary insects as they rose in the reviving sunshine; and high up in the sky hung a solitary eagle, slowly circling over the valley with motionless pinions, on the lookout for some hapless and defenseless quarry.

The grass by the side of the road was still wet with the heavy dew that had fallen during the night, and the apple-trees in the numerous orchards were bending low beneath the increasing weight of the fruit that clustered on their limbs. From every chimney in sight, the smoke rose unbroken by the usual breeze; and the voice of the dairymaid, calling to her cows, sounded clear in the still and perfumed air. The scattered cattle in the pastures cropped the juicy herbage in quiet mood, undisturbed by the shrill neighing of Tom's favorite horse as he came galloping over the turf to greet his master. Everywhere the scene was one of contentment, peace, and prosperity.

These happy and tranquil features of the landscape revived my spirits, and I insensibly grew more and more cheerful under their soothing influence.

Tom chattered buoyantly as we walked, with no apparent thought or trouble on his mind. He talked of our college days, and prophesied my future success; and I was content to let him run on in this hopeful fashion, for I found relief in silence.

"Well, Frank, old fellow, we part here. Yonder lies your road," said Tom, as we paused for a moment on the moss-grown stone bridge that spanned the river and led to the mountain road beyond. "I'm sorry I can not go with you through the Gap, but you know I must go to town to-day for the governor."

"We will say farewell here, then," I replied. "It will be long before we meet again: it may be never."

"Oh, nonsense! we are safe to meet somewhere in the future," responded my companion confidently.

"Let us hope so," said I rousing myself with an effort: "such friendship as ours has been should not be lightly broken."

"You may well say that, Frank. And now good-by. You must not linger here, for you ought to get over the mountain before the sun gets fiercer. Good-by, my dear boy."

"Good-by, Tom. If ever we meet again it must still be as brothers."

"Brothers always!" exclaimed Tom with a kindling eye, as he seized my outstretched hand with his sturdy and honest grip.

"I am glad to hear you say so, for there's no knowing what may happen in these troublous times," I replied, as I adjusted my knapsack, and turned to cross the bridge.

On reaching the turn in the road, a few rods beyond, I looked back for a moment, returned Tom's mute farewell as he stood leaning against the parapet, and then strode forward.

The path to the Gap was at times rugged and steep; but the difficulties encountered suited my present mood, so I struggled resolutely upward and onward. At first I found myself in a deep gorge, as it wound through the dripping rocks that had been cleft by some mighty convulsion of nature in past ages; and the uneven road gave me fresh surprises at almost every turn. The huge masses of stone rose precipitately to the right and the left, like the walls of some ancient castle; their irregular faces being touched here and there with bits of vivid green, where tiny ferns and mountain plants clung in the clefts or drooped from the ridges. Sprays of feathery creepers hung over the rocks at random, their dark leaves brightened by stray bunches of scarlet berries. At the top, hardy trees towered to the sky, their gnarled and twisted limbs betokening many a hard tussle with the howling winds which had so often torn in mad fury over the range.

Passing through this wild gate to the Gap, the road became more steep, the loose rubble rendering my foothold precarious and uncertain. As yet the sunshine had not penetrated the Notch, and the air was damp and cold; so I felt no fatigue, despite my exertions. A dense mass of foliage held this part of the road in close possession; and so wild and virginal did it at times become, that even the pathway was invaded by venturesome vines, as though the forest was jealous of the narrow domain seized by man.

Frequently my passage seemed barred by the immense bowlders that had fallen from the slopes above, thus compelling the road to swerve around their bases, and adding to the savage beauty of the route. It was, indeed, Nature in her wildest mood, and I reveled in the ever-changing rudeness of the scene. My heart grew lighter as I advanced, and I regained all my accustomed spirits.

Thus sturdily climbing the steep and stony road, I suddenly came to an open ledge, which commanded a view of the entire valley I had left behind me. Standing on the smooth rock, as on a shelf hung high on the mountain side, my eyes wandered from point to point, from object to object; and I enjoyed, as one would quaff a delicious draught, all the varied and romantic beauty of the landscape spread out before my eyes. Looking up the valley, the spires of the city of Winchester seemed to be standing almost at my feet, and I could see each of the villages surrounding the city as they dotted the plain below. Farther on rose the dome-like crest of Cedar Mountain, standing sentinel over the broad expanse of field and woodland lying between the twin mountain ranges. Berryville was to my right, and away beyond the town I could distinguish the roofs and steeples of Charlestown, embowered in foliage; while still farther on I caught glimpses of the Potomac River, as its waters glistened in the distance.

On the other side of the valley rose North Mountain, and in the middle ground were the forests surrounding Mount Summit. An irregular line of hazel-bush betrayed the course of Opequan Creek, on whose banks Tom and I had whiled away many an afternoon trying to lure the cautious trout from their deep and shady pools. Right below me stood the Marshall mansion, easily recognized by its cluster of walnut-trees, under whose spreading branches I had passed so many happy hours in the days gone by.

Everywhere, as far as the eye could reach, were broad fields of grain, interspersed with frequent clumps of woods and orchard dots; while in the fields stood noble trees, like emerald gems, their presence adding to the exquisite loveliness of the picturesque panorama.

It was, indeed, a scene long to be remembered for its peacefulness; and as I stood there perched on the mountain ledge, scanning the exquisite landscape, I did not dream that when next my eyes would fall upon it I should find its features sadly changed by the ravages of cruel, dreadful war, — that those fields, now so yellow with shorn stubble and standing grain, would be bare and brown; the patriarchal homesteads wrecked and ruined by angry shot and shell, with unsightly gaps in the long lines of stone now marking the divisions of the land, where heavy cannon had been dragged back and forth as the fierce tide of battle ebbed and flowed; or that these green knolls lying between me and the picturesque towns would be scarred and·torn by lunettes and breastworks.

No, all thoughts of future strife and carnage were absent from my mind, as I took my last and lingering survey of the beautiful valley.

"Good-by, Tom," I shouted, waving my hat over my head; and as I did so the tireless echoes caught up his name, repeating it again and again. It was a happy omen, and I once more sprang joyously into the path on my homeward way over the mountains.

CHAPTER V.

THE HAND ON THE HILT.

"The country rings around with loud alarms,
And raw in fields the rude militia swarms."

UR election was over, the winter had passed, and Lincoln was seated in the presidential chair. The young party which made so vigorous a contest under Frémont had, after four years of persistent endeavor, at length gained sufficient strength to cope with the political organization that had so long held supreme power in the land, but now hopelessly divided on national questions. The East and the West had united in throwing the reins of government into the hands of the new party; but the South, though humiliated by its defeat through the ballot, was still defiant, and threatened to resort to the bullet in defense of her theories and institutions. In assuming this position, she was greatly strengthened by the unwise utterances of Northern politicians; for their words led the Southern people to believe that the North was irrevocably divided in national sentiment: so, while getting ready for war, the South believed that a bold and threatening front would intimidate the less belligerent North.

The political sky was full of strange portents; and the minds of all thoughtful men on both sides of the new geographical line were greatly agitated, for none could tell what a day might bring forth. Scarcely a household in the land but was tempo-

FORT SUMTER BOMBARDED.

rarily divided against itself, so imperfectly were the real issues of the time understood, or their dangers appreciated.

Events crystallized rapidly after the result of the election became known; and before Lincoln had taken his oath of office, several of the wayward States openly revolted. South Carolina impetuously led the way for her sisters, and already the busy note of preparation for the threatening struggle was heard within her borders.

As yet there had been no overt act, beyond the seizure of a fort or two, and a navy-yard. There were many wild utterances, but no blood had yet been shed. A feeling of dread rested upon the nation. Men feared each other, and the ties of personal friendship were visibly loosened.

At length the seven cotton States formally seceded, and the remaining slave States threatened to follow. Then the bolt suddenly fell; and there came a shock which stirred the nation to its very center, and set men's blood running hot in their veins. The national banner and authority had at last been rudely assailed, and a Federal garrison compelled to surrender to the force of arms. In an instant the veil was rent, and the full gravity of the situation stood revealed to the people.

Sumter had fallen, and the harbor of Charleston bristled with secession cannon. The war had at length begun: there was no further hope of a reconciliation. The sword must now decide the quarrel. The roar of cannon drowned the voice of peace. War's angry dogs were let loose.

Such was the attitude and course of events during the spring of 1861. I had gone back to college, and passed the winter in quiet study. As the snow melted under the elms in our college park, and the aged trees were tinged in vernal green, a feeling of disquietude came upon me; for the excited condition of the country had made itself felt, even among the students. It was only a few short months since I had parted from Tom Marshall on the little stone bridge that spanned the winding river under the mountains, yet how changed was the situation! The rapidity with which the quarrel had taken visible shape made this change appear all the more terrible, and my mind wandered from my books to ponder on the possibilities of the future. The college, too, was becoming deserted; for few cared to study the musty records of the dead past while our own history was being made so rapidly before our eyes.

With the news of Anderson's surrender ringing in my ears, I impatiently threw aside my books, and abandoned study. Standing in the streets of New-York City, the next day, I saw a favorite regiment march over its pavements in prompt response to the call of the government.

It was an exciting and extraordinary scene; and my pulse throbbed wildly that bright sunny April afternoon, as I witnessed the fierce outburst of popular feeling. Half a million of people thronged the streets of the great city, and waited in surging masses to see their citizen-soldiery march past. Traffic in Broadway was entirely suspended for the time, and the busy life of the metropolis seemed suddenly diverted from its accustomed channels. From house-tops and windows waved the stars and stripes in endless profusion, while men and women wore the tricolor on their breasts.

All classes of society were excited, for the appeal of the government for protection and support had roused the people to a realizing sense of their danger. The call for troops had broken down many barriers, and the torrent of popular loyalty swept every thing before it.

The banker at his desk had heard the call, and pushed aside his interest-tables to obey it. The physician sitting beside his patient had heard it, and prepared to change the sphere of his duty. The lawyer pleading his client's cause in the courtroom had heard it, and dropped his brief to shoulder a musket in obedience to the summons. The artisan had heard it above the rattle of machinery, and threw away his tools to take up the weapons of war. The clerk had heard it at his counter, and abandoned his yardstick for the bayonet. The artist before his easel had heard it, and turned his canvas to the wall, there to lie untouched until he had done his duty as a soldier. The fashionable idler had heard the appeal in his club-room, and rejoiced, as he pulled off his gloves, that at last he had an earnest object in life. As all these men came together and fell in, shoulder to shoulder, their hearts beat high with enthusiasm; and they marched forward in solid column, fully appreciating the grave responsibility resting upon them.

While the people waited for the militia, thus suddenly summoned from every profession and pursuit in life, a feverish excitement pervaded the crowds. Men who the day before had angrily disputed on political questions, now clasped hands in silent token of their mutual adherence to the government. Bands of young men marched up and down the middle of the streets, singing patriotic songs, being joined in the refrain by the assembled multitude. The expression of feeling was decidedly tumultuous, but it did not seem at all out of place, so abnormal was the occasion, so strange the surroundings. The North was indeed rising in all its might and power, and every man's face wore a look of determination that spoke clearer than words how thoroughly each individual appreciated the crisis at hand.

At length the roll of drums is heard in the distance, and afar off we can see the glitter of the bayonets as they flash in the rays of the setting sun. The police become suddenly active, and push the expectant people back; then the crowd parts, and the head of the column appears. It is the gallant *New-York Seventh*, stripped of all gaudy decoration, but well equipped for active service. With full ranks, the knapsacks giving the command an appearance of solidity not observable on holiday parade, the regiment marches steadily forward to the monotonous beat of the drums. Men in the ranks are recognized by friends in the throng, and earnest farewells are uttered.

"There's Jack! I see him! Don't you? See, right there in the middle," exclaims a young man at my elbow.

"Yes, yes! That's him. That's Jack. Hurrah for Jack! Good-by, old fellow!" and the speaker waves his hat wildly, and unconsciously treads on my foot.

Jack hears his name, sees his friends, and a warm flush of pride mantles his face as he gives a brief nod in response.

"I wonder where Bob is. Isn't this his company?" asks another. "Yes, there he is now. God bless you, Bob! I'll look after mother;" and as he exchanges farewells with his brother, the poor boy's eyes grow dim with manly tears.

"They march better than ever," remarks a bystander critically. "It's positively magnificent;" and he is joined in his cheers by all who hear his words of praise. While the men cheer in their enthusiasm, women weep as they see some loved face vanish; yet they, too, are proud to see their husbands, brothers, or lovers so prompt in answering the call of duty.

Now a tremor runs like a vibration through the vast assemblage, as tidings come that the sons of Massachusetts have been slain in the streets of Baltimore. The New-York soldiers marching down the wide thoroughfare hear the news as they pass; but the column of steel pauses not, and in a moment more it is gone.

The fact that blood has been shed causes men to gaze mutely into each other's faces; for now they realize that at last the seal of peace has indeed been broken, and the pestilence of angry war is upon them. The half-dozen lives sacrificed that day in the Monumental City is but the beginning of the bitter harvest to come.

Day after day I lingered in the feverish city, and day after day saw other regiments pass through its streets. Young men marched in the ranks in their citizen's dress, carrying a musket, content to wait for the uniform yet in the workshop. Others carried knapsacks for the friends they escorted to the place of embarkation. From other cities came fresh bodies of troops, and recruiting banners were flung to the breeze.

It was wonderful to see how men contended with one another

for the privilege of enrolling as volunteers. Veteran officers, who had simply hoped to raise a company, were astonished to find themselves at the head of a regiment. A little band of Mexican heroes started a battalion, and at the end of a week were carrying swords as field-officers in a brigade. Had the government fully appreciated the full extent of its needs at that time, it could have had an army of a million for its first campaign.

Caught up by this whirlwind of martial feeling, I soon found myself in the uniform of a Federal soldier. What mattered it to me which of the States carried my humble name on its rolls, — New York or my native New Hampshire? The loyal States were bound together all the closer that their sons served in each other's regiments. It was not the State color, but the National one, we were to defend.

CHAPTER VI.

DRAWING THE BLADE.

"Then, in the name of God and all these rights
Advance your standards, draw your willing swords."

 IX weeks passed, and we were rapidly learning our duties as soldiers in camp of instruction. The war was indeed assuming grand proportions. In the North the ties of political party were loosened, and men now only thought of defending the integrity of the Union. All of the seceding States had already formed a provisional government, and their armies were actually in the field. Beauregard menaced Washington on the plains of Manassas, and Federal troops were marching to meet him over the roads I had tramped the previous summer. In the Shenandoah Valley, Johnston was in possession, and that beautiful region was beginning its experience of the vicissitudes of war. The Mississippi River was blockaded its entire length, from Cairo to New Orleans; and a Confederate navy was forming in Mobile Bay. In the South-west other opposing armies were confronting each other. It only needed a spark to set the whole train in a blaze.

It was a period of anxious expectation. Armies were rising on every hand with amazing rapidity; ship-yards were thronged with workmen engaged in transforming merchant-vessels into ships of war; founderies were turning out cannon, or casting vast quantities of shot and shell; artisans were learning new trades, for, instead of implements of husbandry, they were fashioning weapons for the battle-field; tender-hearted women wrapped the crisp cartridge, or stitched the uniforms of blue and gray. The pruning-hook was being beaten into the sword-blade, and the simple citizen became a soldier. Throughout the length and breadth of the land a feverish activity prevailed: the pursuits of peace were abandoned for the perils of war. New geographical lines had been drawn, and brother stood up against brother; for Hatred ruled the hour, and pushed Reason from her throne.

Thus had events progressed, when, on a bright May morning, our regiment arrived at Fortress Monroe, near the entrance to Chesapeake Bay, to tread the soil of Virginia.

The scene in Hampton Roads when our steamer dropped anchor was a busy one. Coasting-vessels were lying within gun-range of the fort, waiting to discharge their cargoes, and noisy little tugs were impudently snorting and puffing as they towed the sailing-craft to and fro; while beyond this little fleet of shipping lay a trim frigate, her black hull bristling with cannon. At the long wooden wharf were other vessels, their decks in possession of large gangs of negroes, who, with melodious chants, removed the boxes and barrels of provisions, cases of ammunition, tents, lumber, and hospital stores. On the shore immense sheds were in progress of erection, the carpenters' hammers seeming to keep time with the monotonous songs of the wharf-laborers. Behind all rose the frowning walls of the grim fortress, its grassy parapets crowned with barbette guns. Away to the right, beyond the fort, I could see the camps of the troops that had preceded us. It was a scene full of animation and vigorous action; and, as I watched the huge garrison flag flutter in the breeze over the granite walls of the fort, I realized that at last we were on that mysterious and movable line, — "the front."

All of the men were excited over this entrance upon campaign life: so it was a great relief when our steamer was summoned to the wharf for our debarkation. An hour later we were wading through the deep sand on our way to camp, where we remained for weeks, doing picket-duty on Hampton Creek, diversified by an occasional reconnoissance beyond the deserted village.

The men were beginning to murmur at the lack of active operations, when orders came to attack some Confederate fortifications discovered at a gully called Big Bethel, on the road to Yorktown. Our regiment was to move with others at midnight; and as the extra rounds of ball cartridge were issued, we were told to get all the sleep we could before the hour for starting arrived. A better method for keeping us all awake could not have been devised, as scarcely an eye was closed during the night.

While lying in my tent, listening to the wild surmises of my comrades, my thoughts drifted far away. I had not heard from Tom Marshall since Christmas, when he informed me that even then he was enrolled as a defender of the Southern cause. Now we were indeed ranged on opposite sides of the great quarrel, as both he and Kate had prophesied; and, though I felt strengthened in my own course by the brave letters of my mother, who approved the step I had taken, I was depressed by the thought that our convictions regarding individual duty had placed my friend and myself in such decided antagonism. True, there was little probability that Tom and I would ever meet in the field; and I found some comfort in that belief as I pondered on the possibilities of the morrow.

Midnight came at last, when word was passed from tent to tent for the several companies to form. The order was obeyed with alacrity. It was as dark as pitch when we entered the main road, not even the stars being visible; while the knowledge that we were going to battle made the movement all the more strange and thrilling. It being our first experience of real work, the sense of danger nerved every heart. We had not yet attained the coolness of veterans; but, feeling brave and confident, we obeyed this summons to battle with enthusiasm.

Stumbling along in open column, we pushed on through the darkness silently but eagerly, until, after a two-hours' march, we were led into a bit of woods on the right of the road, and ordered to lie down. As we did so, I began wondering what the result of the approaching engagement would be. Here I lay, musket in hand, among men of whose existence I had been ignorant a few short weeks before; and, as I stretched my tired body on the soft and fragrant earth, I realized the grim earnestness of the situation. In a few hours I might be among the dead, lying motionless on the battle-field, or groaning in an ambulance, sick with pain and loss of blood. Yet a strange feeling of content rested upon me; and, though we were all nervous over the suspense, I noticed no symptoms of coward-ice. Few of us spoke, even in whispers, for silence had been strictly enjoined; and the absence of all sound among so many men was to me more painful to bear than any actual fighting could possibly be.

Suddenly the dull sound of distant musketry somewhere in our rear broke the wearisome silence, and a tremor ran through the ranks; then we heard the rapid galloping of a horse in the road, and soon after learned that two of our regiments coming up had met at a cross-roads, and emptied a volley into each other in the darkness, two or three having been killed, and several wounded. Of course this *contretemps* destroyed all hopes of a surprise, which was a foolish idea from the beginning, and showed how little our officers appreciated the sagacity of our antagonists.

"I tell yez what it is, byes!" exclaimed Dennis Malone, the only Irishman in my company, as he crept into his place in the ranks from some undergrowth in front, "thim rebs beyant are up to snuff. I've bin down among our skarmishers, who are lying on their bellies over there; and by all that's holy, thim divils in the breastworks are out among their big guns wid their lanterns! They'll make it hot for us to-morrer, or my name's not Dinnis."

"Well, this is the first time I ever heard of an Irishman being afraid," said I, as we all laughed at Dennis's speech.

"You know better than that, corporal," retorted Dennis. "It's not afeard I am, at all, at all; but if we don't have the divil's own scrimmage before long, ye may take my head for a fut-ball."

"So you saw lanterns, did you, Dennis?" I replied in a bantering tone. "Are you sure you were not dreaming of the will-o-the-wisps in your native bogs?"

"I'll tell yez what it is, corporal: you're my suparior officer, and I may not know as much about Greek or Latin as yersilf; but, if you think I don't know the difference 'twixt a lantern and a bog-light, I can't say much for yer larnin'."

As the indignant Dennis uttered these words, half a dozen muskets were discharged on our skirmish-line.

"Hurroo! they're beginning the fun. We'll all be kilt before night, or loaded down wid glory!" he shouted, fairly dancing on his knees with excitement and delight.

"Silence in the ranks!" exclaimed Capt. Harding, who commanded our company. "Silence, I say!"

"We'll be as mute as oysters, darlint," responded the irrepressible Irishman, in a sort of stage-whisper. "But why don't yez stop those skarmishers beyant? Shure, they're making the most noise."

Just then one of our cannon, that had been placed in position on a knoll behind us, opened fire, and sent a shell shrieking over our heads.

"Holy mother of Moses! An' what's that?" bellowed Dennis, as he cowered with the rest of us under the awful sound.

"Only a shell, you fool," testily remarked our sergeant. "Haven't you ever heard one before?"

"A shell, is it? I'm much obleeged to you for the information. No, I've never heard one before; and ye were not brought up on that sort of egg-meat, either, Mr. Sargeant."

Dennis's whimsical answer turned the laugh on the sergeant;

"STOP FIRING, YOU FOOLS, TILL YOU GET THE WORD!"

but, while we were enjoying his sally, the guns in the breastworks replied by sending one of their shells crashing through
the trees, and we heard a smothered groan down the line, startling evidence that some poor fellow had been hit.

There was no fun in this, so we again became silent and
watchful, for none knew where the next shell might strike; and
there were more evidently coming, for our artillery began getting to work briskly. By this time it was growing light, and
we were able to see objects about us. Then the order was
given for us to advance through the woods, and I saw that our
line of battle extended across the road.

"I say, Wilmot," remarked Sam Foster, my file neighbor,
"isn't this horrid? Going through these woods, to meet we
know not what, — maybe to get a bullet in one's stomach before
you can tell where it comes from."

"Just my feeling, Sam," I replied. "But if the bullets go
for your stomach they'll find it pretty full already, judging by
the way you punished the hard-tack last night."

"Might as well get killed with a full belly as with an
empty" —

I heard no more of Sam's speech; for at that moment a
terrific roar assailed our ears, and a storm of bullets whistled
over our heads. One or two of the men in the company on
our right went down; and I involuntarily shook myself, half
expecting to find a wound. A minute after, we received
another volley, and there were more men down. Then we
caught a glimpse of the new earth forming the Confederate
breastworks as they frowned on the other side of the narrow
gully. At once nearly every man in the ranks began firing
without orders, much to the disgust of our colonel.

"Stop that firing, you confounded fools!" he shouted
angrily: "wait until you get the word."

But we never got the word; for in a few minutes we were
told to fall back, the shells coming in pretty fast. We did not
mind them much now, for we were beginning to understand that

everybody does not get killed in a battle. The order to retreat disgusted the men; but we obeyed, supposing it to be a change in the plan. As the regiment moved off, my foot caught in a projecting root, and I fell; finding, when I tried to get up, that my ankle was sprained. Here was a ridiculous predicament.

"What's the matter wid ye, corporal? Why the divil don't ye get up? Shure, the rigiment is retrating." And Dennis leaned compassionately over me as I writhed in pain.

"Never mind me, Dennis: go with the boys. I've sprained my ankle."

"Is it lave yer, and ye right forninst the inimy? The divil a fut I'll stir until I see ye get up. It's an illigant excuse I've got, so I have, for staying out here."

"If you gave me a lift, Dennis, perhaps I might be able to hobble off to the rear."

"Shure, an' that wud be flying in the face of Providence. Ain't yer fut sprained on purpose to kape ye out here? Rest aisy a bit where yer are until we see what's going on," replied Dennis, as he began peering through the trees towards the gully.

"It may be a Providence for me, Dennis; but it cannot include you. So, if you won't help me, why, go and join the regiment," said I, angry at my companion's pertinacity, despite its whimsical phase.

"What's good for one, corporal, is good enough for two. I'll tell ye what I'll do. I'll crawl down there and see what they're doin', and then I'll come back and tell ye," replied the fellow, undaunted by my evident anger.

"Precious little good that will do me. What do you want on the skirmish-line? To get a bullet through that obstinate head of yours! Stay where you are."

As I spoke, the line of skirmishers suddenly appeared all around us, as they fell back, at the same time keeping up a scattering irregular fire.

"Halloo! what are you two men doing here?" exclaimed the officer commanding the line. "Where's our regiment?"

"They have moved back, lieutenant, somewhere in the rear," I replied hurriedly. "I've sprained my ankle, and can not walk; while this foolish Irishman persists in staying with me."

"That's bad. But you must get out of here somehow, corporal; for we are changing front, and you'll soon be between two fires. Try and get up," the lieutenant continued kindly, "and we'll help you along."

THE RETREAT FROM THE FIELD.

I scrambled to my feet, and, leaning on Dennis's shoulder, began limping to the rear; the skirmishers now banging away as fast as they could load and fire.

"Well, corporal, an' this is quare work," said Dennis. "Here we are right in the middle of a scrimmage, and neither of us firing a shot. If ye'll rest yersilf against that tree for a minnit, I'll sind both of our bullits into thim divils."

"All right, Dennis. Here's my musket: blaze away," I

replied, laughing at the suggestion. "But mind, if you hit anybody with my ball, it goes to my credit."

"Av coorse. Here's at ye, my darlints," cried Dennis, as he brought his piece to his shoulder, and pulled the trigger, following up the shot with another random one from my weapon.

"Well, how many have you killed?" I asked, as I took back my empty gun.

"Not more than a dozen. Shure, I didn't see any one to shoot at, but maybe the bullits went crooked. Come along, corporal: we'll retrate now in good ordher."

Despite my pain I managed to keep moving, and in a few minutes after entered the field where our regiment was standing in line. As Dennis and I came in sight, two or three of my tent-mates ran forward, thinking I was wounded.

"It is only a sprain," said I in explanation, chagrined at the accident which would prevent my going into action with my comrades.

But there was no more fighting for any of us that day. The field-piece in the road kept up a desultory fire for nearly an hour; and once we heard a loud cheer towards the left of our line, followed by some sharp musketry. Then a lull ensued, and the shells came less frequently. After waiting for another hour, we were told the battle was over.

"What! No more fighting?" exclaimed Dennis. "Shure, we've had none at all, barring those few shots we got in before the colonel stopped our fun."

Just then a fatigue-party passed through our line, carrying twenty or thirty poor fellows who were groaning over their wounds; and we learned that ten or twelve had been killed, including the officer commanding the battery, and Major Winthrop of Gen. Butler's staff. So there must have been serious work somewhere, though we had not seen much of it.

Thus ended our first battle, and it was a fortnight before I could report for duty.

Then came the news of McClellan's victories in West Virginia; and the tide of war drifted for a time into the South-west, with varying success to either side. But all these movements were of secondary importance to the impending conflict in the Virginia Valley near Centerville; and when it ended in the defeat and rout of the Federal army under McDowell, at Bull Run, the Northern people began to understand that the Southerners could fight as stubbornly and courageously as themselves. It was now evident that the war was not to be ended in a single campaign, and preparations were made accordingly.

CHAPTER VII.

THROWING AWAY THE SCABBARD.

"I see you stand like greyhounds in the slips,
Straining upon the start. The game's afoot."

HE spring of 1862 found the two sections still arrayed against each other, with a greatly increased area of operations on both sides. In the West and South-west the names of Thomas and Rosecran, of Sherman and Grant, were becoming known as those of Federal leaders; while McClellan, Banks, Pope, and Heintzelman rose to command in the East. Heretofore campaigns had been conducted almost at random, no concerted plan being laid down. Now all this was to be changed. Henceforth a definite scheme was to be carried out, with three main objects in view, — the enforcement of the blockade along the Atlantic coast, the opening of the Mississippi River, and the capture of Richmond, the Confederate capital. The navy, reinforced and strengthened, was to do the first, the Western armies would attempt the second, while the Army of the Potomac was to accomplish the third part of the plan of operations.

On the other hand, the Confederates, under Breckenridge, Sydney Johnston, and Beauregard, had established a strong line of defense in the West, extending from the Mississippi to the Cumberland Mountains; their right resting on Mill Spring and Cumberland Gap, with the left at Columbus. Fort Donelson and Fort Henry held the Tennessee and Cumberland Rivers, while Bowling Green protected the railroads running south of Nashville. Johnston, commanding the Army of Northern Virginia, covered the James River and Richmond with his left, at the same time threatening Washington. These varied operations, covering as they did so wide an area of territory, betokened a desperate series of campaigns during the summer.

Halleck, commanding the Western Federal forces, had been instructed to pierce the enemy's center, and so open the way to Nashville, and recover a part of the Mississippi-river front, as well as the Memphis and Charleston Railroad, then the main route of communication between the Eastern and Western branches of the Confederate armies. McClellan was to take his command up the Virginia peninsula, and march direct on Richmond; while Banks defended Washington, and Pope operated in the Virginia Valley towards Culpepper. Burnside was at Newbern on the coast, and Gilmore was besieging Pulaski.

In January Thomas repulsed a Confederate assault at Logan's Cross-roads, which compelled the latter to abandon Mill Spring; and in the following month Grant captured Forts Donelson and Henry, these victories being followed by the evacuation of Columbus and Bowling Green. With so good a beginning, the campaign opened brightly for the Federals. It only remained for the Eastern armies to achieve like success, to speedily end the war. But the quarrel was not to be decided so easily.

During the blustering days of March, the Army of the Potomac moved from Alexandria by transports, and landed at Fortress Monroe, being also greatly reinforced by troops from Maryland and the Susquehanna Valley. Our regiment had spent the winter in Baltimore, and took part in a bloodless campaign under Gen. Dix on the Chesapeake peninsula: so we joined the army with high hopes for the future. Promotion had come to many of our officers, who entered other regiments; and I now wore the chevrons of a sergeant.

For the second time in ten months I found myself on board

a steamer lying in Hampton Roads, once more the spectator of a busy, interesting scene. Steamers from the New-England coast, Long-Island Sound, the Hudson and the Delaware Rivers, lay here side by side, their broad decks black with troops impatiently waiting for orders to land. At the old familiar wharf other steamers were being rapidly emptied of their living freight, a constant stream of armed men marching past the forts. A countless fleet of sailing-vessels were also anchored in the Roads, laden with supplies; and in the offing several war-vessels afforded the needful protection. In their midst we discovered the little queer-shaped Monitor, which had only a few days before beaten off the Confederate iron-clad. Towards the mouth of the James River the submerged masts of two frigates, "The Congress" and "The Cumberland," attested the superiority of armored vessels over wooden ones.

The air was raw and cold when our morning roll was called; and the men huddled on the deck in their overcoats, hoping to see the sun shine before we came to land. This hope was gratified; for by the time we received our signal to disembark, the clouds disappeared, and the day grew warm and cheerful.

Already the army was on its way up the peninsula; and as we went into camp on the Newport News road, I could see long lines of troops marching towards our old battle-ground at Big Bethel, their immense trains of wagons toiling through the deep sand in every direction. To us the familiar ground was full of interest, but the pressure of so large an army had obliterated all but the leading landmarks. By the end of a week it came our turn to move to the front, and in the early days of April we entered the camp before Yorktown. Days of inaction lengthened into weeks, and we began wondering at the slow progress made. The army was restive at being thus held in leash in sight of the enemy, though it willingly dug trenches and hauled siege-guns to the batteries.

My Zouave comrades were restless at their confinement in camp: so it was with almost boyish delight that we received orders to go to the fortifications. A day was first spent in the woods, learning how to make gabions and fascines; and the next night we were furnished with shovels and pickaxes. The moon was struggling behind a heavy bank of clouds as we silently marched over an old cornfield, until we reached the high bank of the York River, opposite Gloucester Point. With a few

IN THE TRENCHES.

whitewashed palings from a neighboring garden-fence the outlines of our proposed battery were laid out in an orchard, and the work of digging proceeded merrily. It was something to do at last; and the task was greeted as a positive pleasure.

About midnight I was sitting on the edge of the long pit, quietly watching my platoon at work, when I became aware of the presence of a small group of officers, closely shrouded in their long night-cloaks. The uncertain light given by our lanterns as they stood hidden in the pit afforded me no clew as to the identity of these visitors, though I felt satisfied they were of high rank.

"Good-evening, sergeant," said one of the group, in a musical voice: "you're busy at work, I see."

"Yes, sir," I replied respectfully: "the boys are doing very well, considering."

"They have dug splendidly; haven't they, Marcy?" said the officer to one of his companions. "Look at that cut: it's as straight as a wall."

"Sa-ay, sargeant," cried Dennis, as he wiped his perspiring face, "how many guns are they going to put up here?"

"Four, I believe," was my reply.

"My man," said the unknown, as he leaned against the trunk of the apple-tree, "how do you like digging trenches?"

"Troth, your honor, it's fine fun at the beginning," replied Dennis diplomatically.

"Rather tiresome fun, I should judge," remarked the officer, evidently amused.

"You'd think it fun to have to dig a big hole like this before daylight, right forninst the inimy's guns," explained my Irish comrade.

"Ah! I understand. Marcy, don't you think Warren is going a little too deep?" said the stranger.

"Begorra, an' if we keep on much longer, it's my belafe we'll be in Chiny before morning!" exclaimed Dennis, much to the amusement of his comrades.

"Confound your impudence!" angrily cried the officer addressed as Marcy: "do you know whom you are talking to?"

"Divil a bit! and what's more, I don't care. Shure, ain't we all one color in the dark?" undauntedly retorted Dennis.

"Let him alone, Marcy. The man means no impertinence," said our mysterious visitor.

"Well, general, if you will persist in masquerading in this

way, I suppose we must expect these incidents," replied General Marcy, whom I had by this time recognized as General McClellan's chief of staff.

"Oh, fudge! I like to see and hear what my men are doing, and how they feel," said the general.

"Please forgive Dennis, sir," said I: "he's always getting into a scrape with that foolish tongue of his."

"Forgive him? Why, sergeant, there's nothing to forgive. Good-night, and just tell your Irish friend that General McClellan hopes he will get into Yorktown before he drops through into China;" and with a merry laugh the commander of our army disappeared in the darkness.

The news that "Little Mac" had visited us soon circulated, and it was wonderful to witness the enthusiasm manifested by the men over their general.

The next morning our redoubt was so far advanced that the working-party were entirely under cover, and we continued to finish the details undisturbed by the shells thrown over our heads by the Confederate batteries on the other side of the river. In a week the huge Parrott guns were in position, and we prepared to reply to the favors already received. It was our first experience at real gunnery: so when the four iron monsters were discharged, the stunning reports caused considerable confusion, and we actually forgot to watch the effects of our shells. But the artillery officer directing our movements seemed well satisfied, for he ordered the guns to be again loaded. After a little practice we learned the range; and a day or two after, the artillery captain carefully sighted the pieces, and ordered a broadside. At the simultaneous discharge of our whole battery, we rushed through the smoke of the guns to the ramparts, and saw our four shells explode in a bunch over the water-battery. A moment after, a big column of white smoke rose from the battery, hiding it for the moment from our sight; and the air was full of flying fragments.

"By Jove! boys, you've done it this time," exclaimed the

captain. "Their magazine must have blown up. See! the guns have tumbled into the water, and part of the cliff is falling."

This feat led to our regiment being transferred to the right of the main line, where we remained in charge of the batteries until Yorktown was evacuated.

It was now May; but, though we had been six weeks in the field, our advance had been lamentably slow. Yet, while our confinement in a comparatively small area told upon the health of the army, there was no grumbling. Surrounded as we were by pestilential swamps, disease was rife; and, though we had not seen a battle, the hospitals were rapidly filling. Our general, in protecting us from Magruder's shells, had not cheated Death of his harvest. The army had already lost as many men by malaria as it would have required to seize the earthworks of the Confederates by direct assault.

On the night of the 3d of May, I leaned over the breech of my gun, thinking of the bombardment we were to begin on the morrow. All was silent about me, only the hoarse challenge of some sentinel breaking the silence. The moon was hidden by a heavy bank of clouds; and, in the trenches behind our line of forts, five thousand men lay asleep on their arms. Suddenly a gun was fired from the Confederate redoubt nearest the river, and then another and another followed suit. In a few minutes the batteries opened a furious fusillade, and the air was full of flying shells. It was a magnificent scene; and I forgot my danger in watching the flashes of the guns and the flight of the shells as they rose in front, and fell in the rear, their blazing fuses betraying their passage. Hour after hour this fierce, unexpected cannonade continued, until at length the mortar-shells began tumbling into our parallels. Captain Harding stood near me as one fell.

"Heavens! But this is getting to be a hot place, Wilmot. Tell the men to shelter themselves in the traverses."

"No use, sir. They are all too much excited to lie still," I replied.

BESIEGING YORKTOWN.

"I don't wonder at it: I feel that way myself. I wish we had orders to reply."

"Faith, an' we'd make the divil's own row together," said Dennis, who was, as usual, ready to take part in any conversation near him.

But we never used the guns we had labored so long to get into position; for, as the day broke, two or three negroes came along the river-path, and announced that Yorktown had been evacuated. This changed the whole condition of affairs, for the army was at once set in motion. Before noon, long columns of infantry were pushing forward, being far in the advance by nightfall.

The unhealthy water and the unusual fatigue had at length its effect, for that night I was stricken down with fever. I remember being lifted into an ambulance, and the awful jolting of the vehicle over the rough road, until insensibility deadened my pain. It was with astonishment, therefore, that I found myself, on waking, lying on a rude stretcher in the dark. Trying to discover my whereabouts, a few drops of water fell on my face, which was already dripping wet, and I heard rain pattering on a roof over my head.

"Where am I? Help! Help!" I shouted, glad to find my voice quite strong.

A light glimmered faintly through a window, and I saw that I was lying in an open shed.

"Stop that noise. What's all this confounded row about?" said a voice authoritatively.

"Shure, it's none of us, at all, at all. It's the dead man out in the shed beyant," replied a Celtic voice.

"The dead man? What do you mean?"

"Why, it's the sargeant that you said was dead, and they've put him in the shed. Troth, he's got a good yell of his own, if he *is* dead."

In a few minutes I was lifted up, carried into the house, and snugly wrapped in blankets on a bed of loose hay.

"'Pon my word, sergeant, you've had a narrow squeak of it," said the surgeon.

"How came you to think me dead?" I asked.

"Why, there was every indication of it. That dripping water must have given your system a shock, and so restored animation."

"How lucky the roof leaked! Arrah! who ever heard that a leaky roof was good to bring a dead man back to life?" said the same Irish voice I had heard in the shed. Looking round, I found it was Dennis.

THE DEAD SERGEANT'S YELL.

Wondering at the unexpected presence of my Irish comrade, who seemed always near me, and devoutly thanking God for my escape, I closed my eyes, and fell asleep in the genial warmth of the room. When I awoke the next day, I found the fever gone; but it had left me so weak I could not rise. Seeing Dennis near by, I asked how he came to be in hospital.

"An' do you think nobody but yersilf has a right to be sick?" he asked indignantly. "Shure, while you were lyin' in your tint on the cowld wet ground, a-shakin' wid the faver, I felt me own bones beginning to ache; and they hadn't taken you away long before I tuk sick mesilf, and they carried me here. And that's all there's about it."

"Did you know it was I who lay out there in the shed, supposed to be dead?"

"'Deed, an' I didn't. Faix, if I'd 'a' known it, I'd had a wake over ye, though we'd have to do widout the whishky."

"But I heard you say it was a sergeant," I persisted with the petulance of a sick man. "How did you know that?"

"An' listen to him! As if there's nobody else a sargeant but himself! Oh! but you're proud in your grand sthripes. Shure, they tould me it was a sargeant," said Dennis, coming at last to the point.

"Are you getting well?" said I, amused at my comrade's good-natured loquacity.

"Yis: I'm a thrifle better now that I've found you in the land of the livin'," replied Dennis as he wrung my hand and left me.

I lay dozing on my rude bed all day, being at length roused into wakefulness by the unexpected sight of a woman's face bending over mine.

"How are you getting on, sergeant?" she asked in a soft, kind voice.

"Much stronger, thank you, and a little hungry," I replied, wondering who my visitor could be.

"Come, now, that's a brave sign. Here is some nice soup: see if you can swallow it;" and the tall lady held a spoon to my fevered lips.

The soup was delicious, and I hungrily drank all there was in the bowl.

"There, you will do famously now. But you must lie still, and get strength. I'll see you again to-morrow."

"Who was that, Dennis?" I asked when my visitor had gone. "How did she come here?"

"Faix, she's an angel dropped from the sky, — that's what she is."

"But who is she?"

"Shure, she's the daughter of our old gineral."

"Daughter of our general! what general?"

"Why, ould Shoot-him-on-the-shpot Dix, that we left behind us in Baltimore."

"Oh, I understand! It's Miss Dorothea Dix. I've heard of her labors in the Washington hospitals. But she is not General Dix's daughter, Dennis."

"Well, if she isn't, she ought to be; and her father ought to be a gineral for her sake."

"So," said I musingly, " we have an American Nightingale, have we?"

"I say, Master Frank, the faver's getting into yer head again. Shure, there's no nightingales in Ameriky," replied Dennis compassionately.

"Confound it, man! I was not talking about a bird, but a woman. Did you never hear of Florence Nightingale?"

"Divil a word: who was she?"

"Why, during the Crimean war she went out with a corps of nurses for the English hospitals in the field."

"Well, sargeant, this is a quare world, to call a bird and a woman by the same name. But never mind, Frank darlin', whether they be Nightingales or Dixes, the women are always to the fore, God bless 'em!" said Dennis in a husky voice, his honest blue eyes meanwhile filling with tears.

CHAPTER VIII.

BANDAGE AND LINT.

. . . "And everywhere
Low voices with the ministering hand
Hung round the sick."

YORKTOWN, Va., May 16, 1862.

OTICE. — Every man who is ready and anxious to join his regiment at the front will report forthwith at the office of the medical director.

GEOFFREY WILLIS,
Lieut.-Colonel and Medical Director.

Such was the queerly worded notice I found posted upon the door of our hospital early one morning. I had already regained my strength, thanks to the care of my doctors and a tolerably strong constitution. I found Yorktown greatly changed; for the town had become an immense storehouse for supplies, and the narrow, dusty streets were choked with wagons. Troops still continued to press forward, while steamers carried other detachments up the Pamunkey River towards the White House. The battle of Williamsburg had been fought, followed by a few unimportant skirmishes, so it was evident that a decisive engagement would soon occur.

This aspect of affairs made me anxious to rejoin my regiment, for hospital life was irksome in the extreme. The bulletin of our medical director was, however, so odd in its phraseology that I half suspected a joke; for I knew there were many men who would cling to the easy life in hospital until they were fairly turned out. However, I decided to report for duty. Announcing my intention to Dennis, I was glad to find him as eager to join our comrades as myself. Our house surgeon smiled on being told of our desire to report, and told us to equip ourselves from the accumulated stock of rifles and muskets lying in an out-house. Selecting two breech-loading guns and sufficient ammunition, Dennis and I presented ourselves at

REPORTING TO THE SURGEON.

the medical director's office. There were present on the same errand some twenty or thirty other men, all fully equipped for service.

"So you men are anxious to go to the front," said the director, smiling over his spectacles in an odd manner, as he stood surveying our little group.

Nearly all of the men nodded; and, seeing that I was the only sergeant present, I assumed the office of spokesman.

"We have simply obeyed your order, doctor. I, for one,

would like to join my regiment very much. I presume the rest are of the same mind."

"I'm glad of it. Now, sergeant, you just see that all the men are in good shape for service; then form your squad."

The task of inspection was soon over; and, there being three or four corporals, I organized a little company. It was then quite late in the afternoon; so the surgeon put on his cap, and led the way to the wharf. Arriving there, I was ordered to post sentries, and see that no one went on board the steamer without a pass.

"I'm going to send away some sick and wounded," remarked the surgeon; "and, after we get the steamer loaded, I'll send you to the front."

Wondering why the medical director had not taken a guard from the regular garrison, I established the necessary line of sentinels, content with the fact that it was active duty once more. The embarkation of the sick was a tedious one, and it was midnight before the surgeon in charge of the steamer announced that he could take no more. When he did report the fact, our little medical director stopped the line of stretchers, and turning to me said, —

"Now, sergeant, march your guard on board. You see, I wanted a few steady, willing fellows: that was why I put up such a polite note. You are going to Washington instead of the front;" and he laughed heartily at the success of his stratagem.

My men were delighted at the unexpected change in our destination, and went on board the steamer in high feather. We subsequently learned that on the following day every able-bodied man in the hospitals was suddenly drafted on board a transport, and sent to the army: so we lost nothing by our promptness in reporting for duty.

The passage up the River Potomac was an enjoyable one, despite the suffering by which I was surrounded. As I was sitting in the stern, watching the immense flocks of wild ducks gathering in the stretches of reeds preparatory to their migration northward, Dennis appeared, his face beaming with fun.

"I say, sargeant, what a lot of sarvints that officer has, to be shure!"

"Servants? I do not understand you."

"Shure, isn't there only wan officer aboard?"

"Yes, only one. But what of that?"

"Why, there's a lot of skulkers aboard, and ivery mother's son of 'em sez he's the captain's sarvint."

"Oh! we'll soon fix that," said I. Going to the guard-room between decks, I called out the reserve, and arrested sixteen men who were not on the doctor's books. How they got on the steamer was a mystery. On our arrival at Washington, I reported the fact to the surgeon who received the patients, and was instructed to march them to the provost-marshal's office. There the prisoners were welcomed with cutting politeness, I and my guard being granted passes until the steamer was ready to return.

As Dennis and I wandered down Pennsylvania Avenue, he suggested a barber; saying that his chin felt as rough as a stubble-field in harvest-time. We accordingly walked into the nearest saloon, finding it occupied by several officers. Taking a vacant chair, I was soon in the hands of an attendant.

"Just from the front?" inquired an elderly officer reclining in an adjoining chair, the napkins on his shoulders concealing his rank.

"Yes, sir: we came up on the hospital-boat this morning."

"One of the Sanitary Commission steamers, I suppose?"

"Yes, sir, — 'The Elm City.'"

"Well, and how are affairs getting on there?" continued my interlocutor.

"Pretty well, sir, I believe. When we left Yorktown it was understood the advance was making rapid progress."

"I'm glad to hear it," replied the officer, rising, and disclosing the double stars of a major-general. "Good-day, sergeant."

"Who is that general?" I asked my sable barber.

"Dat gebbelman, sah, be Giniral Wadsworth, de gubernor-giniral, sah, of dis yeah city," was his response.

Entering the street again, we sauntered along the avenue, and at Dennis's suggestion entered Willard's Hotel, where I had stopped while on my way home from the valley.

"We can't sell any thing to soldiers," said the barkeeper, evidently astonished at our ignorance of the regulations; a group of officers at the counter joining in his stare at my demand.

"Not sell to soldiers!" I exclaimed: "why, you are selling to these," pointing to the officers.

"WE CAN'T SELL TO SOLDIERS."

"Oh! them's officers, not soldiers," he replied.

"Begorra, Frank, but he's roight. They don't look as though they ever saw a picket-skarmish, let alone a rigilar scrimmage," remarked Dennis with a merry laugh.

In the lobby we encountered General Wadsworth, who shook his head good-humoredly on seeing us leaving the bar-room.

"Well, boys, how are you enjoying yourselves? Been after something to drink, I suppose."

"Yes, general: we asked for some ale; but as we are only enlisted men, and do not sport shoulder-straps, we have been refused, though there's half a dozen officers in there already half tipsy."

" Well, well, they won't refuse me, so come along," said the old general in a genial way.

"A bottle of champagne and some glasses," said he to the barkeeper, ignoring the salutes made him by the officers. "Now, boys, here's to General McClellan and his army. You'll like that toast."

"Couldn't have a better one, giniral, if you tried for a week," cried Dennis enthusiastically, as he drained his glass.

"Now, sergeant, I'll bid you good-day. Good luck to you both," said the general; and we finished the bottle.

When the military governor left us we were soon surrounded by the officers, and they began pressing Dennis and myself to join them in more drinking. My comrade was nothing loth to do so, and I had some difficulty in getting him safely away.

In due time we re-embarked; the steamer being ordered to proceed at once to the White House, on the Pamunkey River, the new base of supplies for the army. On our arrival I proceeded to the office of the medical director, delivered my papers, and reported myself and guard.

" H'm, so you came on ' The Elm City ' ? " remarked the surgeon, whose lieutenant-colonel's strap indicated that he was a regular-army officer.

" Yes, sir, just arrived, and I'm anxious to rejoin my regiment as soon as possible."

" You can serve the government, sergeant, as well on the steamer as with your regiment," said the old surgeon rather gruffly.

" Perhaps so, colonel; but I would prefer the latter," was my respectful reply.

" You are highly recommended here for hospital duty, and so are your men. It is not often such a compliment is paid to hospital guards. A soldier must always do as he is bid. You will have to remain on the steamer."

"Very well, colonel. If I must, I must; but my comrades in the field will consider me a skulker."

"Never mind what they think. Do your duty wherever you find it," said the director more kindly.

"All right, sir: I always obey orders."

"That's right: spoken like a man. Now, sergeant, you are made an acting lieutenant: so put aside your rifle for the present, and get a sword from that heap over there. You are in military command of the steamer, and I shall hold you responsible for the maintenance of good order and discipline on board."

I saluted in silence, selected my saber, and returned to the steamer, finding it rapidly filling up with wounded men from the picket-lines. While superintending the reception of the remainder, the crusty old medical director appeared on the temporary wharf, and called me aside.

"Now, I want you to pay particular attention to what I'm going to say," he began. "The surgeon detailed to your steamer is a civilian fresh from private practice, and there are also on board a lot of reckless hospital students. I know very well that as soon as you are fairly down the river, this contract surgeon and his helpers will be itching to operate on some poor devil in their hands. Now, the War Department has very wisely established a rule that no wounded man is to have even a finger cut off unless he gives his own free consent; or unless mortification has set in, when of course it must be done to save his life. I want this rule enforced. Do you understand?" and the old officer's eyes twinkled merrily as he laid a hand on my shoulder.

"Perfectly, colonel. If they make any fuss, or resist my authority, I'll clap them under arrest," I replied, laughing at the fun in prospect.

"Capital! You'll do!" exclaimed the old gentleman, turning on his heel, and marching off with a sturdy step, every inch of him a soldier.

The complement of wounded having come on board, we dropped down the stream soon after sunset. About ten o'clock one of my corporals reported that the doctor was insisting on cutting off a patient's hand, despite the man's protests. Surprised to find the director's warning so soon verified, I hastened to the spot.

Entering the ward between decks, a singular scene met my eyes. There were over two hundred pallets in the ward, which was dimly lighted with common ship-lanterns. Near me I could see many of the wounded men sitting up in the uncertain light, excited by the piteous cries of a poor fellow in the center, who was surrounded by a group of men in citizens' dress; two extra lanterns among them shedding a glow of light around the bed. Bounding forward, I exclaimed, —

"What are you doing? What is all this about?"

"Oh! nothing much," replied the surgeon coolly, turning over the instruments in his case: "we're only going to cut off this man's hand, and he naturally dreads the operation."

"Have you asked his consent?" said I.

"No, they didn't, sergeant; and I don't want it cut off just yet," cried the wounded man, looking piteously into my face.

"Don't you know that amputations can not be performed unless the patient consents, or mortification sets in?" I asked the surgeon.

"Oh! what's the use of all this bother? He don't know what's good for him. It won't take us long. Give him the chloroform, Mr. Meredith," replied Doctor Cole.

"You'll not cut off a leg, or an arm, or a hand, on this boat, unless you get the patient's consent. We shall be at Fortress Monroe to-morrow."

"Why, you have no right to interfere. I am the surgeon in charge."

"We shall see, sir."

"Oh, indeed!" said the surgeon sarcastically.

"Corporal Harrison, bring a couple of men here," said I;

and then turning to the surgeon, continued, "Doctor Cole, I simply obey my orders. I am going to place a special sentinel over this man; and the first person who touches him, except to dress his wound, shall be locked up and kept in confinement until we reach the fort. — Corporal, see that these orders are carried out."

This settled the dispute, and I shall never forget the look of gratitude the patient gave me for my interference. I subsequently learned that his hand was saved by careful treatment,

A SURGICAL OPERATION FRUSTRATED.

though he was of course unfit for military duty. On our way down the river, Doctor Cole and his assistants met me with black and threatening looks, until Dennis became frightened; he of course being ignorant of my instructions.

"I'm afraid, Master Frank, thim hospital divils will be afther making throuble for ye whin we get to the fort," said he, as our steamer forged ahead on entering the broad, clear waters of the York River.

"Don't be alarmed. I know my orders, Dennis."

"By the widder Finnigan's black cat, but I'm glad to hear that! Shure, the byes were all worrying at thinking that that murdhering ould doctor wud get the best of ye."

The next morning we dropped anchor in the Roads, the pilot going ashore in a boat to report. Doctor Cole asked leave to accompany him. On arriving at the dock, both proceeded to the office of the medical director, who also happened to be a regular officer.

"I wish to make a grave and serious complaint against the sergeant who commands the guard on board my steamer," began the doctor pompously.

"Your steamer? Pray, which one is it?" inquired the director quietly.

"'The Elm City.' We have only just arrived."

"Oh! 'The Elm City.' Why, I thought that steamer belonged to the government," replied the director.

"Y-y-es, I know. But I'm the surgeon in charge," explained Doctor Cole confusedly.

"Well, what is this complaint of yours?"

"He interfered, and prevented my performing an interesting operation; and he threatened to lock me up if I persisted."

"An operation? What sort of operation?"

"Why, a hand. There were two fingers badly shattered."

"And the sergeant interfered, did he?"

"Yes, he did; and was very impudent about it too."

"Did you ask the patient's consent?"

"N-no. There was no occasion. How did he know what was necessary?"

"And so, sir, you came here to complain of the sergeant. Confound you, sir! he obeyed his orders, which is more than you seem to do. What the devil do you mean by leaving your patients without permission?" thundered the irate director, staring the dumbfounded contract surgeon square in the face.

"I sup-p-posed it was all right," stammered the doctor, bewildered by the unexpected change in affairs.

"Just like you civilians. Now, sir, get back to the steamer as fast as you can, for she's coming up to the dock in a few moments."

I wondered at the changed demeanor of Doctor Cole on his return, and only learned the cause when our pilot narrated the colloquy between him and the director. The latter laughed heartily over my version of the incident, and seemed to relish the grim humor of his White-House colleague. Annoyed at his defeat, Doctor Cole requested to be transferred to Washington. The new surgeon was a far different man; and while I remained in the Sanitary Commission fleet, I had no occasion to again interfere in behalf of the mutilated victims of war.

On our return up the river we were joined by a party of ladies who had volunteered to serve on board the boats, and our next trip was to Baltimore. The wounded men were all desperately hurt, and several operations were really necessary. One poor fellow made up his mind to lose his arm, and submitted quietly to the chloroform sponge. As it was evening, one of the young ladies undertook to hold a candle for the surgeon. Passing the ward on one of my rounds, I was struck by the picture. The still form of the man undergoing amputation, as it lay stretched on the table; the cool, methodical surgeon, as he stood, knife in hand, rapidly cutting the living, quivering flesh; the silent assistant, holding severed arteries with bloody but steady fingers; the steward with basin and sponge, busily mopping up the red life-stream as it flowed from the gleaming knife, — all these features made a group Rembrandtish in its lights and shadows; while in front of the surgeon knelt the fair-haired girl, watching with blanched cheek and dilated eyes the horrible butchery in progress before her. As I approached, the tired surgeon dropped his instruments with a sigh of professional satisfaction, an announcement that the operation was complete. Then for the first time the candle tottered; and as it fell from the girl's fingers she quietly fainted, lying in a confused heap on the cabin-floor. Bravely had she kept up her courage so long as there was any necessity for it; but the moment the tension was relaxed her womanly nature asserted itself, her physical strength departed.

Many a sad scene was witnessed on the steamer during our frequent trips. A big, strong man was brought on board one day with a bullet buried in his skull. He kept talking continually in his delirium, fighting his battle over and over again. From his reiterated words we gained a clear idea of the scene in which he had been an actor. The charge of the brigade upon the guns, the brief hand-to-hand conflict, the struggle for a cannon, all were depicted in feverish language. At last the bullet completed its fatal work; and death mercifully relieved the soldier of his sufferings, as our steamer was tossed by the wild waters of Chesapeake Bay.

This hospital duty became at length insupportable because of its monotony, and I longed to escape from it. The opportunity came at last. We had just returned to the base of operations, and I was strolling idly through the canvas town erected by the sutlers, when I unexpectedly encountered my colonel.

"What are you doing here, Wilmot? Where have you been all this time?" he asked.

I hurriedly explained my sphere of duty, adding that I was anxious to abandon it.

"Why didn't you come up to the front? There were plenty of trains."

"I thought of doing so once, but found a pass was necessary, even to go to the army."

"Confound this red tape!" muttered Colonel Fletcher. "If you are really anxious, sergeant, to join the regiment, come with me: they won't deny a colonel."

"But how can I leave my post? The medical director trusts me implicitly: I would not like to lose his good opinion," said I.

"Oh! I'll manage that. I will write to the confounded doctor, and explain every thing," replied the colonel.

" All right, sir. I'll meet you here on the platform in half an hour, and bring another of our men with me."

" Do so : you'll not regret it," said he, evidently pleased with my decision.

Returning to the steamer, and telling Dennis to get our rifles and knapsacks, we abandoned the old " Elm City," and never saw her again while in the field. That night I was once more among my comrades, who had wondered what had become of me. But the regiment was sadly changed : many a familiar face was missing; and the ranks were growing slender, for the death-roll was already a long one. The men's faces were bronzed by constant exposure, their bright zouave uniforms faded and torn. The *morale* of the regiment was, however, as high as ever : it was one to be proud of.

CHAPTER IX.

A SAVAGE BOUT.

"Twice hath the sun upon this conflict set,
And risen again, and found them grappling yet."

cCLELLAN'S position had now become one of extreme peril. His attempt to push forward towards the city of Richmond, by throwing a part of his force across the Chickahominy River, had been promptly met by the Confederate leader; the result being the disastrous battle of Fair Oaks. Our general now found himself straddling a marshy stream, with no good line of communication between the divided wings of his army. Massed amid an extensive series of pestilential pools and marshes, the large force still under his control was wholly unable to move with that celerity and precision so necessary for the accomplishment of great results; while the health of the entire command was seriously impaired by its long sojourn in the malarious district. Having advanced so far from his base of supplies, McClellan was compelled to use much of his right wing to protect his communications: the result being, that the main body was sensibly shorn of its strength and effective power. The wretched condition of the roads prevented rapid movement of artillery; and we were in no position to assume the offensive, or even maintain a successful defensive line. The momentum of our advance up the peninsula had been lost; and we felt that the army had been placed in a false position in a tactical sense. Still the army had faith in its general, and obeyed every command with a heroism, which, under more favorable circumstances, would have secured victory and renown for both.

Such was the attitude when I resumed my duties in the regiment. McClellan's left rested upon a morass filled with white oaks, while his right occupied some eminences on either bank of the Chickahominy. Though our left was within a few miles of the James River, neither it nor the Pamunkey afforded any protection to our flanks. Out of the one hundred and fifty thousand men that had composed the army at Yorktown, fully thirty-five thousand had been lost by bullet or disease.

My regiment formed part of the right wing under Fitz John Porter, and lay near Savage's Station. The days and nights passed quietly enough; and I enjoyed the change of scene and duty, for this was soldierly work. True, Dennis and I missed the nicer food of the hospital steamer, and my comrade often grumbled over his hard-tack and coffee when he thought of the flesh-pots he had forsaken, but we were otherwise contented, for both had felt out of place away from the regiment. Besides, we knew that we should soon have plenty of warm work on our hands.

On the afternoon of June 26 the camps were startled by a sudden roll of musketry along our picket-line; and the cry, "We are attacked!" ran through the tents as our bugles sounded the assembly. As I took my place behind my company, a terrific burst of artillery and musket firing broke out towards the ravine called Beaver's Dam; and we knew that McCall's troops were being savagely engaged. The attacking force was evidently a strong one, for the fusillade of small arms increased in volume and intensity every moment; and our artillery now began pouring in a deadly fire of shell and solid shot. As we moved up into position, I could see Sykes's regulars pushing forward through a hollow; and, by the time we had entered the edge of a field of growing wheat, they were forming under the shelter of some woods to the right. Our pickets were already busy, and it seemed quite certain that we would soon receive our share of the assault.

"Close up, men! close up!" shouted Colonel Fletcher, "and stand steady!"

There was no need of the caution, for every man knew the importance of presenting an unbroken front. Just then three or four regiments came up from the left to take ground on our right. As they passed in our rear, evidently a little shaken by the terrific volleys they were apparently approaching, our colonel indulged in a grim bit of humor.

"Attention, battalion!" he shouted. "Parade rest!"

The order was promptly obeyed; though the men laughed to see the regiment thus put through holiday maneuvers in sight of the enemy, with a column of troops so disordered behind us. Our colonel's coolness, however, had its intended effect; for the moving column stiffened up, and passed on in excellent shape to the position assigned it.

But I had no time for further observation of its movements; for at that instant the regulars opened a fierce volley, and we began to see the head of the attacking force as it entered the opposite side of the wheat-field. Like a swarm of angry bees, the Confederates poured out of the woods, and engaged the regulars, who soon found themselves outnumbered. They stubbornly held to their ground, however, until a battery galloped up, and, rapidly unlimbering, opened on Sykes's line with solid shot.

Here came our colonel's opportunity. As yet we had not fired a bullet; and, though the men no longer stood at their absurd parade rest, the line was as steady as if on review. The Confederate battery was firing obliquely across the wheat-field, and their balls were flying away from us. Dismounting, Colonel Fletcher waved his hat over his head, shouting, —

"Forward! double quick!"

We saw what was intended, and with a cheer every man

sprang forward on the run. The battery was scarcely six hundred yards away; and, as we dashed through the standing grain, the left gun was suddenly wheeled about for the purpose of giving us a round of grape. As the gunner withdrew his ramrod, and stepped back to his position by the wheel, our colonel yelled out an order to lie down, at the same moment throwing himself flat upon the ground. We followed his example by instinct, and the next instant the air above us was full of whistling missiles. Scarcely had the report of the

CAPTURING A GUN, — GAINES'S MILL.

gun thundered in our ears when I saw our colors rise from among the wheat-stalks; then the regiment resumed its headlong career.

Before the piece could be reloaded, we were among the gunners, and had it in our possession. Our fellows having been instructed in the use of artillery, several of them seized the gun, and slinging it round sent a charge of grape into the body of Confederate infantry coming up to support their battery. A deadly volley of musketry was their reply, and I saw men falling all around me; Captain Parton, who had commanded the company on the right of ours, lying dead almost under my feet, while the lieutenant-colonel had been carried to the rear badly hurt. We were for the moment in a perilous position; but our wild dash had disconcerted the battery, and checked its fire, thus enabling the regulars to advance, which they soon did in splendid order.

The piece we had captured had been overturned in the confusion, and I could see that our right wing was fighting desperately at close quarters for the one next to it. On seeing the regulars coming up in one direction, and the remainder of our brigade in the other, the battery commander limbered up his four remaining guns, and galloped off to the rear, leaving his right section in our hands.

Our reinforcements did not arrive a moment too soon, however; for, as the battery disappeared, a strong force of infantry advanced. Coming up as they did in the corner of the field, the Confederates found themselves confronted by a cross-fire. Being unable to stand before it, they, too, fell back into the woods. The regulars immediately pushed on, and covered our shattered and disordered ranks. The charge cost us fully one-fifth of our number; but it won for the regiment a fame which was some recompense to the survivors, while our colonel gained a brigadier's star for the action.

But the battle was not yet over; for as we fell back with our prizes I saw bright sheets of flame break out on our extreme right, and run along rapidly towards the rear. It was now getting well on towards evening, and the flashes of the musketry made the darkness appear all the more intense. But what could this wheeling line mean?

"I say, Wilmot!" exclaimed Corporal Foster as we stood watching this fresh outburst, "that looks as though we were being outflanked."

"Impossible, Sam! The enemy surely could not get so far round us.'

" Faix, I dunno," remarked Dennis, leaning thoughtfully on
his rifle : " I'm beginning to belave any thing of thim Ribs.
They're loike Mother Maloney's flea : you never know when you
have 'em safe."

The rolling musketry increased in volume and intensity every
moment, and it was evident that our line was slowly falling
back. Then we saw lines of wounded coming towards us,

THE IRISH BRIGADE TO THE RESCUE.

which seemed strange, as Savage's Station lay in the other
direction.

" Forward, ye divils ! " shouted a Celtic voice in the hollow
below us. Looking down, we saw the Irish brigade, General
Meagher at its head, coming along at a jog-trot. Despite the
gathering darkness, I could see that the men's faces were set as
though they knew that something desperate was in store for
them. As the brigade reached the higher ground, I saw the

general turn in his saddle, and wave his sword over his head. The appeal was answered by a wild cheer; and the brave fellows went forward at a tremendous pace, dashing into the woods where the battle was fiercely raging.

Just at that moment our own brigade was ordered to re-form: but the firing along our immediate front was not heavy, so our regiment lay at the edge of the hollow, comparatively quiet; though it was trying work, listening to the shells of a battery posted on a knoll in our rear, for they were firing over our heads, and riddling the woods on the other side of the fields. The night came; yet the scene was full of light, caused by the rolling musketry and the rapid discharges of the four or five batteries still at work. But, despite its desperate resistance, our line was being overlapped more and more every minute, and the Confederates seemed to be carrying every thing before them.

"This is sad business, sergeant," said Captain Harding: "Savage's Station is in the hands of the Confederates, with all our sick and wounded."

"How about our stores at the White House?" I asked, remembering the immense quantities of supplies I had so often seen on the banks of the river.

"Oh! they're all gone, I suppose. We're cut off from the White House entirely now."

"I knew we would get into a devilish mess among these confounded swamps!" exclaimed Burch, our first lieutenant. "Why we ever came here is more than I can understand."

"That will do, Burch. You are always grumbling," responded the captain. "We might as well be here as anywhere else."

"But wouldn't it have been better to hold on to our supplies?" I asked. "Now we have no base."

"True; but they say we are fighting Stonewall Jackson, who has come in from the Valley," replied Captain Harding.

"Yes: we are like rats in a trap," grumbled Lieutenant Burch in his customary dissatisfied tone.

By this time the troops on our right were rapidly falling back; and soon after the Regulars came up, showing that a general retreat of the entire right wing had really commenced. Then orders came from our brigade to move on. As we did so I looked back, and could distinguish the first line of the enemy coming forward in good style. Just at that moment a column of our cavalry dashed across the plain, and disappeared amid the smoke. Forgetting for the time that my regiment was in motion, I stood still, and watched the result of this last despairing charge. In a few minutes a broken band of horsemen came flying back with ten or twenty riderless animals among them. As they galloped past, I also saw that three pieces of a battery were being abandoned for want of horses to drag them off. Finding that the ground I was standing on was becoming untenable, I ran on and overtook my regiment.

We maneuvered to and fro all that night, sometimes on firm solid ground, sometimes in treacherous swamps. Now and then we were saluted by the Confederate pickets, answering them blindly with scattering volleys. Every thing seemed in confusion: none knew precisely where we were, or where we were going. The miserable roads were choked with cannon, ambulances, and wagons; the denunciations of the drivers, and the shrill cries of the affrighted mules, adding to the horrors of the night scene. So great was the press that it seemed as though every vehicle was locked with its fellow. In many instances the artillery, in attempting to pass these trains, became mired in the soft, soggy earth; sometimes being compelled to abandon a gun as it sank almost out of sight. Even the infantry found it difficult to gain firm footing; and, for my own part, I was soon covered with mud and sand. Moving hither and thither in the darkness, we could hear the piteous cries of our wounded; yet we could not help them, and we knew the next moment might see some of us added to their number.

Just then a new feature was added to the scene, for a bright light had suddenly shot up into the sky.

"What can that be?" exclaimed Corporal Foster.

"It must be the stores on fire at the White House," I replied.

"Quite right, Wilmot," said Captain Harding: "Colonel Fletcher has just told me so."

"Then, we're in a pretty fix. But it's just what I expected," said our first lieutenant.

"Why, Burch, at it again!" laughed the captain.

The flames grew brighter and brighter, until the horizon was red with angry light. It was serious business for us, because the destruction of these stores was proof of the critical position of the army.

Then we began our memorable march to the James River. For seven weary days we fought from early dawn until far into the night, marching from the right to the left, each corps and division going into action after traversing in turn the interior line of the army. In this way the line of battle broke away from the right, and was extended on the left. Battle after battle was fought, until we ceased counting the engagements. Along the ridges and hills we formed in line, and withstood the assaults of our antagonists. We struggled through swamps, and waded swollen streams, as we changed one position for another. Amidst a hellish confusion of sounds we fought on: the shrieking shell, the whistling bullet, the dull booming of distant cannonading, the sharp rattle of musketry a few rods away, the groans of the wounded, the frenzied shouts of wagon-drivers, the blows of ax-men, the crash of falling trees, — through it all we marched and countermarched, hardened in feeling, vengeful at heart, fighting with the courage born of despair.

On the second night, after another desperate struggle, orders came for our corps to cross the Chickahominy River. About eight o'clock my regiment was roused up, and sent on ahead to the bridge nearest the line of battle. We were to keep the column in motion; no man being permitted to halt on the bridge, even for an instant. At ten o'clock the head of our division made its appearance, two other columns crossing on the bridges just beyond a bend in the sluggish stream. For four long hours the troops pressed on, the trains holding the center of the road. With a few torches to define the outlines of the bridge, we stood there, urging on the laggards, or lending a helping hand to some half-wrecked vehicle. Wagons, cannon, pontoons, and ambulances, artillery, cavalry, and infantry, all pushed on, pell-mell, with that painful haste incident to a retreat. As the first faint streaks of dawn reddened the tree-tops, French's division came up at a swinging gait. Scarcely had the rearguard reached the other bank of the river when the engineers began destroying the bridge. We were all safely across, and the army was once more re-united. But we had left our dead and wounded behind us, the ground where they fell being strewn with abandoned weapons.

As our regiment moved away from the bridge in search of our brigade, I felt a pain in my right foot, which became at length so irksome, I was glad to sit down, and ascertain the cause. A spent bullet had torn open the counter of my high laced shoe, and bruised the flesh. When I had been hit I knew not, for the excitement and constant movement had prevented my noticing it before. The bullet was safely embedded between the flesh and leather, and I experienced decided relief on cutting out the bit of lead with my knife. I did not dare to unlace the shoe; for my foot was already so swollen, I was satisfied I should not be able to get it on again. Slipping the battered bullet into my pocket, I limped forward, determined to keep up with the regiment as long as possible. Any amount of physical suffering was preferable to being made a prisoner.

What with the pain of my foot, the constant marching, and frequent halts for battle, the next four days and nights passed like a troubled dream. I knew we were in the reserve line at Cold Harbor, and on the left of the main line at Malvern Hill: I afterwards remembered the incessant cannonading which marked the latter engagement, and that once during that afternoon I was roused by Dennis in time to be on my feet when our brigade opened a withering fire on the enemy. Dennis, indeed, insisted that when he slipped into a treacherous hole among the swamps I saved his life by a timely grip of his arm; but I had no recollection of the incident. Beyond the few episodes already mentioned, all was a blank. Wet through to my skin, without food for days, in an agony of pain, my foot feeling as if imprisoned in a vise, and my shoe filled with sharp, cutting sand, I staggered on, half-crazed, until at length, on the 3d of July, our corps emerged from the woods, and we found ourselves in a broad, open field of standing wheat.

"The James River! The James!" shouted hundreds of voices, the welcome cry being taken up and repeated again and again.

It was indeed the James; and, as we moved across the field, I could see the gunboats lying in the stream. Soon after we had halted for camp, our naval vessels began shelling the woods along our front. Despite my pain, I slept soundly through the night, my foot feeling stronger and easier for the rest. Dennis had been missing nearly all of the previous day; but he now re-appeared, his absence explained by the segment of a ham and a bag of biscuit he triumphantly displayed before my eyes.

"Where did you get them?" I cried hungrily.

"Why, whin I found yesterday there was going to be no more foighting, I made up my moind to forage a bit: so I wint down among the wagons and bought these."

"You are sure you bought them?" said I a little doubtfully.

"To be shure. Troth, I'd 'a' shtole thim if there had bin no other way to get 'em. But I came acrost a countryman of moine, — a Munster man, — and he let me hev the whole for a foive-dollar bill."

"Well, he charged you enough for them, though he was a countryman," I remarked, laughing.

"Och! to the divil wid the money! What does it matter, so

THE GUNBOATS IN THE JAMES RIVER.

long as we don't starve?" replied Dennis disdainfully, as he busied himself getting breakfast ready.

"Sergeant Wilmot, you're detailed for guard-duty at the general's headquarters," said the sergeant-major, coming up, and sniffing at Dennis's broiling ham.

"Guard-duty! Why, it's only a few days since I was there on guard," I exclaimed, annoyed at the unpleasant prospect.

"I know it, Frank; but every sergeant above you on my list has been killed, wounded, or is missing. So your turn comes round again in a hurry."

"Very well; but I am in a bad trim for headquarters duty."

"We're none of us great dandies just now," replied the sergeant-major, glancing at his own soiled uniform. "But what's this you've got for breakfast?"

"A bit of ham and some sutler's biscuit. Sit down and join us, Fitzgerald," said I hospitably.

"That's an invitation not to be slighted. I've not had any thing yet beyond a cup of coffee," replied the sergeant-major, sitting down, and joining in the appetizing meal.

An hour later I was marching with my guard to General Fitz John Porter's headquarters, where I discovered that my command did not number over half the strength of the one I had relieved. I accordingly proceeded to the adjutant-general's tent to ask that the number of sentinels might be reduced.

"I have only forty men, sir," said I; "and there are now over twenty posts. Can't we reduce the line?"

"I am afraid not, sergeant. How came they to give you so few men?"

"I don't know. I took all that were detailed."

"Well, you must do the best you can," said the adjutant.

"It will be awful hard work for the men," said I, turning on my heel to rejoin my command.

"Hold on, sergeant!" exclaimed an authoritative voice. Turning again, I found myself before General Porter.

"I've heard your request. It is a very reasonable one: so

use your own judgment. Cut down the posts to ten if you can."

"Thank you, general. The men will be pleased, and do all the better duty," I replied, saluting, and limping away.

"Here! come back, sergeant," exclaimed the general.

I obeyed, wondering what was the matter now.

"What makes you limp? Are you wounded?"

"I got a spent ball in my shoe, sir, on the other side of the Chickahominy; and it has made my foot very sore," was my reply.

"Has any one examined it?" he asked kindly.

"Not yet, sir. I've not dared to take the shoe off."

"But why didn't you report for hospital?"

"Oh! they would laugh at me with only a broken shoe and a spent ball."

"I don't know about that. It may be more serious than you imagine," said the general. "My surgeon shall look at it by and by."

When the surgeon did come, he announced that gangrene had set in, and tortured me with lunar caustic until I thought my foot was on fire. General Porter sent me a good supper, and the next morning gave orders that I should be carried in an ambulance to Harrison's Landing, where the Sanitary Commission fleet were receiving patients. When the new guard arrived I had a sorrowful parting with poor Dennis, and soon after reached the wharf. Halting before the medical officer to give my name and rank, I saw it was the White-House director from whom Dennis and I had run away. The old colonel recognized me at once.

"Ah, ha! So here you are, Mr. Runaway," he exclaimed in a sarcastic tone. "Well, don't you wish you had staid with me?"

"No, indeed, sir. I would not have missed the late movement for any thing," I replied.

"Don't you think you would have been better off on 'The

Elm City,' than tramping through those dreadful swamps, and coming here with a smashed foot?"

"Perhaps so, colonel; but I prefer the swamps."

"I've a good mind to put you under arrest for deserting your post," he exclaimed with a frown on his face.

"Oh, no, doctor! You only arrest contract surgeons, for trying to cut off a man's fingers," I replied saucily, for I knew he considered the incident a great joke.

"Ha, ha! so I do. Well, sergeant, here's your pass. Now go aboard the steamer, and God bless you, my brave boy!"

That night the steamer dropped down the river; and soon after, I entered on hospital life in Baltimore, not seeing my regiment again for some months.

CHAPTER X.

AGAIN IN HARNESS.

"It was a goodly sight
To see the embattled pomp."

In Camp under the Mountains, Va., Nov. 4, 1862.

EAR WILMOT, — I am glad your foot is getting strong, for we miss you very much. You would have enjoyed our campaign in Maryland if you had come out of it with a whole skin as I did; but our poor regiment has suffered terribly. At Manassas we got into an awful hole, and, out of five hundred and forty officers and men, came off the field with less than three hundred. Adjutant Buford was killed almost at the moment we went into action; for he was struck in the chest by no less than five bullets, while we were all scrambling out of a ditch by the side of the railroad. Captain Wayland got a ball in his brain soon after, and we also lost Lieutenants King and Gellett; while among the wounded were Captain Joyce and Lieutenants Butler, Healy, and Martin. So you see, the recruits they have sent us are very welcome: yet we do not muster more than five hundred even now; for at Antietam and Sharpsburg we lost nearly sixty in killed and wounded, and didn't see much of the fighting either. Poor Beaseley was killed at Antietam by an unlucky bullet; and, as you were away, I had to make Phillips our orderly-sergeant in his place, but that won't stand in your way for promotion. Colonel Fletcher is now a brigadier; and as Lieutenant-Colonel Doran died recently of the wound he got when we charged that battery in the wheat-field at Gaines's Mills, Major

Lloyd is now colonel. Captain Purcell wears the silver leaf of a lieutenant-colonel, and your humble servant is major. Sergeant-Major Fitzgerald is to be adjutant, Lieutenant Dickson is captain of Purcell's company, and that old growler Burch is of course your captain. A whole batch of commissions is expected every day, and General Fletcher sent in your name for a lieutenantcy as a reward for running away from that hospital-ship. But you must be in the field to be mustered in as an officer, so the general hopes you will be able to report for duty before we move again. Come right away, and bring a uniform and sword with you. Dennis Malone was made a corporal yesterday, and is always talking of you. I shall expect to see you in a few days. We go into camp to-morrow, near Warrenton. Yours faithfully,

THOMAS HARDING,
Major —th N. Y. Vols.

To Lieutenant FRANK WILMOT,
    Laight-street Hospital, Baltimore, Md.

I had already become impatient of my hospital confinement; and, as I could now walk about, I had already begun thinking of returning to the regiment. Our surgeon shook his head whenever I spoke of it, and urged me to be patient for a few weeks longer, as my foot was still very tender. The major's kind letter, and the announcement that I was to be promoted, decided the question, however; and I insisted on being allowed to go. Finding me determined, the surgeon put my name on the list of convalescents; and the next day I was on my way to the army.

Arriving at Alexandria, opposite Washington, I found the town bustling with excitement, it being the temporary base of supplies. The streets were full of wagons, and long trains of them were moving toward Fairfax, on their way to the army. At the railroad depot, cars were being filled with ammunition, spare cannon and caissons. Everywhere there was bustle and excitement, and it was easy to see that an important campaign was contemplated. Already I caught the influence of army life, and felt its fascination as strong as ever. Clambering to the roof of a train, I had hardly settled myself for my rough ride, when I found the cars in motion towards Centerville.

Events in the field, both East and West, had moved rapidly during my absence from the regiment. Lee left McClellan as soon as the latter had encamped his troops on the James, and attacked Pope, then holding the line of the Rapidan. Pope made a running fight as he hastily fell back before Lee, from Culpepper to Centerville. Washington being threatened, McClellan was summoned to Alexandria with his army. Though it was impossible to win a victory by the union of two half-demoralized armies, the battle of Manassas was fought in haste, and, being lost, was repented of at leisure.

Flushed by success, Lee then boldly crossed the Potomac, and advanced as far as Frederick City, in Maryland, before any check could be interposed. Stonewall Jackson seized Harper's Ferry with an independent column, the garrison surrendering without firing a shot. Startled by this change in the game, the Government placed McClellan in command of all the Federal forces from the Peninsula and the Virginia Valley, when he undertook to drive the enemy back.

By a clever counter-movement on South Mountain, McClellan succeeded in outflanking Lee, forcing him to fall back to Antietam. So well had McClellan got his troops in hand, that when he gave battle at Antietam his onslaught had a momentum which compelled Lee to retreat across the Potomac. The lack of supplies and clothing prevented the Federals entering upon a vigorous pursuit; but when the commanding general did get his army in condition to move, he at once re-crossed the Potomac, his troops full of courage. However, McClellan had scarcely entered on his projected campaign, when he found himself supplanted by Burnside; and he never entered the field again.

In the West, Bragg started out on a raid through Kentucky, but, being foiled in his advance on Cincinnati, consoled himself by declaring Kentucky a Confederate State. The battle of Corinth had occurred during our advance up the Peninsula, and some progress had been made towards opening the Mississippi. Memphis had fallen, and the Confederate lines were being narrowed. Halleck being summoned to Washington, the command of the Western armies fell on the shoulders of Grant, who now held Corinth, Grand Junction, and Memphis.

But the prospect was by no means an encouraging one; for a new levy of troops had been found necessary, leading to a pernicious system of bounties. Even the Confederates were dissatisfied; as their armies were now tasting of the bitterness of defeat, and the severity of the ocean blockade was beginning to be felt. In fact, both sections were learning that the war would be long and tedious.

Despite the half-wrecked condition of the railroad from Alexandria to Warrenton, my ride to the front was an enjoyable one. As we neared Fairfax, after passing through the line of forts occupying the line of hills near Alexandria, signs of the presence of an army multiplied. Enormous trains of white canvas-topped wagons thronged the stony and hilly roads. Painfully crawling up the steep inclines, or plunging madly into the valleys, these wagons covered the face of the country like a colony of ants, indicating by their numbers the extensive scope of the quartermaster's department. Here and there, nestling among the hills, were encamped detachments of troops employed in guarding the railroad; and on our reaching Centerville, I found more forts, more troops, and a perfect sea of wagons. I was at length in the Virginia Valley, and approaching the outskirts of the army. But, beyond the presence of a few cavalry pickets, which were scattered over the plains of Manassas, I saw no large body of troops until we reached Warrenton Junction. This part of the route was full of interest to me, for it was the first time I had seen the ground since the war began. On leaving Tom Marshall, I had sauntered through this section of the country in tolerably happy mood. Now how changed was the landscape!

The country was destitute of timber; the fences had disappeared; and in many places even the dwellings were gone. The smiling roads I had tramped over, with their hedges full of summer flowers, had been obliterated by the march of armed hosts; and where the plow had turned the furrow for a harvest that was never to be reaped, unsightly earthworks frowned over the barren, deserted scene. The ravages of war were visible everywhere, and thousands of dead men lay only half covered by the earth they had fought over. Even the birds were mute, for the thunders of the battles had driven them to the mountains. Brown, bare, and silent, these desolate plains bore striking evidence of the destructive weight of contending armies.

At length I caught sight of tents, and, looking up the valley towards the Rappahannock River, saw that every bit of rising ground was occupied by troops. At the Junction a few of the convalescents on the train left us to join their commands; the remainder going to Warrenton, where the main body of the army was encamped.

By the time our train cleared the confused group of sheds and tents at the Junction, the shades of evening had begun falling. As the light of day faded away, the darkness was strangely tempered by a subdued glimmer, the reflection of which rose high in the heavens. It was caused by the camp-fires of the great army, like the glow over a distant city. I was indeed approaching a city, — one built of canvas, which at an hour's notice could disappear, only to spring up again miles and miles away.

A sharp turn in the road brought our train out of a belt of woods, and a moment after the immense camp of one hundred and fifty thousand men lay revealed before us.

Viewed from the roof of our swaying car, as it rattled over the rudely laid rails, the scene was a wonderful one, even to me, accustomed to such sights. For miles, as far as the eye could reach, up and down the valley, the troops occupied the land. In broad bands, scattered clusters, or dense masses, the

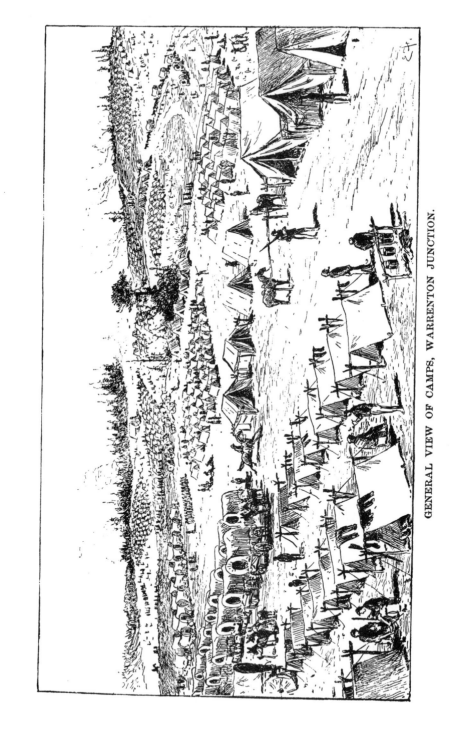

GENERAL VIEW OF CAMPS, WARRENTON JUNCTION.

tents occupied every available bit of ground; and, as every tent was illuminated by the lights within, their outlines were distinctly visible in the gathering darkness. It seemed more like a glimpse of fairy-land than a scene in real life. Thousands of camp-fires lent additional brilliance to the picture; while high above our heads the sky was full of reflected light, which seemed to throw the mountains beyond into deeper and darker shadow. The sounds of many voices filled the air, mingling with the discordant braying of hungry mules, or the more musical neighing of artillery and cavalry horses. Above this confused murmur of sounds, rose the thrilling notes of the headquarter bugles, as they rang out in silvery cadence the usual evening calls; then the monotonous roll of the drums came to my ear, like the bass notes of an organ, as they beat the tattoo. Amidst all these stirring sights and sounds, the train kept on its mad career until the scream of our locomotive-whistle drowned both bugle and drum by its piercing voice, rudely waking me from my reverie to discover that we were entering the town of Warrenton.

On descending to the platform, every bone in my body aching from the effects of my rough ride, I saw it would be difficult to find my regiment in the darkness, so decided to bivouac for the night near the depot. From the drivers who thronged the platform, I learned that the whole army was now massed together, and a general movement daily expected. Wrapping myself in my blanket after a meager supper, I once more slept on the soft earth, waking bright and refreshed early the following morning.

Magnificent as had been the scene over night, the camps were fully as picturesque when viewed by daylight. The sun had just touched the tops of the mountain range, and wrapped them in a mantle of golden light, as I halted on some rising ground beyond the town, and gazed at the wilderness of canvas before me. Right in front lay the tents of my own corps; and, as the mists rose under the warm rays of the sun, they revealed the breakfast fires of the men, while farther on more camps extended until lost in the distance. Noisy as had been the evening, the sounds were now of greater volume and diversity. The bugle and the drum were again active as they summoned the troops to the duties of the hour; and black dots in the landscape betrayed the presence of the assembling companies. Trudging over the dusty road, my heart grew light under the influence of these martial sights and sounds; and I felt a strange feeling of joyfulness at being once more within the limits of the army. The glamour of military life had again fallen on my eyes; and I forgot the cruelty and horror of war in the presence of its pomp and magnificence.

After a walk of nearly a mile, I at length reached our camp, receiving a hearty welcome from my comrades.

The feeling in the army at the sudden removal of General Mc-Clellan, on the eve of a new campaign, was one of great bitterness; for the general possessed that personal magnetism which makes popular leaders. The army entertained a great respect for Burnside, but it was felt that our old commander owed his fall to the machinations of the politicians at Washington. However, we had become seasoned by the heat of battle, and, being soldiers, were content to do our duty under any commander.

To my surprise, the army remained in camp where I had found it, for nearly a week after my arrival; Captain Burch having ample occasion for indulging in his favorite propensity for grumbling.

At last orders came to move; and by the middle of November the entire army was on the march, in three grand divisions, under Sumner, Hooker, and Franklin, arriving a few days after on the banks of the Rappahannock River, near Falmouth. Our pickets reported a strong force of Confederate troops on the other side of the river, and the next day we saw heavy masses occupying the heights beyond the city of Fredericksburg. It seemed foolhardy to attempt the passage of a river in the presence of such an antagonist as Lee, yet that was what our general decided to do.

Two or three days were lost in useless maneuvers, as if to give the enemy ample time to assemble his army, and fortify his position. Finally a feint was made below the town, which came to nothing; the fact being explained by General Fletcher, telling us that there were no pontoons.

"There we go again!" grumbled Captain Burch. "Always some delay. Those confounded pontoons will cost us a thousand lives."

"Yes," said Major Harding; "and when they get you into hospital, I hope they'll mend your temper as well as your body."

The pontoons arriving at last, preparations were made on the morning of Dec. 10 for crossing the river. Scarcely had the pontoon-train made its appearance on the bank, when a furious fire was opened by the Confederate pickets, a few light batteries being also brought into play. Our own artillery then came into action, thus presenting the singular spectacle of a battle being fought across a river for two or three miles of its length. Our brigade was now ordered forward to support and protect the engineers while at work.

We soon reached the place where the upper bridge was being laid: so our regiment was thickly planted in the fringe of bushes along the top of the bank, finding a sharp shower of bullets flying over our heads as we fell into our places.

The engineers went coolly to work, being partially hidden by a fog; and, as boat after boat was launched, it was rapidly placed in position, until it seemed as if the bridge was bodily growing out of the river-bank. Under a galling fire of musketry, these men chopped and hammered as quietly and steadily as they would in a workshop or shipyard; but every few minutes some brave fellow would drop his ax or hammer, and slowly limp away, or be carried off by his comrades. Still the work proceeded with celerity, until it was nearly half-way across.

Then the men found they could no longer stand before the destructive storm of lead that was pouring on the structure. As they retired, the reserve artillery of over one hundred guns began bombarding the city; but even this terrible iron hail did not silence the Confederate riflemen lying so snugly behind the stone wall on the river-bank. Accordingly, a new movement was decided upon: our regiment was to cross the river in boats above the bridge, while another did the same below.

With a wild cheer, our men ran down the cutting that led to the half-finished bridge, and leaped recklessly into the pontoon-boats awaiting us. As we pushed off on our perilous venture, our infantry on the bank behind us began a tremendous discharge of musketry, the batteries on the slopes beyond filling the air above our heads with percussion-shells. This had the desired effect; for the fire of the enemy's riflemen visibly slackened, though frequent cries and groans in our boats showed that it was still effective.

"By the powers above!" exclaimed Dennis, as he crouched at my feet. "This is the worst yit. Whin I 'listed for a soger, it's little I thought I'd ever be a marine."

"Never mind, Dennis," said I: "somebody had to do this. It's an honor for our regiment to be selected."

"The divil fly away with the honor, say I! It's bad enough to be killed by a bullet, but I don't fancy being drownded into the bargain," muttered Dennis in a dissatisfied tone.

The distance from the end of the bridge to the opposite bank was fortunately very short; and as our boatmen verily plied their oars for their lives, we were soon on *terra firma.* As each boat struck the bank, the men sprang into the water, and began clambering up with rigid faces and bloodshot eyes. When my boat came up, I shouted to my men to follow me, at the same instant leaping over the gunwale. In a few minutes more we were at the top of the bank, as with a ringing cheer the regiment drove back the Confederate pickets.

It was sharp work, though, while it lasted; and we could see a column of infantry coming down to meet us. But our supports were prompt in joining us, so we were able to present a tolerably solid front. While we were thus employed, the work

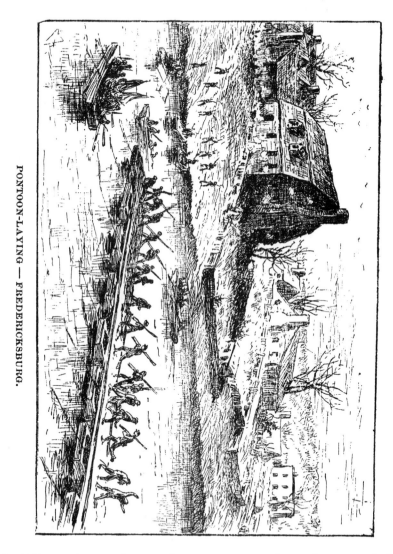

PONTOON-LAYING — FREDERICKSBURG.

of building the bridge had been resumed, and proceeded so rapidly that we soon heard the steady tramp of the advancing columns over its completed span. In half an hour, sufficient troops had arrived to drive in the main line of the enemy, and the number of our forces increased every minute. The river had been seized.

Considering the hazardous duty performed by the regiment, our loss was comparatively light; my company losing only three men, none of them killed, though the companies on the right, which had been the first to cross, suffered more heavily. The dead and wounded were sent back in the returning boats, and word was passed for the men to lie down and rest.

The sun had by this time grown sufficiently strong to dispel the mists, and the slight hoar-frost on the ground also disappeared. The Confederates had evidently abandoned all further effort to prevent our army crossing the Rappahannock, for we now held undisputed possession of the city. Hour after hour I sat on the bank, watching the troops tramping over the bridge, while down the river I could see the other grand divisions moving across. Seeing these thousands of brave men advancing to do battle, I thought of those who would never return; for many of them were fated to find graves on the slopes beyond the town. But they were all in high spirits, laughing and joking with one another as if going to a frolic instead of a deadly engagement.

By two o'clock that afternoon the entire army was over the river, and our pickets were savagely at work outside the limits of the city. The field-batteries that had come over with their several corps were now taking up position on the right and center; while the tremendous mass of heavy artillery assembled in front of Falmouth was again beginning to thunder, sending a perfect storm of shells into the enemy's lines.

We were not slow to understand the tactics of our opponents; for already the heights back of the city were alive with men busily intrenching themselves, the tops of the range of hills frowning with batteries. To face such a line of fire would be a terrible task: still our army coolly prepared itself for the ordeal. As the sun was nearing the horizon, our brigade was called up, and we marched through the streets of Fredericksburg.

Long lines of wounded men were passing to the rear, and the frequent relays of hospital stretchers attested the severity of the conflict already begun. A continuous roll of musketry sounded sullenly on the left; and then we heard a faint and distant cheer, as though some advantageous position had been seized. Beyond this we knew nothing of the results attained. Every house in the city had been abandoned by its inhabitants, the streets being littered with fragments of household property, evidence of the haste with which the residents of the unhappy town had endeavored to save something from the threatening destruction. Shells were falling everywhere, both from our own and the Confederate batteries; crushing in roofs, overturning chimneys, shattering windows, and filling the air with dust and flying splinters. In one street a house had caught fire just before we came up; and a party of pioneers were fighting the flames, which were, however, quite beyond their control.

"Halt!" cried Colonel Lloyd in obedience to a signal given by an officer standing in the street. While we were wondering at the order, a column of white smoke suddenly enveloped the burning house, followed by an explosion. Then we saw the entire building rise in a mass, flying a second after into a million fragments.

"Faith, an' that's the way they do the blasting on the avenoo," exclaimed Dennis, as loquacious as ever. "But it's the first toime I ivir saw a house blown up with gunpowdher."

At that moment we heard our colonel's voice, urging us forward. With a fierce cheer we dashed over the burning wood, and, entering a side street, marched until we were nearly clear of the town. There had been some mistake, however, for we came to a position already occupied by troops: so the brigade faced about, and, turning down a narrow lane, started towards the right near the river-bank. This movement brought our regiment in the rear of the column. As we were about entering the lane, an aide came tearing up the street, wildly gesticulating with his sword as he leaned over his horse's head.

"Halt! halt!" he cried on coming within speaking distance. "For God's sake, colonel, bring your regiment, and follow me."

The order was promptly obeyed; and away we went after the staff-officer, wondering what new peril was threatening. As we reached the main street leading to the bridge, I caught sight of a mob of men running disorderly towards us down the hill. It was a panic-stricken regiment.

"Stop them! for Heaven's sake, stop them!" exclaimed the aide hoarsely. "Stop the cowards, if you have to shoot them down!"

"Halt!" shouted our colonel in a stern voice. "Fix bayonets!"

The rattle of steel was heard, and the men without further orders gathered in solid line to receive the fugitives. I now saw that it was one of the new regiments; and I noticed a mounted officer, probably their colonel, riding in the midst of the mass, slashing furiously right and left with his saber.

Those who were in the advance saw our leveled bayonets barring their passage to the river; but it was too late for them to stop, the pressure behind being so great, that, despite efforts of our men, several of the dazed fools were impaled on the rows of glittering steel. For a second our column of veterans gave way before the impact of the flying regiment, but soon recovered its ground, and the disgraceful rout was checked.

The colonel, evidently an old army officer, was fairly beside himself with rage, and continued to ply his saber savagely on the heads of his men, as he bitterly cursed their cowardice. Finally he dropped the point of his sword, and burst into tears.

"My God! I'm disgraced for ever!" he exclaimed in a choking voice. "Curse you, for a lot of cowardly curs! You deserve to be led out and shot, every man of you."

"How did this happen?" asked Colonel Lloyd. "Why did they break in this shocking way?"

"I had just got them into line with the rest of our brigade," replied the discomfited commander, "and we were advancing in tolerably fair shape, when a shell burst over the battalion on our left, and knocked over a score of men. At sight of this my left company wavered, and, before we could check them, finally broke, and ran towards the rear. The whole regiment followed suit, like a flock of sheep going over a wall. If you hadn't happened to be at hand, I doubt if they would have stopped this side of the river."

"Well, don't be discouraged," said Colonel Lloyd: "it's their first fight, I suppose. When they really get under fire they will do well enough."

"Curse them! Only let me get the cowards fairly within range, and I'll take them into the very jaws of that hell yonder!" exclaimed the old veteran impetuously.

"Colonel, the general wishes you to bring your regiment back to the line," said another aide, riding up.

"How the devil am I to get them there? They'll be all running away again."

"I'll help you," replied Colonel Lloyd quietly. "Just you start them, and we will follow."

By this time the routed regiment had partially regained its formation; the men apparently beginning to be ashamed of themselves, for they listened to the vituperations of their officers in abject silence. Obeying the command of their colonel, the battalion broke into column and marched up the hill, we following at a short distance.

I could not help pitying the poor fellows in the ranks, for they were evidently destined to be severely punished for their conduct. By stampeding, many a man now moving toward the battle-field had sealed his own death-warrant; for I knew very well that the regiment would be pushed forward without mercy.

Entering a side street, the disgraced regiment moved out over the field beyond the town, marching in tolerably steady order towards the position assigned it. On, on, it went. A gap in the line opened, but the doomed battalion passed through. A fierce volley of musketry burst from the low foot-hills, and I saw the regiment begin to melt before the terrible storm of bullets. The colonel waved his sword a second, then reeled in his saddle, and fell dead beneath his horse's feet. It was a terrible example, but a necessary one; but sad to see so brave a colonel sacrificed for his men.

Colonel Lloyd now gave an order, and we started back to find our own brigade, but were again stopped by instructions to act as a sort of provost-guard in the streets of the city; the battalion being soon scattered by detachments, busily employed in protecting property and driving stragglers towards the front.

The firing along the main lines had now greatly slackened, and it was evident that some change was being made in the disposition of the assaulting columns. Heavy bodies of infantry were seen moving towards the extreme left, while others reinforced the center under Sumner. It grew dark soon after, and though the troops were in constant motion far into the night, they moved in silence, the only sounds that came to the ear being the pattering shots of the opposing pickets, as they kept up an aimless fire amid the darkness.

Our company was now summoned to escort some prisoners to the rear, so we saw no more of the army until it had retreated across the river. We were thankful for our escape, though our captain grumbled as usual because we had missed the disastrous engagement which shattered the army and drove its general from his command.

CHAPTER XI.

A FEINT.

"Behold in awful march and dread array
The long-extended squadrons shape their way."

URNSIDE had been succeeded by Hooker, and the winter had passed quietly. The woods and forests which had hidden the corps and division camps when first established had now all disappeared, for the axes of the soldiers had swept away every tree and shrub for their fires. The entire country was bare, not even the shade-trees in the fields being spared. Barns, out-houses, fences, trees, all were gone: even the gardens were obliterated. The ravages of war had withered every thing.

With the beginning of February, signs of a new campaign became visible. Supplies of every kind poured into the lines of the armies, the hospitals were rapidly emptying, and the ranks of the regiments filled up amazingly. Then the grand review — the usual prelude to a general movement — took place.

It was a clear, warm morning when our brigade started for the rendezvous of the army on the plains of Falmouth, opposite Fredericksburg. On our arrival, we found the entire command on the ground, preparing for the review. The plateau selected sloped gradually to the river, with here and there a few slight dips in the ground on the right. The cavalry were in front ranged in solid masses, by regiments and brigades; and as our regiment took up its allotted position, I saw that the infantry to the right and left were rapidly forming in like order. There were four lines, two corps in each; the regiments standing like blocks with their colors in front, while the batteries of artillery were placed in the open spaces between the divisions. Our brigade happening to be stationed on the highest point to the left, I could see the whole army as it stood marshaled in grand array, on a plain fully two miles square.

The sun was shining bright and warm as orders came for the men to rest, the slight breeze being just sufficient to stir the heavy silken folds of the regimental colors as they waved in their tattered elegance. It was a scene for the genius of a Vernet, with all its martial glory, and wealth of color. The bright rays of the sun flashing on a hundred thousand bayonets and sabers, as they were moved at the word of command; the picturesque field-batteries, the dashing cavalry, and the long, dark lines of infantry; the parti-colored banners of the corps, division, and brigade commanders, bearing their strange devices of star, crescent, and cross,—were the salient points in this living, animated picture. It was war in all its pomp and circumstance; and as I watched the sunlight play in dalliance on the burnished steel of gun-barrel and bayonet, or followed with curious eye the passage of the clouds, throwing their soft shadows over the assembled host as the breeze carried them swiftly over our heads, I began to feel all that warm delight and enthusiasm that comes so naturally to a soldier at a time of holiday and parade. Here was a mighty army, ready for combat and campaign, marshaled in all its massive strength and power. As my eye wandered over the striking scene, my cheek glowed at the brilliance of the scene and the magic of the hour; though I knew this grand review to be but the prelude to a long summer of fatigue, danger, and privation.

We had arrived about the hour of noon; and, so well timed were all the arrangements, there was no confusion, no hesitation. Regiments and brigades and divisions formed with a pre-

REVIEW BY PRESIDENT LINCOLN—FALMOUTH, OPPOSITE FREDERICKSBURG.

cision due to long practice and perfect discipline, so that the several corps fell into line with marvelous rapidity. As we thus prepared for the final ceremony, I could see on the heights beyond Fredericksburg (which a few weeks before we had vainly tried to win) long brown lines. It was the Confederate Army of Northern Virginia gazing at its opponent in the field. There, no doubt, were the eyes of Lee, of Longstreet, and of Jackson, all fixed upon us. Seldom has an army moved in review before such spectators. There was no battle threatened, though the two armies were face to face. We were enjoying the brighter side of military life: the darker aspect was to follow in the near future. Let us enjoy our holiday while it lasts. In a few weeks we must meet those brave men in butternut, in a death-struggle. Both armies were equally brave; and while the one paraded to receive the President, the other watched with curious eyes the splendor of the pageant unfolded before it. As I leaned on my sword, waiting for the signal that was to tell us that the review had commenced, I wondered if Tom Marshall was on those heights; and my thoughts wandered back to the happy days in the Valley, and I saw again the old homestead, the sweet, saucy face of Kate. Thus meditating on the past, and the change that had taken place, I was recalled to the duties of the present by the report of a field-piece. It was the signal.

On the extreme left of the front line I had noticed a tall flag-staff, from which fluttered a huge ensign. As the sound of the gun died away, the flag fell and rose again. Then we saw the flash and smoke of another cannon; and, as its booming came to our ears, a third was fired. An aide now went galloping along the front of the cavalry. Next the bugles sounded the "boots-and-saddle" call, and I saw the eleven thousand horsemen mount their steeds. Scarcely had the lines grown steady, when a battery stationed near the river began firing the national salute. On the instant we heard a hoarse command, and a broad flash of light swept along the cavalry corps as the men drew their swords from their scabbards. Amid the smoke of the saluting battery, I saw a tall figure on horseback ride toward the center of the line. It was the President; and at his side rode an officer we knew to be General Hooker, while behind them galloped his brilliant staff. As the President rode forward, color after color fell in obedience, and now and then a solitary sword dropped as the generals tendered their salutes. On, on, galloped the brilliant *cortége*, until the rolling ground hid it from our sight.

Then the infantry bugles began their clamor, and our lines grew rigid. When the President came riding back, there were more flashes of light as the brigades presented arms, and the colors waved tumultuously in the increasing breeze. Up one line and down the other galloped the chief of the people, and I could distinguish Mr. Lincoln's face as he drew nearer and nearer our line. To the shrill note of bugle, and the measured roll of drum, our corps now stood ready to give salute.

" Present — arms ! " cries our colonel hoarsely ; and, as the men's muskets pass from their shoulders to the front, I lower the point of my sword, and for a moment see a tall form crowned with a high black hat, and an erect soldierly figure, gallop past, side by side ; and now the staff go thundering by.

"Shoulder — arms ! " and the men remain like so many statues, until I hear the clatter of hoofs behind us. As these sounds die away, the order to rest is again given, and we watch the closing scenes. By and by the cavalry get into motion, wheel swiftly into column, and begin counter-marching to the left. Next the lines of infantry break into column; and an hour after our own turn comes, and we are in motion. As we reached the route of marching review, I could see, over the heads of my men, a long line of troops extending over two miles in the distance, moving toward the reviewing stand. At length we come to a signal-flag. We are approaching the President as he waits to see the army march by in solid, impressive array.

"Guide right, shoulder arms!" cries our colonel over his shoulder; and a minute after our regiment pushes forward with steady, swinging step. Following our colonel's example, I drop my sword in salute, and once more catch a glimpse of the President's face as he raises his hat in honor of our tattered, faded colors. Then comes the order to quicken our steps; and, as we dash on at a headlong pace, we know the review is at an end for us.

The days lengthened into weeks, until at midnight of an April Sunday we learned that the long-contemplated movement would begin at daybreak. The campaign had at length commenced, and the troops were in high spirits as they prepared for the march. Extra ammunition and ten days' rations were served out: so we knew that it was a long and fatiguing march we were entering on.

We were on the road by three o'clock, and kept moving forward, with few halts, until four in the afternoon; having by that time reached the summit of a hilly ridge we recognized as leading to the fords on the upper Rappahannock.

"I say, Wilmot, I'll have to sup with you to-night, for that confounded pack-horse of mine is somewhere in the rear."

"All right, major: you are quite welcome," said I.

"I come to you, Frank, for I know you are always well provided," continued Major Harding, throwing himself beside the little fire where Dennis was cooking supper.

"Shure, major, ye know ye're quite welcome," said Dennis. "But we've only got some fried bacon and an omalate to offer ye."

"Bacon and omelet! why, Dennis, that's a supper fit for a general, let alone a poor major who has lost his baggage. But how in the name of wonder, Wilmot, did you manage to carry eggs on this hurry-scurry march of ours to-day?"

"Oh! I know nothing about it," I replied. "I am so accustomed to Dennis's surprises that I positively forgot to inquire. — How did you manage, Dennis? Tell the major all about it."

"Well, ye see, major dear, whin thim ordhers came for us to move last night, I had just been down to the sutler's and got three dozen eggs; and as the leftinant and me only ate a dozen for our breakfast at daybreak, why, I saved the rest for our supper;" and here Dennis gave his frying-pan a turn, believing that he had fully explained the whole matter.

"But how did you save them, corporal? You couldn't carry two dozen eggs in a haversack over twenty miles without breaking them all," persisted Major Harding.

"Shure, I broke every one of 'em before starting: they carried safe enough after that," replied Dennis.

"Will you never come to the point?" said I. "What do you mean by breaking eggs and carrying them afterwards?"

"Well, ye see, leftinant darlin', I broke the eggs in a pan, and thin poured them into a canteen, and our march stirred them up illigantly for the omalate;" and, as Dennis spoke, he gave the mess a clever toss in the air to turn it.

"Who but an Irishman would have hit on a plan like that?" remarked the major, taking the boiling coffee-pot off the fire.

"It's glad I am, major, that you think all Irishmen aren't fools," said Dennis, dishing up the rude omelet.

"Fools!" replied the major, "I never saw an Irish fool in all my life. No, Dennis, Irishmen are far from being fools; though I must say they lack wisdom sometimes."

"That's what they used to call at school a distinction without a difference," said I. "But come, let us eat Dennis's canteen omelet before it gets cold."

"An don't be afraid of it. Shure, there's more left where it come from," added Dennis.

"Well, major," said I, after we had discussed our supper, "what does this movement mean?"

"It's intended to be a secret at present. But enough has leaked out to show that it is a flank movement on Lee's position. We are to be joined at the ford above by the Eleventh and Twelfth Corps."

THE MARCH TO CHANCELLORSVILLE.

"A flank movement, eh? Then, that accounts for our early start and this hurried march, our small supply-train, and so many rations on the men's shoulders."

"Yes," assented the major; "though it don't explain the absence of my pack-horse."

"Oh! never mind: he'll turn up in the morning."

"I hope so, for we are to make a bold push to reach the Rapidan."

"The Rapidan! why, we can scarcely do that."

"We must. General Fletcher said those were the orders. We are to cross the Rappahannock at Kelly's Ford, and then make a forced march to the other river. If we succeed in doing what is laid down for us, Lee will be surprised in more ways than one."

"I hope so," said I. "It would be a splendid stroke."

"Yes, indeed. But I'll bid you good-night, Frank: I'm in command of the pickets to-night."

The corps was roused without sound of bugle or drum before daylight the next morning; and as the sun began reddening the eastern horizon, we were already on the road. We made a long and painful march that day, over a rough and stony road; finally halting at nightfall a mile or two below Kelly's Ford. Our start the third morning was not so early; but we reached the ford by nine o'clock, finding the other corps already across the river, and waiting for us to join them.

As we descended the long winding road down the hill towards the pontoon-bridges, I saw that the column was a complete army in itself. Besides the three corps of infantry, I could discern a strong force of cavalry in the advance; and we passed some of the reserve artillery as we stumbled down the steep incline. Here were, at least, fifty thousand men of all arms: so the movement was indeed an important one. Hurrying across the frail bridge, our corps was soon bivouacked in the fields reserved for us.

While the men were thus resting, Gen. Meade made his

appearance at the head of his staff. When the men of his old corps caught sight of their commander, they greeted him with a joyous cheer. As the hurrahs rose in the still morning air, they were caught up by the other corps, and repeated with vigor. The general seemed surprised at first, but, soon recovering himself, spurred his horse forward as if to escape the enthusiasm of his troops; but the act only intensified the ardor of the welcome. The gray-haired and spectacled veteran then rose erect in his stirrups, rode proudly through the surging lines, and, lifting his cap high above his head, galloped bareheaded out of our sight. The scene vividly recalled the McClellan days to my mind.

But there was no time for cheers or ovations; for, soon after our general disappeared, the entire force was put in motion. Our corps was destined to strike Ely's Ford, the other two being headed for the Germanna. The distance across the tongue of land lying above the junction of the Rappahannock and the Rapidan was scarcely twelve miles: so we reached the latter stream by sunset, halting in the stony road for our pontoon-train to come to the front. The stream proved too strong for our frail canvas boats, so the idea of a bridge had to be given up. Orders were accordingly passed along the line for the men to prepare to wade the river, swollen though it was. The scene that ensued was a hilarious one. Officers and men marched sturdily into the river, until nearly all were breast high in the cold water; being compelled to hold their weapons, ammunition, and food above their heads.

It was quite dark when our brigade began crossing. Laughing and shouting to each other, the men plunged into the icy water as though they were schoolboys on a frolic. There were no lights to illumine our watery path; and as I waded I thought of Bunyan's description of the River of Death — but here Death stood waiting on the other side of the river. Many a man now laughing merrily was destined to fill a soldier's grave in the tangled woods beyond.

It was very cold as we emerged from the water, and clambered up the steep and slippery bank: so our general was compelled, despite the needful secrecy of our movement, to permit fires, in order that his men might be in condition to fight on the morrow. We had gained a foothold, however; and, as our presence must be revealed at daylight, a few hours made but little difference.

Gathering fence-rails and brush-wood, the troops built big

CROSSING ELY'S FORD, RAPIDAN RIVER.

fires, and danced merrily in the grateful heat. Wild shouts and occasional cheers made the night air vocal; and as I stood drying my clothes I could see by the lurid light of our fires that the remainder of the corps was still making the passage of the river, it being midnight before the rearguard got across. Up the river there was more light, showing that the other corps had also been compelled to ford the stream.

Finding my uniform thoroughly dried, I followed Captain

Burch's example, and wrapped myself in a blanket for sleep. But the men were too excited for rest, and they gathered round the fires discussing the movement.

"I tell ye what it is, b'yes," exclaimed Dennis, — "ould Meade's a trump. Won't Lee wake up in the mornin' whin he hears our guns bangin' away at his back door!"

"You're right, corporal," replied Sergeant Foster. "But I'm afraid they'll see our fires."

"Well, an' fhat if they do? Shure, Hooker will be moving in on their front. Thin we'll have the Ribs between us."

"Of course the main body will be moving. But if those bridges hadn't failed us we would not have needed those fires," replied the sergeant.

"Arrah! thin we'd have missed our hot coffee," said Dennis.

"Bother your coffee!" retorted Foster. "Wouldn't it be better to lose our coffee and make a complete surprise?"

"Stop that talking," exclaimed Captain Burch pettishly. "You men had better go to sleep instead of bothering your heads about our general's plans."

"All right, captain darlin': shure, won't we find it all out in the morning?" said Dennis; having, of course, the last word, as he coiled himself before the fire, and lapsed into silence and slumber.

The fires began to smolder, the darkness grew heavier; and I finally fell asleep with the shouts of the artillerists and wagon-drivers sounding in my ears as they urged their horses and mules through the river. When I awoke again the sun was shining bright and warm above the trees.

CHAPTER XII.

FOREST STRATEGY.

" Attempt the end, and never stand to doubt :
Nothing's so hard but search will find it out."

 HEN our column got in motion, after a hurried breakfast, we found the road from the ford in the possession of the artillery and our trains : so we pushed bodily through the tangled undergrowth on either side. After struggling forward for an hour the corps emerged from the labyrinth of vines and creepers into a dilapidated plank-road, which intersected the dense woods on a line as straight as an arrow for two or three miles ahead. Passing a cluster of half-ruined houses, known as Robertson's Tavern, we pressed on until late in the afternoon, when the command was ordered into bivouac among some young oak-woods. By this time we had lost all trace of our bearings. As yet there were no signs of the enemy, so the situation was becoming both exciting and interesting.

The next day was Friday, the first of May, and the fifth since we had broken camp at Falmouth. It was evident that the expected battle would soon occur ; for our movements were now slow, and marked with caution and deliberation. We were early on the move, marching slowly up the road for a mile or two, when we suddenly entered the fields around the Chancellor mansion, where I learned General Hooker had established his headquarters. Here we found the Second Corps massed, and General Fletcher informed us that the Third would probably be up before dusk.

"Then this is the main body of the army," I remarked.

"Yes," replied our brigadier. "Being largely reinforced, we have changed positions."

"But, general, I thought we were to attack Lee on his flank."

"That was the intention when we crossed the river," replied the general. "But something has changed the plan."

"We seem to have wasted much valuable time since we reached this side of the river: why is it?"

"Wiser heads than yours have asked that question, Wilmot. Even generals do not understand it."

The column now began moving across the open ground, and our brigadier spurred forward to his position in the line. Turning sharply to the left, we passed the Chancellor House. On the piazza stood General Hooker, his clean-shaven face wearing that look of supreme confidence so characteristic of the man. Leaning against one of the pillars the general watched our corps march past; but he received no greeting from the men, for there was a feeling in the ranks that a valuable opportunity had been lost. Citizen soldiers are quick to perceive errors and resent them; for when men come out to fight for principle they want no experiments, and will not tolerate indecision or timidity on the part of their leaders. The army had begun to doubt its general, so it was not surprising to see a corps pass him in silence. Once across the fields, we entered a road that pierced a bit of woods on the right, soon after crossing a marshy creek, and again came into some open country.

As the head of our division emerged from the woods, I saw a few dots of smoke, and knew from the sound of the dropping shots that our line of skirmishers were going into action. In the hollow just behind them I noticed the first division under Griffin forming in regular line of battle. General Sykes, our division commander, then galloped forward to select our position, we following him on the run. Scarcely had we quickened our footsteps than the guns of a Confederate battery opened a rapid fire on our advancing column from the edge of the woods at the other end of the fields. At first we received shells, which flew high above our heads; but finding the distance too short they sent us solid shot, almost at point-blank range.

Whiz! whiz! whiz! went the iron balls; and a dozen heads near me involuntarily ducked as the flying missiles flew close. Bang, bang! whiz, whiz! now the shot came faster and faster; but they did no harm, so the men trotted along with steady, rapid step. At last the gunners got the range. As our regiment passed over a rise in the road, I saw that the shots had taken effect ahead, for there were several men down; and when we reached the spot where the balls had plunged through the ranks of the leading brigade, there were six or eight men lying dead in the roadway, and twice as many writhing in the ditches on either side. But it was no time for faltering, so on went the division at a headlong pace.

As we passed these dead and dying men, our brigade left the road, and began forming in line of battle in the field; the woods on our right being occupied by more troops. It now looked as if we were going to engage the enemy in earnest; for the skirmishers were firing furiously, and our batteries began shelling the woods in front.

"Halt! Lie down!" cried Colonel Lloyd, as he caught the call from our division bugler. We willingly obeyed the order, for our sharp run down the road had winded the men. The rest was of short duration, however: for the lines in the woods on our right began to move forward; and our leading division advanced steadily across the fields, closely following the skirmishers, who seemed to be rapidly driving in the Confederate pickets. We were soon called to our feet again, and the line marched forward in support; the third division coming down the road and taking position behind us.

"Lieutenant Wilmot," said Major Harding, as he galloped

along the rear of our regiment, "the colonel desires you to take a few men, and set fire to that hut by the roadside: General Fletcher thinks it helps the enemy's batteries to get our range. Be quick about it, for those confounded guns are doing a great deal of mischief."

"All right, sir: I understand," was my reply as I summoned three or four files to fall out of the ranks. Though I had purposely omitted calling Dennis, I was not surprised to find him at the head of my little party, as we ran towards the hut.

"I didn't call you, corporal. Why did you come?" I asked.

"Av coorse ye didn't. Shure, didn't ye know I'd come widout callin'?" replied Dennis naïvely.

"You should always wait for orders. You are constantly doing the wrong thing."

"Arrah, leftinant darlin'! don't be angry wid poor Dinnis. Don't ye know I'd walk through fire and water to sarve ye?" And the cunning fellow spoke in the wheedling way he always adopted when found fault with.

I said no more, finding it useless; though I felt provoked, for it had become a recognized fact in the company, that, wherever Lieutenant Wilmot went, Corporal Malone was sure to be near at hand.

We had only a short distance to go, and on reaching the hut of course found it empty and deserted. It had evidently been a negro-cabin, for there was only one room with a sort of rude loft overhead. The logs composing the walls were old and dry; and my men busied themselves in collecting some broken fence-rails, to build a fire near the chimney. Standing in the doorway, watching the progress of the work over Dennis's shoulder, I was startled by a sudden crash on the roof, — a few of the rafters and rough shingles tumbling about our ears.

"Marciful powers! An' what was that?" exclaimed the corporal, ruefully rubbing his cheek, which had been struck by a piece of a broken rafter.

"It was another of those troublesome round shot," said I.

"The general was right in thinking this shanty a fair mark. Hurry up, boys, and get a fire going."

"Begorra! an' if that ugly bit of iron had come in at the windy instead of the roof, some of us wud be dancing a jig by this time," remarked Dennis.

"Or lying dead on the dirt floor," said I. "But there, that will do. The logs are in a blaze. Come, men, let us join the regiment."

Scarcely had my party emerged from the hut, when we heard another cannon-ball go whizzing through the air, followed by a crash which told us it had struck the blazing hut. This time the projectile had hit the side wall, and torn a ragged gap between the logs. It was a narrow escape. We had left the hut just in the nick of time.

"The saints presarve us, but we'd the blessed own luck that toime!" exclaimed Dennis as we all involuntarily shuddered, and gazed at the shattered wall. "Troth, an' that hole will make an illigant draught for the fire, anyhow."

"The deuce take you, Dennis!" said I, laughing. "Only an Irishman would have thought of that. We have had a lucky escape, men, and must now overtake our regiment as soon as we can; for here comes the third division on our heels."

But there was no need of any hurry: for before we reached our command the line had halted, and did not advance any farther; the evident intention being to make a feint in strong force, and so maneuver for position. The artillery-practice continued for half an hour on both sides, with very little result in casualties, and then slackened until only two or three of our guns were at work. While leading my party back to the regiment, we had passed over the abandoned position of a battery belonging to Gen. Griffin's division; the deep furrows cut in the sward by the wheels of the pieces showing that it had been in action there. A broken caisson lay on the ground, and the dead body of an artillerist beside it told the story of a Confederate shell. The sight presented by the torn and disfigured corpse was a horrible one, but we had no time to reflect upon the man's fate.

After reaching our places in the ranks, there was a great deal of marching to and fro, to very little purpose as it seemed to us; and it was quite dark when we were given an opportunity to rest, finding ourselves among some young pines towards the left of the fields. The men contented themselves with a few of their crackers, no fires for coffee being permitted. After waiting for over an hour, we received orders to fall back to the creek we had crossed during the day; and on reaching it the corps formed in line along its banks, the others marching to the rear, straight up the road to the top of the hill, on the crest of which they began erecting a strong line of breastworks.

"There'll be no coffee for us, Master Frank," said Dennis, as he sat beside me after our line had been formed.

"Of course not," I replied. "We can not have fires: they would reveal our position."

"Well, if we can't have hot coffee, we'll be contint wid cowld chocolate," responded Dennis mysteriously.

"What do you mean now, Dennis? Some more of your commissariat surprises?"

"Shure, a cracker and a chunk of chocolate cake will be better than nothin'. I've got a bit in my haversack I saved for a rainy day like to-night;" and Dennis handed me a generous share of the cake.

"Upon my word, Dennis, you're a genius! This couldn't be improved. I really don't know how I should fare if it wasn't for you."

"Oh! I'm a janius, now, am I?" replied the corporal in an injured voice. "Than, why the divil do ye always be a-scoldin' av me because I always thry to kape near ye, loike this afternoon whin we burned down that artillery target of a hut?"

"Well, well. I'll not find fault with you any more, Dennis. But now that you are a corporal, I don't think it quite right for you to be my cook. You know I can not induce you to accept payment for the service."

"An' is it money ye wud offer me? Don't ye always pay for the extras we get, and haven't I the same as yersilf? Share and share alike was yer own words. Troth, Master Frank, an' I'd often go hungry, as the rest of the boys sometimes do, only for you."

"Oh! if you balance the account in that way, I've no more to say. But what's this? You have two haversacks now. One seemed enough this morning. Where did you get the other?"

"Why, I stumbled against it down the road, a bit; an' it's half full of sugar."

"And are you going to keep it?" I asked.

"How the divil can I foind the owner now?" he cried. "It's an officer's, because there's so much sugar. As for kapin' it, there's Bobby Wilson, he lost all his coffee and sugar whin we wint swimmin' in the river. I'll give him half of it, and share the rest among the boys. But I'll kape the shpoon, though."

"Ah! there's a spoon, is there?"

"Yis; an' an illigant silver shpoon it is too; an' it's got one of those things on the handle, we used to see on the quality's coaches in dear ould Dublin."

"I suppose you mean a crest?"

"Yis. That's it. There's a crown wid a shield undher it."

"A crown! Then it's an old relic. Was probably picked up in Fredericksburg last December."

"Maybe so," replied Dennis; "but I got it in the road, so I'll kape it."

At that moment Colonel Lloyd walked along the line, cautioning his officers to keep their men awake, but silent. He also directed that the men put their knapsacks on. This was proof to us that an attack or a movement was anticipated.

As I lay on the carpet of decayed leaves, I could hear the men whispering among themselves, their half-distinct words making the enforced silence all the more oppressive. Two hours passed; and I was almost forgetting the order about keeping awake, when Dennis clutched my arm.

"Hist, leftinant! Didn't you hear any noise?"

"No. Did you?"

"I thought I heard a twig snap, beyant there, across the creek."

"You must have been half asleep, Dennis, like myself. A broken twig don't signify much."

As I spoke, however, the sound of a man slipping and floundering into the water could be distinctly heard.

"There, now!" exclaimed Dennis, "I knew it was a man."

"It must be one of our stragglers trying to find the road," I replied.

"Now, yeou uns! North Carry-lin-ians, there! From fower ranks to tew ranks, right smart. G-i-t-t!" cried a strange voice among the trees on the other side of the creek. It was the Confederate line advancing upon us!

The effect was electrical; for on the instant, and with one impulse, the men of our brigade sprang to their feet, and poured a sudden and murderous volley across the creek. As the crash of the guns died away, we could hear infantry precipitately retreating among the trees and brush. Then followed the groans of the wounded.

Our brigade volley set the rest of the corps to emptying their muskets, and it was several minutes before the fire slackened. As we received no counter volleys, it was evident that the Confederates had been misled by our fires on the hill, and walked unwittingly into our line while forming their own. As our position was now revealed, orders came for the men to cut clubs with their hatchets, and hammer on the standing timber. This and the felling of a few trees by ax-men made a very good imitation of a chopping-bee. Whether it deluded our antagonists, or not, we could only conjecture.

Midnight came without any more alarms or musketry, and we received orders to move silently to the rear.

"What's up now, major?" said I as my old friend passed me, while the men were getting ready.

"We are going to fall back, and take a fresh position. The main line is on the hill," he replied: "we have only been acting as a blind."

"There seems to be a great deal too much of these feints and blinds," I remarked.

PASSING THE SLEEPING CORPS.

"Why, Frank! are you taking a leaf out of Burch's book?" said the major.

"Oh! I'm not grumbling; but the men are not fools, and they are getting tired of this forest strategy."

"Well, well. Let us be patient. Mind, the orders are to make no noise."

The movement was executed very silently. So careful were the men, that they carried their tin cups in their hands lest the utensils might rattle against their bayonets. Stealthily the fifteen thousand men composing the Fifth Corps marched up the steep hill, leaving no sound behind them. There was something weird in this hurried, silent movement of so many armed men, whose muffled tread had a ghostly sound. There was no moon, and the stars were hidden by clouds: but there was sufficient light reflected from the watch-fires on the hill-top for one to distinguish the outlines of the trees on either hand; and I almost fancied there were leering faces on their shadowy trunks, for my eyes were haggard from want of sleep.

Half-way up the hill, we passed a new picket-line; and I ascertained from a sentinel that it belonged to the Eleventh Corps. On the crest there was an excellent barricade, behind which the main line of the corps was sleeping in long, double rows. Pushing across the fields, we passed some more troops lying in reserve, and next half a dozen batteries snugly parked. With the exception of a few sentinels scattered about here and there, all the men were fast asleep. Leaving these dreaming warriors, the corps now entered a belt of pine-woods; and, passing down a narrow road for nearly a mile, we went into position and line-of-battle. A picket-line was thrown forward; and then the exhausted men flung themselves on the ground, and slumbered.

CHAPTER XIII.

A NIGHT OF TERROR.

"O night! when good men rest, and infants sleep,
Thou art to me no season of repose."

AWOKE finding the day far advanced. Every thing had been quiet along the lines during the night, save a few muttering shots from some distant picket-post. No orders had been received; and, hidden as we were among the pines, no one seemed to know our exact position in the line, while a few impatient spirits began to imagine that we had been forgotten. To me the prevailing silence was oppressive; for I could not forget that these dense and tangled woods contained nearly a quarter of a million of men ready and eager to fly at each others' throats. Once I fancied that I heard distant cannonading; but, as no one else could distinguish the sounds, I soon forgot them.

"Well, Harding, what's the news?" said Captain Burch about sunset, as the major strolled over to where we were lying on the crisp pine-needles carpeting the ground.

"Good news," replied the major. "They say the First and Sixth Corps have crossed the Rappahannock below Fredericksburg, carrying every thing before them."

"Then that *was* cannonading you heard, Frank, after all," remarked Captain Burch.

"I thought I was not mistaken," said I. "But, major, how far have they carried every thing?"

"They've already taken the city and a portion of the heights beyond, and are still pressing the enemy hard."

"Then, why the devil don't we get to work here?" exclaimed the captain, finding fault as usual. "Why, we haven't fired a single shot to-day, and scarcely heard one, either."

"There's a good deal in what you say, Burch," replied Major Harding. "But I make it a rule never to criticise. There may be good reasons for this inactivity. We don't know all the circumstances attending our movements."

"I don't care. I think it's a"—

Neither Major Harding nor myself heeded the close of Captain Burch's angry exclamation; for at that instant a sudden and terrific crash of musketry broke out on our right. Judging from the constancy and volume of the volley, it was quite evident that something serious had happened.

"What can that be?" said the captain, forgetting all his spleen in the surprise of the moment.

"A sudden assault by the enemy, no doubt," replied the major. "Well, Burch, you can't grumble now at not having something to do. We are likely soon to have all we can attend to. By Jove! that musketry is simply terrific,—awful work going on somewhere! I wonder where it is."

The fusillade of small arms continued with unabated intensity and vigor for several minutes more, until it seemed to be coming, like a mighty wave, nearer and nearer; while the racket was now increased by rapid cannonading. Affairs were beginning to look serious, and both officers and men fell into line without orders. There was no telling when we should be called upon to assume our share of the conflict. As we stood silently listening to the roar on our right, an officer of our brigade-staff rode up, his horse plunging and crashing through the trees.

"Colonel Lloyd, we are to move to the right. Please make haste! The whole corps is in motion."

" By the right flank! forward! " shouted our colonel, " double quick! "

We obeyed the colonel's order, as the aide disappeared to repeat his instructions down the line; and dashed through the trees in column, the low dead branches of the pines whipping and cutting our faces until we were half-blinded. Finally we came to one of those wide paths so common in Virginia woods; and as our regiment entered it, I could see that for nearly half a mile ahead the road was full of hurrying troops. Here the pace became even more rapid; and our colonel seemed half-mad with furious excitement, as he urged us to make more speed. Something terrible must have happened to cause this headlong rush of the corps.

" I say, Wilmot, what can be the matter? " gasped Captain Burch as we ran panting side by side together.

" Why, the enemy must have come up in heavy force from some unexpected quarter," I replied, fairly out of breath with our long hard run.

" They're always doing something of that sort," grumbled the captain.

" Keep moving, boys, keep moving! " cried Major Harding cheerily, as he swerved his horse to avoid trampling upon an exhausted man who was falling out of the ranks.

" Troth, major, we're not letting much grass grow undher our feet, anyway," replied Dennis hoarsely, the sally causing a laugh among the men.

The musketry increased in vigor and fury as we proceeded, and I knew that in a few minutes more we should be on the scene of conflict. The rapid firing of the batteries, the cease-less rattle of small arms, and the shrieks of flying shells, gave ample token of the severity of the engagement: so it must be a moment of peril for our army.

All of a sudden the road ended in a bit of open ground, and the next moment our regiment was in the midst of a harrowing scene of confusion and terror.

The field was the same we had crossed during the previous night, when abandoning our masking position on the creek. Then we had moved diagonally over it towards the left of Hooker's line: now we came out into a sort of pocket where the woodmen had cut a little deeper into the forest. In this sheltered field lay several batteries of our artillery, evidently a part of the reserve, all huddled confusedly into one corner.

Rushing impetuously into the open ground, we found our passage impeded by tumultuous masses of disordered troops, struggling furiously, madly, among themselves. It was not yet dark: so I could see that here in this nook were thousands upon thousands of panic-stricken men, fugitives who had broken in the presence of the enemy, acting more like a flock of frightened sheep in a pen than trained soldiers. Many had thrown aside their weapons in their frenzied flight, each man only intent on his own temporary safety. It was part of the Eleventh Corps, which being taken in flank had fallen back in dire disorder.

Looking over the heads of these frenzied men, I saw, in the red light which follows sunset, the Confederate lines, as they coolly, steadily advanced over the field to seize their expected prize, the field-guns and the broken division. But they were too late; for at that moment the old Fifth Corps tore its way through the mob of fugitives, and faced the enemy in solid line of battle.

It was a terrible task, though, to push as we did through the confused mass of panic-stricken men; and I remembered afterwards that more than one musket had been clubbed, and used to clear a path for our advancing columns. Though they were our comrades, the men of the Fifth knew that they had put the army in sudden peril, and so for the moment treated them as enemies.

The right of our corps, being the first to arrive on the scene of disaster and dismay, of course bore the brunt of the desperate hand-to-hand struggle which ensued. When our brigade

THE ROUT OF THE ELEVENTH CORPS, CHANCELLORSVILLE.

came up, we were sent to the center of the large open field to support the artillery; and a weary time we had of it. But the Confederate advance had by this time been checked: the abandoned breastworks were partially retaken and held.

Nothing is more trying to the nerves of even a veteran soldier than a furious battle at night. The darkness conceals the foe, and adds to the difficulty of executing the necessary movements. Uncertainty and doubt weigh upon the hearts of the bravest; while the impossibility of ascertaining your precise position increases the sense of danger, which becomes exaggerated because unseen. Laboring under these influences, as the brigade stood to arms in the field, I became oppressed by a dread I could not easily shake off. It was indeed an awful moment. What the end would be, no one could tell.

It soon grew quite dark, the stars being hidden by the sulphurous clouds of smoke that enveloped the battle-field; and our eyes were blinded by the frequent flashes of the guns as they maintained an incessant shelling of the woods in front. It was curious to see, as the scene was illuminated by these rapid artillery-discharges, the frantic efforts of the officers in the shattered corps, as they strove to restore order and discipline among their men. They made but little progress, however; and, a body of cavalry coming up, both officers and men were driven into a corner, and held there until daylight.

As we took our position behind the batteries going into action, I began to think that we were being surrounded; for shells sputtered and hissed over our heads from almost every point of the compass, until it seemed that the missiles would, the next minute, come tearing through our ranks from the rear. But I soon lost all sense of danger amid the sights and sounds around me. The deafening roar of cannon, the fierce though monotonous rattle of musketry, the detonations of exploding shells, and the crash of falling trees, made a hellish Babel of sounds; yet there was a strain of music in the dreadful din that accorded with the scene and the hour. Under the crash and swell of this mighty orchestra of war, there was an undertone equally trying to the nerves. Fierce curses were uttered by excited officers as they gave their hoarse commands, and with them there came to my ears the pitiful cries of the wounded who were falling all around me in the darkness.

Leaning on my sword, listening to all these discordant sounds, the groan of one of our men, dying almost at my side, thrilled me with its mournfulness. Once I was thoroughly startled by the screams of a disabled and plunging horse attached to one of the caissons just in front of our regiment. It was indeed a night of terror. For three long hours we stood thus, in the very midst of a passionate combat, passive, yet ready to act, losing men every moment, but firing no shot in return. At length the woods caught fire from the shells, thus adding a new element to the scene of destruction and carnage.

"My God! this is awful work, Wilmot!" exclaimed Captain Burch in an awed tone. "Here we stand idly waiting to be shot down like cattle. Curse those cowards! A pretty pickle they've put us into!"

"You ought to be happy, Burch, at having so much good reason for grumbling," said I.

"There's altogether too much to grumble about. I don't like such large doses."

"By the right flank, forward!" cried out our colonel.

We obeyed the order, and moved a little farther to the right; but soon after the regiment was sent back to the left. As we halted the second time, a fresh battery dashed up, and unlimbered on the ground we had just abandoned. Bang, bang! went two or three of the pieces, the increasing clamor deafening me. The battery discharged its guns with great rapidity; and as the men loaded by the light of their own pieces I saw that they were firing at point-blank range, showing that the enemy's lines were close at hand. Using shell and solid shot at first, the gunners soon began throwing grape and canister into the edge of the woods; and orders were passed down our line to form and stand steady. Twenty minutes passed without any volleys from Confederate rifles, and the battery was withdrawn with the same celerity observable when it went into action. As it disappeared, our brigade moved obliquely forward to take its place; and, as we did so, I stumbled over the body of a man that had been crushed out of shape by the ponderous wheels of the retiring guns. While we were thus engaged, two other batteries on our left wheeled their pieces round to the right, and began a furious shell practice across our front; the hissing of the balls being startlingly distinct.

"Now, men, steady!" shouted our brave colonel in the darkness. "When you get the word, remember and fire low."

As he spoke, a shell burst over his head; and, before the light was extinguished, we saw both horse and rider go down. A cry rose from the ranks; but it was soon checked, for our ears were gladdened by the sound of Colonel Lloyd's voice as he disentangled himself from the dead animal.

"I'm all right, boys," he shouted cheerily, his words being drowned by a spontaneous cheer.

At that moment Major Harding rode up, and surrendered his horse to the colonel, who at once remounted, and controlled the enthusiasm of the regiment.

All at once, and without warning, we received a volley of musketry right in our faces, and a score or two of the men fell beneath it. Kneeling quickly at the order, we began pouring in a steady, merciless fire towards the woods. The cross-fire of our artillery was now redoubled in fury and intensity; but, a few minutes after, orders to stop firing were given.

There now seemed nothing more for us to do; the Confederates changing front, and renewing their assault farther down the line. So we lay in position during the remainder of the night, listening with curious ears to the progress of the battle as it ebbed and flowed around us. I longed for the daylight, even if it brought with it a fiercer struggle; for then we should at least be able to see our antagonists, and so lose the feeling of uncertainty which now oppressed every heart. Standing in the midst of the fight, we remained silent under the shells thrown into our devoted ranks by distant and unseen Confederate batteries, our own guns maintaining their part in the stubborn midnight duel.

Sitting down on the cold earth, I at length fell asleep from exhaustion and fatigue, despite the turmoil prevailing all around me. I did not wake again until rudely shaken by Dennis, who thus warned me that the regiment was moving. As I followed the command off the field, in the gray of the morning, I noticed one of my men still sitting on the ground. Going up to rouse him, I was shocked to find him dead, his breast torn open by the fragment of a shell.

CHAPTER XIV.

BEATEN DOWN.

"The beaten soldier proves most manful
That, like his sword, endures the anvil."

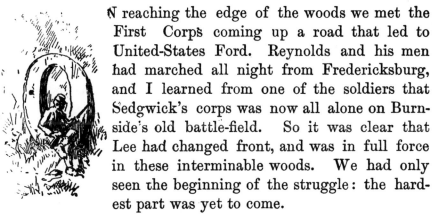

N reaching the edge of the woods we met the First Corps coming up a road that led to United-States Ford. Reynolds and his men had marched all night from Fredericksburg, and I learned from one of the soldiers that Sedgwick's corps was now all alone on Burnside's old battle-field. So it was clear that Lee had changed front, and was in full force in these interminable woods. We had only seen the beginning of the struggle: the hardest part was yet to come.

Knowing this, the silence prevailing at the moment was ominous. Even the pickets were hushed, and it seemed as if both armies were sleeping. Rubbing my eyes to keep awake, I could scarcely realize that we had passed through so noisy and turbulent a night. Though I was surrounded by all the ghastly evidences of battle, our struggle in the darkness seemed more like a phantasmal dream than stern reality. Weary and sleepy I staggered on, careless alike of the present and the future.

" Where are we going now, major ? " said Captain Burch, as our old friend appeared on foot beside us.

"We are to act on the reserve again," he replied. " Having had such a hard night of it, I suppose they consider the corps entitled to a rest. It won't be a very long one, I fancy; for things don't look altogether right, to my mind."

"Why, major!" I exclaimed banteringly, "you are borrowing a page from Burch's book now. Surely you are not getting discouraged?"

"'Discouraged' is not the word: 'anxious' would be better. You know, Wilmot, I'm not given much to croaking; but we are now acting entirely on the defensive, which seems strange after our successful flank movement. I can not understand it," and the major shook his head mournfully.

"I must confess to the same feeling," said I. "There seems to have been a sad bungle somewhere."

"You have just hit it, Frank. 'Bungle' is the only word for it. We do seem to have the worst of luck, and always get tied up."

"That's because our generals waste so much time getting ready," said Captain Burch.

"There's some truth in that," replied the major.

"Oh, well! it's not our fault, so we must make the best of it," said I. "You are a little out of sorts, major, being on foot again."

"Perhaps so," he replied, laughing. "I confess I do feel a little out of my element, off my horse; but Colonel Lloyd needs him now more than I do."

"You came near being made a lieutenant-colonel last night," said I. "That was a narrow escape for our colonel."

"It was a close shave, indeed. But I don't want any promotion to come through my friend's death."

Neither Major Harding nor myself thought that one year later he would find himself suddenly made a colonel on that very ground. The future is mercifully hidden from mortal eyes.

Our division now formed the extreme left of the corps, and the rear of our column had just entered the woods when we were ordered to lie down under the trees in line of battle. Worn out as they were, the men gladly obeyed; and in a few minutes scarcely one of the fifteen thousand was awake. As for myself, I had barely stretched my limbs on the carpet of dead leaves when my eyes were locked in tired slumber.

How long I slept, I know not; but when awakened suddenly by a tremendous volley of musketry, the sun had risen high in the heavens. So great was the crash, I almost fancied I felt the ground quake under me. The outburst had brought the whole corps to its feet; and as we stood listening to the fearful, vengeful rattle of small arms, we knew that the enemy was

ARTILLERY GOING INTO ACTION.

again making a desperate effort to pierce our lines. Precisely where the attack was being made, I could not at first determine, for our movements during the night had confused me. It was, however, quite near: that was certain. For several minutes the corps stood listening with bated breath to the awful, rolling sound, yet it lost none of its incessant vigor: on the contrary, it grew in volume until fully fifty thousand muskets were engaged. The minutes went on: yet at the end of an hour the terrible, incessant volley continued, the roar of the battle being

made more maddening by terrific cannonading. Being hidden
in the woods, we could see nothing; and though accustomed as
we were to being held on reserve, I felt my nerves thrill at the
painful suspense.

"Be the powers, leftinant! an' that's a moighty big scrimmage going on beyant, wherever it be!" ejaculated Dennis, as
he eased his knapsack against a tree.

"You are right," I replied: "there's desperate work afoot.
That musketry is very heavy."

"Where is it, anyway?" queried the corporal.

"I know as little as yourself; but, as near as I can judge, it
must be where we lay all night."

"Begorra! an' it wasn't much laying down we did lasht
noight," grumbled Dennis. "Shure, it was the divil's own
dance we had of it, from first to last."

The musketry now became even heavier and more fierce than
before: the battle seemed to be coming nearer and nearer. So
long a time had elapsed since it began, the affair was becoming
monotonous. The men were now lying down again, some of
them even asleep, despite the convulsion of arms going on
barely half a mile away.

"Come, Wilmot," said Major Harding: "let us go to the
edge of the woods, and see what is going on."

We passed up the road to the left of the brigade; finding ourselves, in a few minutes, on the wide field, among a group of
officers, all watching the movements. As the major and myself
emerged from the woods, a couple of our corps batteries came
thundering up, and, passing us at a hand gallop, speedily unlimbered on the open ground. A minute after the guns opened
a shell fire, at long range, over the tops of the trees in front,
their trunks hidden by a great bank of smoke. The entire field
was now a scene of terrible confusion. Ammunition-wagons
were being hurriedly unloaded in the center, the boxes of cartridges moving on men's shoulders in the direction of the engaged line; while hundreds of wounded men were streaming to

the rear, a long string of stretchers accompanying them. Neither the major nor myself could distinguish the troops at work; for the ground was covered by a dense white smoke, the line of breastworks being marked only by a fierce and angry light playing through the sulphurous vapor. It was the constant flash from thousands of muskets, and so continuous was the fusillade that the flame never died entirely away. As we looked, a brighter, blinding light appeared for an instant in the field, and I knew that one of the ammunition-wagons had been set on fire by a Confederate shell. The air was a moment after filled with a perfect cascade of fragments: the body of a man rose amid the flame and smoke enveloping the vehicle, and then came tumbling headlong to the ground. The horses attached to an empty wagon near us took fright, dashing wildly into the woods, their progress only being stopped by the trees; while the ill-fated driver was hurled from his seat, and killed.

Still there was no slackening in the murderous musketry, the struggle increasing in fury until the woods in which the opposing lines were fighting actually caught fire. A blinding smoke soon covered the whole field, and penetrated the entire forest. Among the trees beyond where the wagon had been wrecked, two or three dozen coatless surgeons were at work, their arms bare to the shoulder, all busy at their horrid task of amputation. Rude tables had been erected in irregular rows, and on each lay a mutilated soldier losing a part of his shattered and bleeding body. Groans and piteous cries resounded in these forest shambles. It seemed as if hell itself had come on earth for a time.

"Those fellows of ours are fighting manfully, aren't they?" said Major Harding to me.

"Yes, indeed. The attacking force must be a strong one. I wonder why they don't order us up."

"All in good time: we'll have our share before long. The battle has scarcely begun."

"But those men can not stand that sort of thing all day."

"No," replied the major; "neither can the Confederates. Unless our line gives way soon, Lee will be compelled to slacken his fire and withdraw his troops. But come, Wilmot, we must not stay here: our corps may soon be moving."

Orders for us, however, never came; the corps lying there idle all day. For four long hours we sat and listened to the ceaseless musketry, it abating no jot of its angry fury. The flames in the woods spread, until the smoke became so suffocating that we were compelled to hug the earth for air to breathe. Still the battle continued. Though it had been begun at eleven o'clock, and my watch now told the hour of three, there were no signs of the conflict ending. About four o'clock the firing began losing its strength. Once broken in volume, the volleys slackened rapidly, and there came brief lulls, followed by fiercer outbreaks. We knew that the battle was nearing its end. Was it a victory, or a defeat, for the Federal side?

The lulls in the musketry grew more and more frequent, the artillery paused, and finally there came a period of comparative silence. At this moment the Third Corps appeared in the road on our front, when we learned that a part of our established line had been abandoned. The men were weary, and they told us of heavy losses. Their faces were blackened by powder, and many exhibited traces of bullets in their clothing. One gray-haired man had a watch in the case of which a rifle-ball had left its mark. A young, boyish-looking sergeant showed me a daguerreotype of his mother, a bullet being embedded in the center of the picture. He had carried it in the breast-pocket of his blouse, where lying over his heart it had undoubtedly saved the wearer's life. Throwing open his shirt, the proud boy revealed the imprint of the embossed case on his bosom.

"I wouldn't take the best farm in our county for that picture," said he. "Mother always said she would pray for me, and this is an answer to her prayers. God bless her! I've felt like crying ever since I found this bullet. That would look nice for a sergeant, wouldn't it?"

"I don't think so," I replied. "It's natural for you to love your mother."

"Of course it is. Well, we made a good square fight of it, anyway. Good-by, sir: I must be off;" and the little hero ran after his comrades. The troops marching past seemed astonished to learn that we had been idle so near them. Though they made no complaint, we felt humiliated at having been kept out of the engagement. After the Third, came a part of the Second Corps; and we understood that the line was to be extended on the right.

"You'll have to stand the next assault," remarked an officer to me as I gave him a drink from my canteen, "so keep your powder dry."

As the rear of the column slowly straggled by, a group of mounted officers appeared. It was General Hooker and his staff. Our men began cheering him; but he held up his hand, and the noisy salutation died away as quickly as it had been begun.

"He's wounded!" cried out a score of voices as the general put his hand to his head and slightly wavered in his saddle.

"No, no, boys," responded the general quickly, "not wounded, only a little stunned: I'll be all right by and by."

The men gave a hearty, gladsome cheer; the general galloping forward to escape their enthusiasm.

Now that the road was clear, our bugles sounded the advance; and we moved forward to a line of breastworks hitherto occupied by our pickets. A dead silence had by this time fallen on the woods, and the fighting seemed to be over for the day. We had, however, been in position only a few minutes, when our ears were saluted by what seemed scattering musketry. No attack was made on our line; and I leaned against the breastwork, listening to the singular sounds, conjecturing what this strange, intermittent firing could be.

"I say, Wilmot, that's a queer sort of musketry," remarked Captain Burch. "It don't sound much like picket-firing, and there's not enough of it for breastwork fighting. I wonder what it means?"

"I am as much puzzled as yourself, old fellow. I never heard the like of it before."

"The fire out yonder must be growing stronger; for there's less smoke, and I feel the heat more. I hope it ain't coming this way, though that would be just our luck," continued the captain, in his grumbling way.

"It would be odd indeed," said I, "if we were compelled to retreat before the flames instead of the enemy."

"There! Don't you hear the fire crackling?" interrupted the captain. "I do plainly. As sure as you live, Wilmot, the fire *is* coming this way. We shall be burned up or burned out."

As he spoke, a sergeant belonging to the pickets came scrambling over the pile of logs and earth.

"What's the matter, sergeant? Are you wounded?" I asked.

"No, sir: I'm all right. But I thought this was the Hundred and Fortieth: where are they?"

"A little way to the right. But why have you come in?"

"Why, the woods are all on fire out there, and we're going to dig a trench to keep it from spreading: so I've come in for more men and some tools. Do you know the woods over there are all full of wounded?"

"Good heavens! Is it possible?" I exclaimed in horror. "Can't you save them?"

"Too late, I'm afraid. That's been tried already. Why, we calculate there are two or three thousand dead and wounded, both Federal and Confederate, lying there under the burning trees," said the sergeant, disappearing in the direction of his regiment.

"That accounts for the queer musketry, Wilmot," remarked the captain. "It's the fire exploding the muskets lying on the ground."

" Very likely," I replied ; " but I'm thinking of the wounded. It's horrible to think of those hapless men being burned to death. I'll go and see the major."

On my telling Major Harding the awful condition of affairs, he decided at once to rescue the wounded. He soon gained the approbation of our brigadier : so, with a force of nearly a hundred volunteers, he and I started for the abandoned battle-ground. Crossing the field where we had watched the progress of the engagement, we found it entirely deserted by both armies, but thickly strewn with *débris*. Knapsacks and canteens, muskets, cartridge-boxes and bayonets, shattered artillery caissons, and broken wagons, dead horses and men, lay scattered on the ground in dire confusion. In the distance, towards the Chancellorsville House, I could distinguish a body of infantry which I recognized as a Confederate line. As we were not going within range of their rifles, our party pushed boldly across the corner of the open ground. On reaching the left of the line occupied by the Third Corps, we found the irregular dropping musketry fire still going on ; and the ominous roar of the advancing flames betrayed the rapidity of their progress. As we proceeded, I could hear the screams of pain and frenzied appeals for succor uttered by the hapless wounded, who seemed doomed to a dreadful fate.

" Come, men ! into the woods with you, and pick up every live man you meet ! " cried the major. " In with you, boys ! Leave your muskets behind you. — Lieutenant Wilmot, you remain here, and see that the rescued are placed in safety."

The men quickly unslung their knapsacks, and, sticking their bayoneted guns into the ground, disappeared among the trees, led by Major Harding. In a few minutes some of them returned, carrying groaning men ; and I busied myself in seeing them comfortably disposed of at a safe distance from the fire. In doing so, I saw that our fellows were making no distinction ; for the blue and the gray came side by side as they had fallen. The Confederate infantry we had seen across the field now

began firing at us: but after a few rounds they apparently discovered our errand; for they at once ceased, giving a wild sort
of cheer to encourage us, their yell sounding strangely amid the
crackling of the flames. In a few minutes we had thirty or
forty poor creatures in the field, who loudly cried for water,
water! We gave them what we had, and I sent for some am

BRINGING OFF THE WOUNDED.

bulances. As I gave the order, Major Harding appeared, his
face and hands black and grimy.

"It's no use, Frank. We can do no more. The fire has got
such headway, we can't face it and live. Heaven help those
poor wretches! we can do nothing. My God! it makes my
blood run cold to hear them scream;" and, as he spoke, the
stout-hearted officer threw himself on the ground, tears coursing
down his besmeared cheeks.

It was indeed a hopeless task; and, as our party re-assembled,
every man's face grave and awe-stricken, we listened silently to
the cries of those beyond all mortal aid. Curses and yells of
pain, piteous appeals and spasmodic prayers, could be distinguished; but though we could hear their voices. we were cut off
from them by a wall of fire. The flames roared more fiercely·

the cries grew fainter, until at last they were hushed. Looking into the burning forest, I saw that every shrub, tendril, and sapling was being consumed: even the monarchs of that wild region were scorched and killed by the fire. No human being could live in the presence of so fierce a heat; and as the fiery torrent rolled on madly, swiftly, we stood and watched its progress, knowing that in those few fleeting moments hundreds of brave men who had struggled in mortal combat with each other, amid the tangled growth of vines and trees, had now passed through a horrible death together.

The ambulances soon arrived, when the men set to work placing the rescued men in them. On turning toward the row stretched on the earth, I found three already dead, and a fourth quietly slipping away into the dark valley. Before all of the ambulances were dispatched, seven were dead; their bodies being left on the ground where we had laid them.

"Wilmot, you and I have seen some tough scenes since we entered the service," said Major Harding, as we marched back to our regiment; "but this last experience is the toughest of them all."

"Yes, indeed!" I replied. "It's bad enough to find your comrades falling all around you, not knowing when it will be your own turn; but to see helpless men burned to death, and be unable to save them, is simply awful."

There was no more fighting anywhere along the line, so the day passed into night without further disturbance. At sunset news came that Sedgwick was moving on the heights behind Fredericksburg, which explained the silence of the Confederates along our own front. The fire in the woods died away, and the night proved a quiet one for us.

The next day and night we lay in position, hearing Sedgwick's guns, and wondering why we made no aggressive movement. In the morning we learned that Sedgwick had been beaten back. The intelligence was received by the men in silence, for they knew that Lee had now crippled both wings of our divided army. Our general had missed his opportunity. Still the troops waited confidently for orders. None came, however; and after sunset we were surprised by the appearance of the entire reserve artillery, moving silently, secretly, along the road. The wheels of the caissons and guns were swathed in blankets, and the batteries took the road to the ford.

"A retreat, a retreat!" were the words that ran along the lines.

It was indeed a retreat. Lee had out-maneuvered Hooker. We were now to fall back across the river.

The artillery having disappeared, infantry came next, a whole corps, followed by more cannon. Then we received orders to build large fires along the lines of our position. This movement had a double purpose, — that of deceiving the Confederates, and affording light for the marching columns. The troops continued moving far into the night, and I learned from a staff officer that the advance had already crossed the Rappahannock. No orders came for our corps, so we continued to hold our line of battle. A heavy rain set in; and the men gathered round their fires, discussing the situation. A feeling of despair was in every heart, for all knew the honor of the army had sustained a blow difficult to recover from.

The retreat of the other corps lasted until after midnight; the silent, mysterious march of so many armed men, as they plodded on through the rain and mud, being an appalling spectacle, for demoralization was already visible in the ranks. About two o'clock in the morning, word was passed down the line to increase the fires: so our men proceeded gloomily to tear up the breast-works, now useless, and heaped up the friendly logs until the woods seemed to be again in flames. By this time the army had disappeared: we were evidently alone in the forest; the task of covering the retreat had fallen to us. Scarcely had the fires been freshened in their generous glow, when our corps was put in motion. Leaving the blazing line, we struck off through that part of the woods where the field

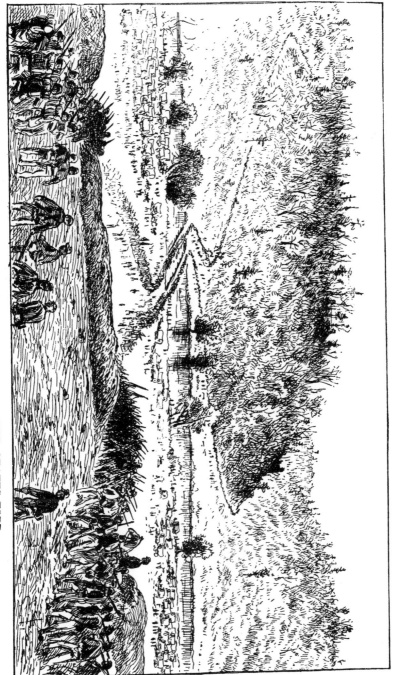

RETREAT ACROSS THE RAPPAHANNOCK.—UNITED STATES FORD.

hospitals had located on that terrible Sunday. On we went, stumbling in the darkness over ghastly heaps of human legs, arms, and hands, grim evidence how active had been the implements of the surgeons. Among these dreadful proofs of the cost of war, lay many a corpse, unburied, uncared for.

As the day dawned, we emerged from the woods, having followed no regular path, being guided solely by occasional cut saplings and blazes on the larger trees. In a field near the ford, the ground thickly sprinkled with clumps of young pines, we found the main body of the army hurriedly crossing the river. In a few minutes the corps fell into line to hold the approaches to the ford. The men, finding their muskets wet and rusty, began snapping caps in harmless fusillade as they endeavored to dry the nipples.

While they were thus engaged, General Meade, our corps commander, came slowly riding along the line.

"What the devil are you doing, men?" he exclaimed in an angry tone. "What's all this noise for?"

"Shure, gineral," replied the irrepressible Dennis, "we're only thrying to dhry our guns a bit. Faith, an' we couldn't fire a shot if thim divils should come at us now."

"Well, you could give them your bayonets," responded the general wearily.

"Yis, sir: so we can," retorted the corporal, determined as usual to have the last word. "But if it's all the same to you, gineral, we'd loike to give 'em bullets as well."

"Officers, see that your men do not waste too many caps," said the general, endeavoring to hide a smile as he rode on.

By noon all of the other corps were safely over the Rappahannock, when it came our turn to cross. As yet we had seen nothing of the enemy beyond a few horsemen who appeared on some rising ground in the direction of Fredericksburg. On moving down towards the ford, we found the road leading to the pontoon-bridge in a terrible condition; the pressure of so many thousand feet, and the heavy wheels of the artillery and wagons, having cut up the soft wet earth until it was a perfect sea of mud, through which we floundered up to our knees. The river itself was also greatly swollen by the rain of the previous night, and the last remaining bridge seemed in instant danger of being swept away. Several hawsers fastened to trees on either bank held the swaying structure in position, but we were compelled to wade through the increasing freshet before reaching the precarious bridge of boats. Our brigade happened to be the last to cross; and, being detailed to bring up the stragglers, Dennis and I were on the bridge when the engineers cut loose the fastenings on the western bank, and sent the pontoons swinging round in the angry, foaming current. For a moment I imagined we had gone adrift.

"Begorra, Master Frank, an' I don't loike these rivers at all!" exclaimed Dennis, endeavoring to keep his foothold. "Ivery toime we get on thim, the wather tries to dhrown us. Shure, I volunteered to foight on the land and not in the navy."

"Silence, you fool," said the engineer officer in charge of the bridge. "Stand ready, all, to jump when we near the bank. Keep cool, there's no danger."

"Thank ye for the information, sir," replied Dennis in a low tone. "Couldn't ye give us a feather-bed to jump on? The wather's dreadful cowld."

"If you give me any more of your impudence," cried the engineer wrathfully, "I'll fling you overboard."

"Do as you are bid, corporal," said I. "Captain, give the word when you are ready, please."

He nodded in silence, as he watched the bridge swing round.

"Stand ready to jump, now — jump!"

My little party instinctively obeyed, finding themselves waist-deep in the icy water; but in a few moments all had floundered safely ashore.

The road up the steep bank was blocked with broken wagons, and the woods were full of men. There was no longer any cohesion, any discipline. Corps, divisions, and brigades had become inextricably mingled together. Regiments melted to a company, some even losing their colors for a time. Officers and men straggled into the woods to cook such food as remained, rank being forgotten for the moment; for all seemed reckless as to the future. Though the army was safe from pursuit, the bitter feeling of defeat was uppermost in every man's mind. Demoralization reigned supreme. The magnificent army that had a few weeks before passed in proud array before the President was now humbled and shattered.

Dennis and I scrambled up the rocky defile, and on reaching the heights above plodded forward through the mud in hopes of overtaking our regiment. But, after a weary march of a few miles, we lost all trace of the corps in column, though the men composing it were thronging the forest on either hand.

"Halloa, Wilmot! where are you going to?" cried a familiar voice.

Turning to see who spoke, I saw our major lying on the ground in front of a fire, near the roadside.

"Why, I'm seeking the regiment, of course. Where is it?"

"Everywhere. The whole corps seems to have gone straggling. I sprained my foot among those confounded rocks at the ford below, and had to halt here. Come, sit down and rest."

"This is an awful state of affairs, Harding," said I, accepting his invitation; Dennis at the same time preparing to cook some coffee.

"You may well say that," replied the major. "But the men will soon get over it. In a few days the army will be all right again."

"I hope so, though it's dreadful to see a whole army broken and scattered as ours appears to be."

"Oh! don't get down-hearted, Frank. We have need of all our courage now. It's the fortune of war."

Finding that Major Harding's sprain was a severe one, Dennis and I shared his bivouac for the night. The next morning he was able to walk with tolerable ease: so we started quite early for our old winter-quarters, picking up such of our men as we chanced to overtake on the way. That evening we reached our old camp with nearly one hundred muskets, while others were still plodding on. We were greeted most heartily by

RETURN TO THE ABANDONED CAMPS AT FALMOUTH.

Colonel Lloyd, he being evidently glad to see so many of his men once more. No reproof for our absence was uttered; it being considered the most natural thing in the world, in presence of the general disorganization. Indeed, the colonel informed us that he had ridden into camp with scarcely fifty men at his horse's heels, while others had been coming in all day.

Our party comprised nearly all the missing since our roll-call on the battle-field, and on the following morning there were no absentees unaccounted for. The army was already resuming its old formation.

CHAPTER XV.

A PAUSE.

"The war, that for a space did fail,
Now, trebly thundering, swelled the gale."

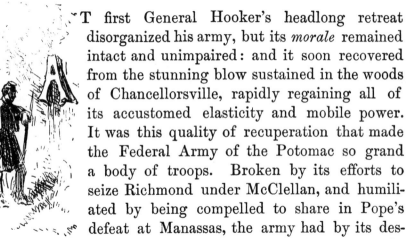 T first General Hooker's headlong retreat disorganized his army, but its *morale* remained intact and unimpaired: and it soon recovered from the stunning blow sustained in the woods of Chancellorsville, rapidly regaining all of its accustomed elasticity and mobile power. It was this quality of recuperation that made the Federal Army of the Potomac so grand a body of troops. Broken by its efforts to seize Richmond under McClellan, and humiliated by being compelled to share in Pope's defeat at Manassas, the army had by its desperate valor clutched a decisive victory at Antietam, only to find itself hurled by Burnside against an impregnable position at Fredericksburg. Following Hooker, it had halted on the verge of destruction amid a labyrinth of virgin woods; and, now after a few short weeks of rest, was again ready for the field, undismayed by the reverses of the past, only remembering its victories and successes. Though the army had been greatly weakened by its losses, it longed to meet the enemy.

April and May passed with the army still in camp, but June at last brought the threatening movement. A reconnoissance by Sedgwick revealed the fact that Lee had assumed the initiative; and on the day we learned the news, Pleasonton's cavalry corps began marching past our division camp. The next morning the entire army was in motion. Our corps was thrown along the line of the Rappahannock River, above the junction of the Rapidan; and we lay in scattered brigade camps until the middle of June. A cavalry engagement between Pleasonton and Stuart, on the plains of Brandy, unmasked Lee's movement towards the Shenandoah Valley, thus compelling Hooker to attempt a counter-stroke. He accordingly set his columns in motion along the interior line.

It came my turn to go on picket-duty a few days after the cavalry fight; my command receiving ten days' rations, for all knew that the corps might take the road at any moment. Outpost duty was to me a decided relief from the stagnation of regimental camp-life and routine. It was therefore with positive pleasure that I rolled up my overcoat and blankets, — my faithful friend and follower Dennis making a perfect packhorse of himself with a tremendous stock of provisions.

"Av coorse it's a heavy load now," he replied to my remonstrances, "but it will be loighter before we're relaved; and besides, Master Frank, we haven't fur to go."

"Have your own way, Dennis, as you always do," said I, knowing how futile argument was with him.

"To be shure I'll hev me own way," retorted Dennis. "You're an officer, and I'll obey your ordhers to the death, but whin it comes to carryin' coffee and sugar and a thrifle of a ham or two, it's me own back's the masther."

Bidding my brother officers adieu, I set out with my detail for our post of duty. The day was bright and warm; but the woods were delightfully cool and shady in their fresh young foliage, our narrow path under the trees being fringed with wild flowers, fragrant and beautiful. The twitter of the mating birds overhead, the soft hum of the insects, and the splash of a brook as its waters went tumbling over the steep bank into the river, sounded in my ears as I marched at the head of my little column, until I almost fancied myself in my native woods; the heavy tread of our party and the clink of steel alone destroying the illusion.

We were to relieve a part of the pickets lying a few miles above the junction of the two rivers; and, as the post was scarcely three miles distant from our camp, we were not long in reaching our destination. On finding the officer in command, I discovered, that, though I had an equal number of men, I was expected to cover a longer line than his; the pickets of the other brigade having been, for some unexplained reason, entirely withdrawn, consequently I was assigned to the entire division line. As the retiring pickets had been on duty for five days, I expected a similar period of service. It was a matter of indifference to me, however, for we had an ample supply of food; the men seeming to share my delight at escaping from camp duty and drill. Going over the ground to be guarded, I ascertained that we held fully a mile of the river, so, while posting my sentries, was careful to caution the men to keep up frequent communication with each other, and avoid giving needless alarms.

Having occasion to change the location of the reserve post, I directed Sergeant Foster to pick out a suitable position, while I arranged the line. By noon I had accomplished the latter to my satisfaction, and, after seeing the old picket-guard sling their knapsacks and depart, for camp, turned my footsteps towards the center of our extended position. The spot selected by Foster for our reserve bivouac lay among some immense rocks that had evidently been piled up on the river-bank, in chaotic confusion, by some mighty convulsion of nature. Admirably adapted for defense, and approached by a rude path which wound around the bowlders at the top, the little rocky nest was entirely hidden, though we had a complete view of the river, both above and below the bend. The dense undergrowth that overhung these disrupted rocks formed a leafy canopy above our heads, completely sheltering us from the rays of the sun.

I found my men quietly awaiting me; and, as I at once approved of the sergeant's choice, they were not long in making every thing snug and comfortable. There was ample room for two hundred men; and, as my whole command was scarcely half that number, there was plenty of elbow-room for those off duty.

Dennis soon fixed a quiet corner for me; while others busied themselves in gathering a stock of fuel for our watch-fires, finding an abundant supply in a heap of dry drift-wood deposited at the foot of the rocks by the frequent freshets on the river.

Leaning against one of the massive stones forming the ramparts of our natural fortress, I gave myself up to reflection. Gazing on the swiftly moving river, its current narrowed and deepened in the bend by the intrusive, unyielding presence of these conglomerate rocks, and watching the shifting shadows as they played on the angry surface of the turbulent stream, I thought of the weary marches and thrilling battle-scenes I had participated in. The toil, perils, and excitements attending army-life gave zest to the present, and led me into bright anticipations for the future. I knew the approaching campaign was to be a severe and protracted one, but my heart beat high with hope as I forecast the probable scope and result of the movement.

"Leftinant, dinner's ready," said Dennis sententiously. "Shure, ye must be hungry by this toime."

I laughed as I turned to obey the summons, for with it had flown all my dreams.

The time passed quickly, and we had been three days on picket-duty without any incident happening to disturb us. There were no challenges during the night, no signs of the enemy by day. Indeed, I began to suspect that we were guarding the river against nobody; for the Confederate pickets, who had maintained a pleasant intercourse with our predecessors in exchanging coffee and tobacco, were now no longer visible. In this belief I was joined by Lieutenant Martin, commanding the pickets on my left, and we communicated our suspicions to the field-officer who visited .us; but he failing to share them, we continued as much on the alert as though the opposite bank were fringed with hostile riflemen.

I had just returned from an inspection of my line on the afternoon of the fourth day, having found every thing provokingly quiet and uninteresting. The evening was deliciously cool, the breeze down the river being laden with the perfumes of the forest; and I experienced a fresh degree of pleasure in viewing the romantic scene after supper. Carelessly lounging over the top of a bowlder, smoking my pipe, my thoughts began drifting away again; and I had wholly forgotten my surroundings, when Dennis suddenly touched my arm exclaiming, —

"An' what the divil was that?"

"Confound you, corporal! what do you mean by startling me like that?" said I, angry at the unwonted interruption. "What are you staring at, you idiot?"

"Why, I thought I saw a man down there on the other side," he replied, not noticing my reproof, so intently was he peering across the river.

"It seems to me, Dennis, that you are always seeing somebody or something," I retorted sarcastically. "Hang it, man, be quiet! I see no one; and, if I did, he can not eat us."

"Troth, an' we wud be a tough mouthful. But, if ye didn't see him, Master Frank, I did. Yis: there he is now."

"Where?" I whispered, now thoroughly aroused.

"Why, over there, by that big birch-tree. There he is, sitting down on that flat bit of rock, for all the world like a big brown toad;" and Dennis pointed excitedly towards the upper end of the bend.

Following the direction of Dennis's finger with my eyes, I saw that he was right. A man was there, sure enough, sitting among some rocks at the river's edge, as motionless as if made himself of stone.

"It must be one of the Confederate pickets," said I: "they are beginning to show themselves again. Tell Sergeant Foster I want him."

In a few moments Sam was by my side.

"Sergeant, take your rifle, and pass along our line to the right. See that the men are on the lookout. There's a man down there on the opposite bank, and no doubt more above and below. Tell Sergeant Coulter to take the left and do the same."

The two sergeants disappeared on their respective errands; while I continued to watch the stranger, Dennis and the rest of my reserve scattering among the rocks for the same purpose. There was no need to enjoin silence, for all seemed to appreciate its necessity.

The sun had gone down, but there was sufficient light left for us to discern the man crouching under the trees. I had noticed that he had no musket; and, as I watched him, I wondered what he intended to do, for it was now evident that his presence on the river had a definite purpose. Ten or fifteen minutes passed, yet the man made no sign or movement; and I was getting somewhat impatient, when he rose to his feet, and, turning round, dragged a log of wood from under the bushes, silently launching it into the water. As he did so, I saw that he had a revolver slung around his neck.

"Begorra! he's going to cross," whispered Dennis, over my head. "Shall the b'yes give him a volley?"

"No, no! Let him come, and we will capture him. Pass the word for no one to fire."

As I uttered the words the Confederate placed himself astride of the log, and plunged boldly into the stream. It was evidently an old experience, for the fellow guided his log so adroitly that the current was carrying him straight towards our position. I saw that he intended to land among the drift-wood under the rocks: so, hastily calling on three or four of the men nearest me, I crept down the bank to receive our visitor. By this time he had reached the middle of the river, coming swiftly towards us, evidently unconscious of the reception awaiting him. As he neared the pile of drift-wood, the daring voyager shifted his right leg off the log, and, sitting sideways, made a sudden leap for the landing. So accurately had he judged his distance, that as he abandoned the log he was able to scramble up among the loose chips and sticks forming the *débris*, soon rising to his feet.

"Surrender, sir. You're my prisoner!" I exclaimed as I rushed forward to seize the intruder.

I was, however, too precipitate; for like a startled deer the Confederate turned before I could lay hands on him, and with a jeering laugh leaped lightly into the river.

THE CONFEDERATE SPY.

"Fire!" I shouted.

At the same moment, I felt the mass of dry wood give way under my feet; and I fell into the water, hearing my men's muskets ring out a spattering volley as I took my involuntary bath. The current being so rapid, I believed I must swim for my life under the shower of bullets my men were sending after the fugitive; but the next instant my outstretched hand caught a friendly branch, so I was able to draw myself up to a safe footing. Scrambling over the rocks, I saw the Confederate gain the opposite bank in safety. As he reached the shore he waved his hand derisively, and then disappeared among the trees.

"Are you much wet, lieutenant?" asked Ferguson, one of the men who had accompanied me down the path.

"Up to my waist. But that's no matter: it's losing that impudent scamp that annoys me."

"I don't see how we missed hitting him," remarked Ferguson. "There must have been twenty bullets sent after him."

"You all fired too hastily, and he was going with the current. I am glad, though, that he escaped unhurt," said I, squeezing the water out of my pantaloons. "It would have been a shame to shoot him like a rat in the water."

"Why, you told us to fire!" replied Ferguson reproachfully.

"I know it. It was on the impulse of the moment. So brave a man deserved to get off." And, as I spoke, I led the way up the crooked path to our rendezvous.

Stripping before a fire, I soon dried my clothes, and then made a tour of my line. The incident caused considerable excitement among the sentries, each man offering his own explanation; but I was convinced in my own mind that we had missed a scout who was endeavoring to get through our lines.

The following day, word came along the chain of sentinels that Lieutenant Martin wished to see me. On joining him, I found the young officer much excited.

"Do you know that the corps has broken camp and marched away?" he exclaimed as soon as we met.

"Impossible! They would not go away without recalling us."

"But they have, though," retorted the lieutenant. "And all the pickets on my left are gone too."

"Indeed! How did you find out all this?"

"Why, I got out of coffee, and sent one of my men to camp for more. He came back, saying the troops had all disappeared. He also discovered the absence of the pickets down the river."

"This is a nice fix," said I. "Tell your sergeants to keep a sharp lookout while we go and see the officer on the right."

Sending one of my men ahead to notify the officer above of our coming, Lieutenant Martin and myself followed. Half an hour later we met my messenger, who reported that there were no pickets above. This was startling news, for it was quite evident that through some blunder or accident we had been overlooked and forgotten. The question was, what were we to do? My brother lieutenant, having only recently received his commission, naturally shifted all the responsibility to my shoulders, as his senior in rank.

"I tell you what," exclaimed Martin, after we had discussed the matter for some time: "my men discovered a horse and equipments concealed in the garret of a house near our post. You take him, Wilmot, and ride over the camps yourself."

"A capital idea. That horse must belong to the scout we missed capturing last evening."

An hour later I was riding through our deserted camp, finding that the corps had indeed abandoned us. The fires were all dead and cold, so the column must have moved the previous day, if not before. My course was therefore clear: we must follow and endeavor to overtake the main body. Strictly speaking, I ought to remain until recalled; but I knew that it would be ridiculous under the circumstances.

Early in the afternoon I had assembled both Lieutenant Martin's pickets and my own. Forming the force into four companies, we soon organized a little battalion.

"Martin," said I, "you will please act as lieutenant-colonel, and take the rear of the column. Sergeant Foster is to be our adjutant, and the other sergeants will command the companies. Corporals, take the line of file closers."

"All right, Colonel Wilmot," replied Martin, laughing at the oddity of our position.

"Now, men," I continued, "we must do our best to overtake the corps, so I shall expect you to move rapidly. If any one falls out and straggles, he does so at his own risk. Forward, march!"

We were a tolerably strong body; and, though the men were somewhat excited over the novelty of our situation, I felt confident they could be depended upon in case we fell into any danger. Dennis, at his own urgent solicitation, was given command of the advance-guard, and I also threw out a few flankers to prevent surprise. These precautions taken, we trudged merrily forward. At the end of two hours we struck the main road, finding it ankle-deep with dust: so I ordered my men into the fields, and moved briskly on. We knew that forced marches would be necessary to overtake the army; and, the men knowing that their only safety lay in keeping well together, I had no trouble in holding my little column in tolerably good shape.

After marching eight or ten miles, we halted at night-fall in a clump of woods in the vicinity of a small brook, a few fires only being permitted. Our sentinels being undisturbed during the night, Lieutenant Martin and myself managed to get some sleep, though both of us naturally felt very anxious. At daybreak the men were roused, and after a hasty and scanty breakfast we again hurried forward.

We were now in a wide tract of open country, broken here and there by tiny bits of woods; but there were no signs of any large body of troops. The day was a very hot one, and the men began to feel the effects of our rapid pace; but I urged and encouraged them as best I could, finding them cheerful and responsive to my appeals. At noon we made a halt of an hour, learning at a house near by that Federal troops had passed the day before; but, they being horsemen, I could not tell how far the corps was in advance. Marching steadily on until the sun began to creep down the western sky, we came at length to a cross-roads, where I halted my wearied command to decide our future route. Both of the roads betrayed the passage of troops, but which to take was a perplexing problem.

"Halloa!" suddenly exclaimed Lieutenant Martin, as we stood debating the question. "There's cavalry coming," and he pointed down the road to the right.

"Attention, battalion!" I shouted, leaping into my saddle.

"Lieutenant, let the men form behind that fence, and see that every musket is ready. Courage, boys! We may have to fight: if so, we must give a good account of ourselves."

A brisk cheer was the only response, as the men obeyed orders, and rapidly fell into line. The cloud of dust raised by the advancing cavalry came nearer and nearer. The moment that was to decide our fate was almost at hand.

Despite my outward coolness, I was very nervous; for it seemed hard to be overpowered and made prisoners, as we might be, when another day would probably place us safely within the lines of the army. But, as the approaching cavalry was evidently not a very strong force, I determined to fight, if necessary, for our liberty.

By this time the column had discovered our presence; for it halted, and threw out a few troops to reconnoiter. Scarcely had these men emerged from the cloud of dust that enveloped the main force, when I discovered they were Federals. Immensely relieved, I rode out on the road, and hailed them.

"Who are you?" shouted a sergeant as he unslung his carbine.

"Union troops," I replied, "trying to find the army."

The sergeant wheeled his horse, and, followed by his comrades, galloped back to the column. In a few minutes the entire body of horsemen advanced, and I saw there were three or four squadrons.

"How came you so far in the rear?" demanded the major as we met in the road.

"We belong to the Fifth Corps, and were left on the picket-line," was my reply.

"By Jove! this is a lucky meeting," said the major in a gratified tone. "Why, we were coming after you! The mistake was only discovered to-day. You did just right, lieutenant, in coming on: we shall now be able to overtake the army to-morrow."

This was delightful news, for I had no desire to be an independent commander any longer. My little battalion gave a rousing cheer as the cavalry rode up: and we were soon trudging on over the road in high spirits, every knapsack being taken by the riders in order to lighten and ease my men.

While Major Stephens and I rode forward at the head of the combined column, I learned from him that the army was concentrating towards Centerville, and that it was understood that Lee's advance was already beyond Winchester, heading for the Upper Potomac. Another invasion of Maryland was intended, and we would soon be on the old ground where the army had maneuvered the previous summer under McClellan.

An early start the following morning enabled us to overtake the rear of the army, when my men took back their knapsacks, and Major Stephens bade me good-by. There was no further need of his protection, and he was all the more anxious to get forward on learning that Pleasonton was moving his corps towards the Loudon Valley. It took us another day to catch up with our brigade, our safe arrival being considered quite an event. General Fletcher seemed glad to see us; but how we came to be abandoned, or who was to blame, I never knew, for there seemed to be a desire at headquarters to forget the incident.

I found the army in regular campaign order; and after a week of almost constant marching we crossed the Potomac at Edward's Ferry, and advanced to the line of the Monocacy River, halting at length on the outskirts of Frederick City in Maryland.

CHAPTER XVI.

MOVING TOWARDS BATTLE.

"His marches are expedients to this town,
His forces strong, his soldiers confident."

OW the great army lay in camps around Frederick City. As yet nothing was definitely known regarding the movements of the Confederate army, beyond the fact that Lee was already overrunning the rich and fertile valley of the Cumberland. We learned that his advance had reached the Susquehanna River, near Harrisburg. All was doubt and uncertainty about our own programme. For two years we had marched hither and thither while the gigantic game of war was played by our several commanders, and now waited patiently for the signal that was to hurl our columns against the antagonist we had so often met before. Every man in the ranks, whether he carried a bayonet or a sword, knew that a great and decisive battle was at hand; yet all felt prepared to stand the issue.

I had been ordered to see a culvert in the road near our camp properly repaired. While overseeing the fatigue-party, young Jenkins, General Fletcher's aide, rode up.

"Have you heard the news, Wilmot?" said he, reining in his horse to avoid my men.

"News! no, I've heard nothing. We rely on you fellows of the staff for that article," I replied with a laugh. "What is

new now? Are we going to move to-night, or to-morrow? If
to-night, I must hurry up and finish this culvert."

"Oh! we won't march to-night. You must know that
Hooker has been removed, and Meade has been given the command of the army. That's news, isn't it?"

"Yes, indeed. Where did you hear it?"

"Down in Frederick, to be sure. General Hooker started for
Washington at noon. We are to have the official orders to-
morrow. Every thing is in confusion at headquarters, and no
wonder: this constant change of commanders plays the very
devil with the army."

"You are quite right, Jenkins. We are like the shuttlecock
in the old school-game."

"Well," replied the young aide, gathering up his reins, "it's
a comfort old gray-haired George has got it this time. If he
only does as well at the head of the army with his spectacles as
he did with our corps, we men of the Maltese cross will have
good reason to be proud of the old man."

"Three cheers for General Meade!" cried one of our men.

The call was responded to most lustily.

"You see, Jenkins," said I, "the new commanding general
will be popular in the old Fifth. But who's to be our new
corps general? I hope it's one of the regulars."

"You have your wish, old fellow. Sykes takes the corps,
and Ayres carries his long black beard to the head of our division. But I must hurry on, or my brigadier will hear the news
before I reach him."

Thus came another of those changes which so often tried the
temper and *morale* of the Army of the Potomac. General Meade's
order was read to the troops the following day; the men smiling grimly as they listened, for these veterans had learned by
bitter experience how often political intrigue had crippled and
paralyzed the army. Contrary to all previous usage, General
Meade refrained from issuing dramatic bulletins, evidently
appreciating the fact that his troops were not apt to be roused

into temporary enthusiasm by empty words or loud-sounding phrases. Simple and direct in his announcement, the new commander won the confidence of his army at once, finding them responsive to his touch when the emergency arrived.

No sooner was the change formally announced, than we began moving. Corps after corps broke camp with accustomed celerity, marching rapidly through the narrow streets of Frederick, or skirting the old-fashioned town to the right and the left. Our corps was among those to pass through the quaint little, city, which we found crammed with the *impedimenta* of war. Wagon-trains choked the side streets, waiting in helpless confusion for the marching columns to pass, and clear the road. Small bodies of cavalry, on escort-duty, forced their way through the crush of vehicles, while excited staff-officers galloped to and fro, carrying orders to the front or rear. At the door of almost every house in the main street, lounged groups of mounted orderlies, the men holding their reins in their hands in anticipation of a sudden call for duty. General officers were abundant, showing that we were approaching army headquarters; and at every window I saw the wondering faces of women, as they watched with bewildered eyes the busy and martial scene before them. The fluttering of the tattered banners and colors, the brazen blare of the bugles, the shrill notes of the fifes, the reverberating rattle and roll of the drums, gave life and sound to the picture, as regiment after regiment, brigade after brigade, division after division, pushed forward with steady measured step to the music.

Marching on the flank of my company through the queer, ancient-looking town, with its picturesque gables, its crooked, half-paved streets, I imagined myself in some European hamlet. The residents even seemed strangely foreign, for they appeared to take but languid interest in our movements through their streets. The Federals were in possession to-day, to-morrow it might be the Confederates. Either way they were pushed to the wall, compelled to wait until the tide of war drifted away from them, and left the town to its wonted peace and quiet.

With these fancies passing through my head, our regiment came to an old tavern that stood in the heart of the city, its wide piazza filled with general staff-officers, their broad shoulder-straps glittering in the glancing afternoon sunlight. From the balcony above drooped the flag of the army-commander, and under its waving folds stood General Meade. The hot-tempered but good-hearted veteran had checked the head of his old corps in their wild greetings to his familiar face: so we continued to march before him, proudly, silently, with no other recognition from our old commander than the occasional lifting of his cap as the regimental colors fell in silent salute to his rank. I only saw him for a moment, but I thought his eyes glistened behind his glasses as he watched the corps march past. Erect and motionless the new leader of the mighty army stood beneath his great banner as if on parade. As the general thus watched the passage of the long column of bayonets, I caught brief glimpses of Warren's nervous features, and Webb's smiling bearded face as he nodded in reply to some remark of Hunt the artillerist. A moment more, and we were gone, soon after entering the open country beyond the town.

Our route now lay to the right; and as the sun went down we crossed a stone bridge which spanned the romantic winding Monocacy, soon finding ourselves on a high ridge overlooking the little city. As we marched forward over the macadamized road, I noticed two other columns of infantry moving through the fields below us; but they were too far away for me to distinguish the corps symbols on the staff ensigns. In the road under the ridge, between us and the distant infantry, moved the reserve batteries of artillery, in ponderous, massive array; the rumble of the heavy wheels coming sharp and distinct to my ears through the still air, as the pieces jolted over the stony roadway. Far away beyond the town glistened the white tops of the endless supply-trains, and beyond them, again, the rays of the setting sun were caught by the shining muskets of more troops in rapid motion; while straight ahead, on our own road, I could see the cavalry under Pleasonton and Kilpatrick as they cantered gayly onward in advance of the whole army.

It was evident by all these signs that before many days we would reach the expected battle-field.

"An' whare are we going, leftinant, annyhow?" asked Corporal Malone as he trotted along at my elbow. "When are we goin' to foight?"

"You are as wise on that point, Dennis, as I am. We will know soon enough where the battle is to be fought, when we get there."

"Arrah! any fool knows that, Master Frank. But I hope we won't be long getting there, for this knapsack is a thrifle heavy for convanient marchin'."

"We must not be impatient, Dennis," said I. "When it does come, the battle will bring death to many of us."

"Av coorse. That's the forthune of war, more's the pity. But the b'yes are getting used to that, like the cat we gossoons used to throw into the Liffey just for the fun of seeing it crawl out agin."

"Ah, Dennis! you're the same light-hearted Irishman, no matter what happens. Here you are, far away from the Liffey, fighting in a strange land, you hardly know what for."

"Shure, foightin' comes as nateral to an Irishman as his mother's milk. And as for knowing what we're foightin' f'r, ain't it for liberty or death, as my countryman Pathrick Henry said in the good ould days whin the red crass of England was furninst him?"

"Well," said I, laughing, "I never heard Patrick Henry called an Irishman before, though the name is suggestive."

"To be sure," responded Dennis confidently. "Though he never trod the ould sod, he was a thrue Irishman, wherever he was born."

"He proved himself a brave man in perilous times; but he was an American, and stood up to defend his native land, while you have no such incentive."

"That's a big word I don't precisely understhand," responded Dennis, hitching uneasily at his knapsack. "But shure, I've left dear ould Ireland for ever, and may as well die on the battle-field as in my bed. It's the land of liberty, anyhow."

"Too much liberty sometimes. If there had been less, this war would have been avoided."

So saying, I lapsed into silence, seeing the evening deepen into night, as we moved slowly onward. At nine o'clock the corps halted for bivouac in some open fields.

The two succeeding days were toilsome ones; for we marched constantly from early dawn until dusk, over dusty roads, past fruitful fields of wheat or corn, across rickety wooden bridges too weak to bear the artillery, through thriving and peaceful villages, until we reached the border-line between Maryland and Pennsylvania. Each night I had flung myself on the ground too tired to care for the supper Dennis so cheerfully prepared for me; and I began, like him, to long for the approaching battle. Any thing was preferable to these fatiguing, exhausting marches, through rolling valleys or over steep mountains. My feet were sore, my head seemed bound by a band of iron. My old wound, too, was beginning to make itself felt at almost every step, until it required all my pride, and strength of will, to keep me in my place.

Late in the afternoon of the first day of July we reached the picturesque town of Hanover. Near the cross-roads were lying the bloated carcasses of half a dozen cavalry horses, evidently slain in a brief skirmish between Pleasonton's and Stuart's troops, a few hours before our arrival.

Close to the road, near the scene of the cavalry fight, stood a farmhouse, at the gate of which was an old-fashioned pump and horse-trough. The pump-handle was in constant motion, as the weary, foot-sore soldiers flocked around it to quench their thirst with the delicious water that flowed into the mossy trough.

Coming up and waiting for my turn to drink, I noticed a sunburnt, gray-haired man, leaning over his rude gate, watching the troops. He was dressed in a faded, well-worn suit of homespun, having no doubt spent the day in the hayfield; and I could see that he was pleased that his pump was doing such good service.

THE CONFEDERATE GRAVE UNDER THE ROSES.

"Good-evening, sir," said I to him, removing my cap, and mopping the perspiration from my face. "It's rather hot weather, this, for marching."

"I 'spose it 'tis, though I never did any marching," was his brief response.

As the old farmer uttered the words he moved a little; and my eye was attracted by a new-made grave among a clump of rose-bushes, just inside the fence. Wondering at the sight, I ventured to ask the reason for its being there.

"Whose grave is that?" said I, pointing to the mound of fresh earth.

"A reb's," he replied laconically. "One that got killed in the fight the horsemen had here to-day."

"Indeed! and so you buried him."

"Yes: buried him myself. They left him lyin' in the road, out thar, just as he fell. I could do no less, you know."

"Of course! but why did you make your rose-garden a graveyard?"

"Wa-al, it was the wimmen that wanted it so. Yer see, stranger," and the old man's voice trembled and grew husky, "yer see, I had a boy once. He went out with the Pennsylvany Resarves, and fou't along with McClellan, down thar among those Chicka-oming swamps. And one day a letter come. It was writ by a woman; and she told us as how a battle had bin fou't near her house, while she and another woman lay hid all day in the cellar. When the battle was o'er, them wimmen came out, and found our Johnny thar, his hair all bloody and tangled in the grass. So they digged a grave in the soft earth of their gardin, and buried my boy right amongst their flowers, for the sake of the mother who would never see him agin. So when I saw that poor reb a-layin' out thar, all dead and bloody in the dust of the road, I sed I'd bury him. And the gals, they sed, 'Yes, father, bury him among the rose-trees.' That's why I did it, stranger."

Then the poor old father's voice was choked by a smothered sob, while a faint cry behind him betrayed the presence of a sister to the dead hero lying in his garden grave near Richmond.

"Indeed, sir," said I, feeling my own throat tighten over the sweet pathos of the little story, "I can appreciate the love you bear your dead son. It must be some consolation to remember what you have done for the man whose body lies there under the bushes."

"Yes, stranger: that 'ere grave ain't much," — and the old

man turned to look at the rude mound his hands had made, — "it ain't much, but it will be something to remember our Johnny by."

Bidding the farmer good-by, I hastened after the regiment, my eyes dimmed with tears, but my spirits strangely strengthened by this touching instance of human love and forgiveness.

CHAPTER XVII.

A NIGHT MARCH.

"Now was the noon of night; and all was still,
Save where the sentinel paced his rounds."

UR corps went into camp just beyond the Pennsylvanian town of Hanover, in a wide field of ripening wheat, which was trodden flat as the divisions of infantry marched over it to their respective positions. The farmer owning the land seemed the picture of despair, as he stood at the gap in the fence, watching with astonished eyes the ruthless destruction of his grain. The unfortunate farmer becoming troublesome, I was stationed in the road with a guard for the double purpose of keeping him quiet, and at the same time preventing our men from straggling towards the town, its modest church-spires being visible beyond a strip of woods on our right.

"I say, Mr. Officer," cried the man, as I pushed him aside with my sword to let the column pass, "you've no right to go in there. That's my wheat them soldiers are treading into the dirt."

"Oh! we won't argue the question of rights," said I: "when on the march, as we are, armies can not stop for trifles. At any rate, your grain is doomed: so stand aside, sir, and let the troops go on."

"But that's wheat. Do you understand? Wheat! Almost

ready to cut too. Why didn't that general of yours take his men into the meadows? The grass there is all mown. Why does he spoil my wheat?"

"My good man," I replied, "I know it seems hard to destroy your wheat-crop; but don't you see that our artillery and wagons are going into the meadows? Had we gone there, they would have been compelled to take your wheat-field, and ploughed ground is too soft for wheels. Besides, they need the hay for their horses and mules."

"I'm a ruined man," groaned the distracted farmer. "Why, now they are carrying off my fences! What are they going to do with them?"

"Burn 'em, me darlint," said Dennis, who had, as usual, chosen to join my temporary guard. "Shure, thim rails makes illigant fires."

"Fires! Burn them! Why, they'll tear down my house next."

"Come, come, my friend. There's no use your staying here, for you can not stop the destruction of your property. You had far better see the general, and get his certificate of the damage done. The government will pay you for it."

"That so? Well, if I get the pay for it I don't care how much they take," exclaimed the farmer, as he started across the fields to find General Sykes.

"An' do ye think Uncle Sam will pay him?" queried Dennis, a look of blank astonishment spreading over his fun-loving face.

"One of these days, I suppose, though there won't be much haste about it," I replied as we fell in the rear of the brigade to rejoin our regiment.

Our expectations of a quiet night's rest were, however, doomed to be disappointed; for the men had scarcely finished pitching their little shelter-tents when the bugles sounded the ominous call to strike them again for the march. In less than an hour after we had entered the wheat-field the entire corps was in rapid motion.

The sun was dropping behind the range of hills we had crossed during the afternoon, as we entered the main road. We soon learned the cause of this sudden, unexpected movement; for word ran along the line that the Confederate army had been encountered in force at a village called Gettysburg, that there had been a heavy skirmish by the First and Eleventh Corps under General Reynolds, and that the general himself had been killed, so the engagement must have been a determined one. Indeed, Major Harding told me that General Sykes had received peremptory orders to march all night, and, if possible, reach the scene of hostilities before daylight: we had therefore a tramp of twenty-odd miles before us. This was nice news after the thirty-six miles we had traveled since sunrise; but the necessity was evidently an urgent one, for the officers were instructed to keep their men well together.

Tired and exhausted as I was by the fatigues of the past few days, since leaving Frederick City, the knowledge that we were now hurrying to the battle-field gave me fresh strength; while Dennis was bursting with delight at the prospect of another scrimmage, his sallies keeping the company in excellent humor.

As darkness fell we entered a string of villages, the inmates who were gathered at their gates being wild with enthusiasm over our coming. Stalwart men stood unweariedly pumping water for the thirsty troops, while the women handed more fortunate soldiers broad slices of bread-and-butter with rich draughts of pure milk. Over the gateways hung lighted lanterns, and from the limbs of apple-trees the stars and stripes fluttered in the cool night air. Our veterans cheered lustily as they passed under the flags, while the villagers waved their hats and handkerchiefs to the men passing onward to do battle for them. It was an exciting and wonderful scene.

Many a touching incident I witnessed during this memorable night march. Young girls shed tears as they watched the brothers of other women march on to possible death; while many a soldier, begrimed with dust and exhausted by fatigue, thought of the old home where he had left his own loved ones. Stopping for a moment at the gate of a dwelling, I noticed a young mother leaning over it with her chubby child in her arms. Above the woman's head swung a couple of common stable-lanterns, their soft light falling full upon her face. The child was crowing with delight at the strange pageant, as it watched the armed host pass on.

"I beg your pardon, ma'am," said Jim Manners, one of my men, as he dropped the heel of his musket on the ground, and peered wistfully into the faces of the mother and her child, — "I beg pardon, but may I kiss that baby of yours? I've one just like him at home; at least, he was when I last saw him two years ago."

The mother, a sympathetic tear rolling down her blooming cheek, silently held out the child. Jim pressed his unshaven face to its innocent, smiling lips for a moment, and then walked on, saying, —

"God bless you, ma'am, for that! God bless you!"

Poor Jim Manners! He never saw his boy again in life, for a bullet laid him low the next day as we made our first charge, and he found his grave on the field where so many thousand brave fellows fell. As we buried him in the twilight, I remembered the kiss he had given the stranger's child, drawing from the incident another lesson of the depth of human love.

So rapidly did the corps march during the night, that, about one in the morning, we had arrived within striking distance of the position assigned us; then came the welcome order to lie down and rest. As the column halted in the darkness, the men threw themselves on the narrow strips of sward by the roadside, sleeping in long rows as they lay wrapped in their blankets and ponchos.

For me, however, sleep was not so easy. The excitement of the night march, and the pain of my swollen foot, as the tender flesh of my old wound rebelled against the strain put upon it,

combined to drive slumber from my eyes. As I lay on my
blankets, gazing at the stars, my thoughts were busy with the
past, back to the days of my boyhood when there was no
dream of civil war in the land. I saw in fancy the quiet old
home, as it stood under the shadows of the big elms, while the
face of my dear mother, who at that moment might be praying
for the safety of her boy, seemed to be close to mine. Then I
thought of Kate in her native valley; and we were once more
galloping over the picturesque roads, the woods resounding
with our light and joyful laughter.

But how different were these fancied scenes from those around
me! A confused murmur of sounds came to my ears amid the
darkness, for the movements of troops had by no means ended.
The low, monotonous rumble of artillery ran along the ground;
and, as I leaned on my elbow, I could distinguish the outlines
of the heavy guns and their caissons, as the batteries moved
slowly forward to some advantageous position selected for
them. Now and then a hoarse command was uttered, followed
by a sudden increase of speed; and the earth under me trembled and shook with the jarring motion of the wheels as they
were jolted over the deep ruts in the road. Then came a
curious clattering sound, which my accustomed ear knew to
be caused by the hurrying movements of cavalry, and soon
after a long column of horsemen passed up the middle of the
road, by the side of which my comrades were so calmly sleeping. Silently yet rapidly these mounted men rode by, their
heavy sabers jingling in musical cadence as their horses' hoofs
thundered on the soft earth.

"Steady, men!" said an authoritative voice; and the column
slackened its pace for a minute or two, only to be put into
swifter movement by the sharper cry of, "Forward!"

The cavalry gone, I began to hear the creak of more wheels,
and saw, in the fields on the opposite side of the road, the faint
outlines of the ammunition and supply trains going into park to
await further orders. As I saw wagon after wagon move into

line with its fellows, their white tops glistening in the uncertain starlight, I knew we were still in the rear: the projected battle-ground must be some distance beyond.

Listening to all these confused sounds, I realized the majesty and magnificence of war, the fascination and romance that surround the soldier on actual field-service. The masses of infantry, the columns of swiftly moving cavalry, the ponderous field-batteries, and the interminable supply-trains supplied the principal features of the wild picture, which had a solemn dignity about it one could not ignore. To the inexperienced eye the confusion would seem inextricable; but I was aware that there was a system in it all, that a decided, persistent plan of operations was being carried out.

Then I thought of the uncertainty of my fate during the next few hours. Thousands of brave soldiers, who had passed scathless through many a hard-fought battle, would on the morrow see their last fight, make their final charge, and from living men, full of daring ambition and fervent hope, become mere clods of clay. Many a fine fellow would, in the flush of his manhood, be lying the next night cold and stiff on the field; and beside these fated ones there were others, who, though still alive, would be writhing in pain from wounds that might yet end in death.

Despite all these horrors that I knew were to come, there was a glamour over my eyes; for I began once again to glory in anticipation over the turmoil and fierceness of the approaching struggle. I even forgot the grave issues at stake, so readily does the trained soldier become hardened in his trade. It mattered but little to me at that moment, whether slavery was crushed, or the Union of the States preserved. I recked nothing of the ends in view. It was only the tremendous game of war I felt an interest in: beyond that, there was no thought of the future.

It is this feeling that molds the soldier into a true hero, and explains the motives of so many brave men passing from country to country, from camp to camp, only eager for and intent on employment in the field of danger. To these soldiers of fortune, the cause they fight for is of secondary importance. What they seek is the exhilarating excitement of battle, the shock and clash of arms: their whole aim is to join in some headlong, desperate charge. The spice of danger is the great charm that possesses them, for to your true soldier the fear of death never comes. He may experience a nameless dread at the first moment of going into action; but, that once over, he is cool and collected, yet full of daring and momentary rage. The glare and smoke of battle intoxicate him: the shadow of death that hovers over him is lost sight of in the brightness and grandeur of the scene in which he is an actor.

O War! War! How natural thou art to mankind! How slow would be the progress of history or civilization, did not thy torrent of fire and blood sweep aside every obstacle, thus doing at a single stroke what years of diplomacy would fail to accomplish!

Lying thus on the moist and fragrant earth, with these confused fancies flitting through my brain, I thought once more of Tom Marshall, and wondered if he were still alive. It was now almost three years since we had parted on the bridge, but beyond the one letter received from him in college I had heard nothing from or of him.

"Oh that this struggle were over!" I exclaimed, forgetting all about the romance of war. "Would that to-morrow's battle were the last!"

With these words on my lips, my tired body succumbed at length to fatigue, and I sank into a dreamless and heavy slumber.

CHAPTER XVIII.

CHARGE AND COUNTER-CHARGE.

" The shout
Of battle now begun, and rushing sound
Of onset, ended soon each milder thought."

HEN the bugles of our corps rang out the reveille, the sun had already risen clear and warm, throwing long red streaks of light over the fields and woods. Leaping to my feet, I found every thing already in commotion. Thousands of little camp-fires were blazing in the fields, as the men prepared their frugal breakfasts ; the lines of stacked muskets alone showing the position of the different regiments and brigades. The mists were rising in rifts and circling wreaths under the combined influence of the sun's rays and the heat of the countless fires, only lingering among the tree-tops of the adjacent woods. The atmosphere was, however, still raw and chilly ; the heavy dew that had fallen during the night making the grass quite wet.

In every direction there were signs of intense activity. Troops were moving up, the wagons had already drawn out of park, and the hum of many voices mingled with the neighing of horses or the bellowing of mules. It was, indeed, a true battle morning, the beginning of a struggle the result of which none could forecast. As I looked about, watching the marching columns or listening to the careless laughter of the soldiers

near me, I realized that many a joyous fellow, now only intent
on his hard-tack and coffee, would never see another sunrise or
respond to the familiar reveille.

"What are you thinking about, Wilmot?" asked Captain
Burch. "Getting nervous over the battle?"

"Not at all. It was the thought that so many lives must
be sacrificed to-day."

"It will be a tremendous fight, no doubt," remarked the captain. "Some difference from our first battle at Big Bethel, eh?"

"That was only a brief skirmish, Burch, compared to what
we are going to have here."

"Leftinant, the coffee's ready," said Dennis. "Won't you
come too, captain?"

"Of course I will," replied the captain. "I am as hungry as
a wild-cat."

The scene by daylight was far different from what I had
imagined it to be in the darkness. To my surprise, I saw we
were near a cluster of houses, the outskirts of Gettysburg. It
had evidently been a beautiful spot before the remorseless tread
of the army came to crush out its smiling features. The fences
had disappeared for fuel, a few scattered posts alone marking
where they had stood; even the hedges were destroyed as
wagons and cannon had been cruelly driven through them;
and a barn near by was a complete wreck, the boarding having
been stripped from the frame to strengthen a bridge over the
creek for the passage of our artillery. Ruin and destruction
had begun: the iron heel of war betrayed its presence everywhere, the ruthless despoil of property attesting the unavoida-
ble severity of all military operations.

Although our corps had not yet received orders to move,
other troops were on the march; for a column of infantry
was hurrying across the fields to our left, their artillery passing up the road we had occupied during the night. As the
guns rumbled along, I noticed that they were stripped and
ready for action. Far away in the rear I could see another

corps coming up, heading to the right. The army was girding up its loins for the struggle.

While Captain Burch and I were quietly sipping the coffee Dennis had provided, an ominous rattle of musketry began beyond some woods in front, showing that the pickets of the opposing armies were already at work. This was the overture to the terrible concert; these dropping shots sounding musically in our ears, as their sharp patter rose and fell. Before we had finished breakfast the rolling musketry grew heavier; and a battery opened a desultory fire for a few minutes, only to lapse into silence again, as the picket duel slackened, and finally ceased altogether.

Our bugles now began their brazen clamor: so I hastily swallowed the last of my coffee, and, buckling on my sword and revolver, answered the call for our regiment to fall in. A few minutes after, the entire corps was in motion. We went forward for about a mile, when the head of the column turned off into a piece of open woods, on the right of the road, where the line of battle was formed. As no skirmishers were thrown forward, I knew we were still on the interior line, so flung myself on the ground while the corps awaited orders.

An hour passed in silence, our brigade being moved a few hundred yards to the left to straighten the line. While thus occupied, an aide galloped up, and distributed General Meade's order to his army. On the brief address being read by Fitzgerald, our adjutant, we learned that our general intended to give all the honors of the battle to his soldiers, relying on their steadfast courage to successfully carry out the simple plan of operations he had decided upon. We were reminded that to win the battle was to shorten the war, that to lose it would entail fresh sacrifices on the army and the nation. Our antagonists were as brave as ourselves: so it would require all our heroism, strategy, and strength, to obtain a victory. Such was the simple, unpretending appeal of our general; and it was curious to observe the effect it had upon the men in the ranks.

Every face wore a look of resolution, every hand grasped its musket more firmly. It was evident our leader had shrewdly touched the right chord this time. The battle was already half won.

This brief ceremony over, the different brigades were formed in masses; and the corps marched slowly, deliberately, *en éche-lon*, through the woods into some scattered fields. Finally we entered a bit of open country; and, as the command passed obliquely over some rising ground, I caught a glimpse of the main line, the outlines of the batteries in position being clearly defined against the cloud of white smoke raised by the incessant skirmish-fire now going on. Here we were halted, word being passed that we were again to occupy our old position of reserve.

It was evident that the battle would soon begin in earnest, that we were only to be summoned when a decisive blow was to be dealt. It was an old experience with us. Finding that no further maneuvers were contemplated, the men threw themselves on the soft earth, and fell asleep. Having passed so wakeful a night, I slumbered with the rest.

I had been asleep some hours, when the headquarter bugles rang out the alarm; every man springing instinctively to his feet, as the shrill notes sounded in their ears. The sharp call was repeated again and again, as the several commands took up the refrain, the entire corps standing to arms before they had ceased. Then I saw General Sykes gallop forward with his staff over the field; and the next moment our division began following him towards the main line, now fiercely engaged from right to left.

"What's the matter?" I inquired of Major Harding: "where are we going?"

"Away to the left, somewhere," he replied: "our line has got doubled up there. At least, so said the aide who brought the orders. He must have come right through the line of fire, for his face was bleeding badly when he galloped up."

"How 'doubled up'? I don't understand," said I.

"General Fletcher sent our colonel word that Sickles at the head of the Third Corps has got into a hole; so I suppose we are going to his assistance."

"Close up, men, close up!" shouted Colonel Lloyd, turning round in his saddle. "Major Harding, keep the men well up together there, in the center. We shall be on the double-quick in a minute."

The crisis was assuredly a critical one; for, as we were getting the column into tolerably good shape, the voice of our colonel was again heard. Looking up, I saw him standing in his stirrups, waving his sword, and urging the regiment forward on the run. By this time we had entered a narrow road, with thick hedges on either side; and I saw that the first division, under Griffin, was moving over the field on our right in columns by brigades, as though anxious to reach the scene of conflict before us. We went on in this pell-mell fashion for over a mile, still obliquing to the left; the shells from the Confederate batteries beginning to fly over our heads as we advanced. But their guns had not yet got the proper range, so we managed to hold together pretty well.

All at once a deafening roar of rapid cannonading broke out near the head of our column, as the corps batteries, galloping furiously forward, unlimbered and went into action. The musketry we were approaching now grew more intense and vengeful. It was quite evident that before many minutes we should be in the midst of the *mêlée*.

"General Fletcher! For God's sake, hurry up your brigade!" cried a young staff-officer as his horse leaped over the hedge into the road. "Make haste, sir, or you will be too late."

As he uttered the words in a passionate manner, the speaker once more plunged his spurs into the dripping flanks of his foaming steed, and galloped off to urge haste on Griffin's troops. He was but a boy in years, though a veteran in courage; and I watched him admiringly as he dashed across the field. He had ridden scarcely a dozen rods when I saw a puff of white smoke break over his head, showing that a shell had burst; while at the same instant the doomed officer reeled in his saddle, and then fell headlong with his horse to the ground. Both had been killed. The young soldier was at rest: the remainder of the battle must be fought without him.

But I had no time to reflect upon his fate, for just then we were called to face our own. As we reached the crest of a rise in the road, the situation of affairs was revealed at a glance. Below, in a narrow sort of glen, was massed the left of the Third Corps, fighting stubbornly, but confusedly, with a strong force of the enemy. Colors waved tumultuously amidst the wedged mass of men, while mounted officers wildly endeavored to restore order, and reform the shattered ranks. A merciless fire of musketry and grape-shot was being poured into the flank of the devoted corps, and for the moment it seemed as if the enemy were carrying every thing before them.

General Fletcher, our brigade commander, was now riding at the side of our column, uttering some orders; but so deafening was the roar of musketry and cannon, I could only understand by the look on his face, and the movement of his sword-arm, that he was urging us forward. At that moment thirty or forty men came hurrying by in a body on their way to the rear. Those in the center were carrying a stretcher on their shoulders, and I caught a glimpse of a velvet cuff among the blankets.

"Who is it?" cried two or three of our men.

"General Sickles," was the whispered reply.

"Much hurt?"

"Leg shattered by a shell. May be dying."

As the hospital party disappeared, our division rushed forward with a wild hurrah, in columns by brigade. Soon piercing the confused lines of the enfiladed corps, we threw ourselves in front, and began forming in line of battle. My regiment happened to halt at the edge of a small clump of woods, lying a little way to the right of the Little Round Top; and as we fell into position, the entire brigade opened a well-directed volley on a heavy force of Confederates coming upon our front.

Scarcely had the men begun emptying their muskets, when an order came to cease firing and prepare to charge. Hastily reloading their pieces, our men stood pretty steady under the galling practice of the enemy's batteries. It was a painful period of suspense, to wait thus for the word; but it was of

GENERAL SICKLES, WOUNDED.

brief duration, for just then, the bugles sounding the advance, away we dashed across the rocky hollow.

Right in front, on the other side of the glen, stood a battery of some three or four wide-mouthed Napoleon guns. It was to take or silence these that the brigade was sent forward.

"God bless you, Master Frank!" exclaimed Dennis earnestly, as he seized my hand. "We mayn't see each other alive again. Be jabers! but this *is* the divil's own scrimmage."

I returned the honest corporal's grasp without a word, for we were already on the move.

As we crossed the glen at a mad, headlong pace, the guns of the battery opened on us with a murderous discharge of grape and canister, at close range. But we were now going down hill, so escaped the greater part of the shower of iron pellets, which went whistling over our heads; though a good many men dropped. Before the gunners could reload we were upon them, and a desperate hand-to-hand fight ensued. The dash of our brigade was so sudden, and our progress across the glen so rapid, the movement was a surprise for the Confederates; consequently the battery fell into our hands before their infantry supports could come up. On reaching the muzzle of one of the guns I found myself confronted by a tall gunner, who having seized a musket made a lunge at me with the bayonet. Instinctively warding off the thrust with my sword, the point of the fellow's bayonet became entangled in the guard, and I felt it pierce my fingers. Before I could recover myself, Corporal Malone sprang to my side, and drove his own bayonet through the throat of my brave antagonist, who, with a groan, fell to the ground as the piece became our prize.

The other regiments had meanwhile pushed on to either side of the battery, and engaged the attention of the enemy's supports: so we enjoyed a brief breathing-spell. Looking about me, I saw that the battle was now raging furiously on our right, the headquarter flag of General Sykes being in the very midst of the fierce *mêlée*. The bright flashes of the muskets illumined the clouds of powder-smoke, and revealed the ranks of the combatants as they struggled, foot to foot, for the mastery. It seemed strange that we should so suddenly have nothing to do in the center of so hot and deadly a combat, but our respite was only a temporary one.

While Griffin's division was uttering a wild, triumphant cheer, on seeing the Confederate line stagger and begin to give way, the left of our brigade fell off in the direction of the Round Top; and in a minute after our regiment followed in its turn. I then saw that the face of the hill was in the hands of a considerable force of Confederate troops. Nothing daunted, the head of the column gave a rousing cheer; and up we went over the loose, slippery rubble. The Confederates made a gallant effort to hold their vantage-ground, but we outnumbered them; and though it was a terrible task to clamber up the rocks in the face of a galling fire, we accomplished it, and were in a few minutes at the very top, with the enemy in full retreat.

It was with a frightful loss, however, that we had won the position; for the rocky hill was thickly strewn with our dead and wounded. As I looked about me, trying to discover who were missing, my first thought was of Dennis; for the timely aid he had rendered me over the brass gun in the glen was not to be readily forgotten. I remembered, that, just after we had begun our awful climb through that storm of bullets, I had lost sight of him: so I glanced anxiously along the line of my company, hoping to see his face. As I did so the brave fellow appeared by my side.

"The saints be praised, an' I foind ye all roight and safe!" was his joyful salutation. "But what's that? Yer face is all bleeding. Are ye much hurt?"

Putting my hand to my cheek, I was surprised to find it covered with blood, for I had felt no wound. Then I remembered that a shell had burst over our heads when half-way up the hill. A chip of it must have grazed my cheek. The wound was, however, very slight.

"Oh! it's nothing, Dennis," said I, "only a scratch. Are you all right?"

"Iviry bit of me is here," responded the corporal quaintly; "though at one toime I thought I was a goner. Down by that big stone below, which we had to go round, I fell behind, for me fut shlipped; and I found mesilf all alone, forninst a big feller who had hid behind the rock. Begorra! before I could say 'How are ye?' he sthruck his murdherin' gun into me face. I belaved mesilf a dead man; but just then a bullit kem along, and tuk him by the side of the head. He forgot to pull his trigger, so I come up and left him."

As Dennis finished his speech, Colonel Lloyd appeared.

"Wilmot, have you seen any thing of Adjutant Fitzgerald?" he asked.

"No, colonel, not since we left the glen," I replied.

"I hope he's not hit," said the colonel.

"Well, I think he is," remarked Captain Burch : "I saw him stumble and fall just as we passed through that line of alder-bushes below."

"Some of you run down and find him," said the colonel.

Half a dozen men darted over the crest of the hill towards the alders; soon returning with the adjutant, who was evidently badly wounded.

"Well, Fitz," said I, leaning over the poor fellow, as they laid him down, "what is it? Where are you hit?"

"Somewhere in the chest," he responded faintly : "I don't exactly know where. But I'm afraid it's all up with me."

"Don't say that, Fitzgerald," exclaimed the colonel. "Ah! here's the doctor. He will soon put you to rights."

Surgeon Humphrey's face wore a grave look as he gazed at the wounded officer. Kneeling down, he opened the adjutant's coat and shirt, then silently rose to his feet.

"It's mortal," he whispered to me, with a mournful shake of his head. "Who is to tell him?"

The dying man had, however, narrowly watched the surgeon, reading his own fate in the averted face and whisper.

"Well, doctor? If I'm going to die, why don't you say so, and be done with it?" he exclaimed petulantly.

"I'm afraid you are badly wounded, Fitzgerald," replied Surgeon Humphrey; "but I'll have you carried to the rear, where you will rest easier."

"No! no! Let me stay here with the boys. Let me die with them around me. Ah! I shall never form the parade for them again. Good-by, colonel. Good-by, Frank : you'll find my mother's address in my note-book here. When I am dead, Frank, write her how I died, and tell her my last thoughts were of her. Dear old mother! This will be sad news for her. You *will* write, Frank, won't you?"

"Yes, Fitz, if I live," I replied.

"Ah! yes, I forgot. This fight isn't ended yet. If not you, Frank, some one else must do it."

As the adjutant uttered the words in a faint, weary manner, a loud cheer rose from the glen.

"What's that?" he exclaimed in a stronger voice, trying to rise. "What's that cheer for?"

"The enemy has fallen back. We have regained the lost ground," replied the surgeon as he wiped the dying man's damp brow.

THE DYING ADJUTANT.

"That's good. Lift me up, Frank. Let me see them once more."

We lifted him tenderly, and he took a long and wistful look into the glen. Griffin had taken up a strong position, and was now holding his line intact. Though full of smoke the scene was readily understood by Fitzgerald.

"Thank God! we have driven them back," said he. "I'm glad to know that. Good-by, boys! Good-by, Zou-zous! Don't forget Tom Fitzgerald when he is gone. Good-by, Frank! Remember — my — mother. — Re — mem — ber — mo — ther."

And as the brave spirit fled, we laid the dead body on one

side to prepare for continuing the battle. Orders had been passed down the line for the men to imitate their fellows on the lower ground, and build breastworks out of the loose stones so abundant on the hill-top. In a few minutes a low, irregular wall rose in serried outline along the crest of the hill; while the pickets, half way down, dug little pits with their hands in the rubble to protect them from the bullets that were still whizzing about their ears.

As I was watching the men build their rude stone breast-work, Dennis touched my elbow, whispering, —

"I say, leftinant, there's Gineral Warren. Maybe ould Meade ain't fur off."

"Where?"

"Right over there. Don't ye see him sitting on that stone beyant?"

"Yes: now I do. I wonder what he is doing here."

"He's looking to see if there isn't a chance for another scrimmage," muttered Malone. "Shure, he's niver so happy as when there's a rigilar row."

While he was speaking, the general rose from his seat, and approached me.

"Lieutenant, do you know General Crawford when you see him?" he asked.

"Yes, general, quite well," I replied.

"Well, he's waiting with his division down there," pointing towards the road over which we had advanced an hour or two before. "I want to give him an order, and have no aide with me."

"I'll go with pleasure," said I, thrusting my sword into its scabbard. "What is your message, general?"

"I want him to charge over that glen again. Don't you see they are forming to storm this hill? We must anticipate their charge by one of our own."

"Would't it be better for me to bring General Crawford here? You can explain the situation to him."

"Yes," replied General Warren. "If you can do so quickly. Otherwise tell him to move forward at once, and charge on that line to the right of those rocks;" and he pointed to the spot where we had advanced on the battery.

"All right, sir," said I, running along the ridge.

I had gone some fifty paces towards the rear when I met a mounted officer, his horse carefully picking his way over the loose stones. It was General Crawford.

"I was sent to look for you, sir," said I to him. "General Warren wishes to see you."

"Where is the general?"

"Just above, sir. I'll show you the way," I replied, retracing my steps.

"What! haven't you gone yet?" angrily exclaimed General Warren as I re-appeared. "Didn't I tell you" —

"Here is General Crawford, sir. I met him coming to meet you," I interrupted; for I well knew how quick-tempered the general could be.

"Oh, all right! I beg your pardon, lieutenant. — Why, Crawford, where in the devil's name have you been?"

"Where you left me," replied General Crawford quietly. "Having received no orders, I came to see if we were needed."

"I want you to take four or five regiments into this Devil's Glen, as these men have aptly named it," said General Warren. "It's a hot place, though. Are your men in good spirits?"

"Never better. They are really impatient at being kept standing idle under fire."

"Well, lose no time in taking them in. Send out a heavy skirmish-line, and charge with your main force. Break up that movement of the enemy before they get too strong. Do you think you can do it?"

"If it's possible for any troops, general, the Pennsylvania Reserves can do it," said General Crawford somewhat haughtily, as he stroked his luxuriant side-whiskers.

"They ought to fight well on the soil of their own State,"

muttered General Warren grimly, as he returned the salute of
our third-division commander, who immediately disappeared.

A few minutes after, the Bucktails Regiment came forward
in close skirmish-line; and on looking towards the road I saw
several regiments moving to the front. Rapidly forming in
line of battle, the Pennsylvanians dashed forward with a loud
cheer, their general at their head with one of the colors in his
hand. Battery after battery opened fire on the heroic bat-

BUCKTAILS GOING INTO THE DEVIL'S GLEN.

talions, wrapping them in flame and smoke, until a loud cheer
announced the success of the hazardous movement.

It was now getting dark, and we fancied the day's work to
be over. But in this we were mistaken; for, as Crawford's men
fell back, the Confederates gathered fresh strength, and made
another bold and desperate move.

Above the dip in the ground where the road ran, one of our
field-batteries had been placed, though it was not visible to the
enemy. Our line seeming to be weak just there, they made a

dash upon it in the gathering twilight; evidently expecting to pierce our line, and so cut off the Round Top.

The rapid fire of our skirmishers, as they lay in the glen, was the first intimation we had of an attack; but orders came running down the line at the same moment for our men to reserve their fire until they saw something to aim at.

"That comes from Warren," remarked Captain Burch. "I remember how he swore at Big Bethel because our green troops banged away before they were within range."

On came the Confederate column in the uncertain light, and we were beginning to see a dark mass moving silently, swiftly, towards the narrow road; when suddenly our battery on the knoll opened a tearing broadside of grape and canister. As the flashes of the guns lightened up the scene, I saw that the entire glen was swarming with men. Now was our opportunity; and as the battery sent another shower hurtling through the air, our infantry fired a deafening, blinding volley into the surging columns. Exposed to so heavy and unexpected a fire, the Confederates wavered a moment, and began falling back. Then the two brigades of regulars rushed out on the charge. We again held possession of the glen.

This ended the fighting on the left of Meade's line for that day; and the darkness soon put a stop to the incessant fusillade all along our front, from the Round Top to Culp's Hill. But we knew the battle had come to no definite result: we should have it fiercely renewed the next day.

CHAPTER XIX.

A MIDNIGHT ADVENTURE.

"And thousands had sunk on the ground overpowered,
The weary to sleep, and the wounded to die."

IGHTFALL found me asleep under the lee of a bowlder, when I was awakened near midnight by Colonel Lloyd. He informed me that a reconnoissance by a small party had been ordered to be made along a sunken road by the side of a creek considerably to the left of our position. Signs of some mysterious movement had been reported by the pickets: so I had been selected to command the little expedition, consisting of twenty or thirty volunteers, for the purpose of ascertaining the scope of the enemy's maneuvers.

"Pick out your men carefully, Wilmot," said the colonel, "and run as little risk as possible."

"Rather a good joke, colonel. Order a fellow off on a bit of dangerous duty, and tell him to run no risks!" I replied with a laugh.

"I promised General Fletcher I would caution you, Wilmot, when he mentioned your name in connection with this movement. You are to find out all you can, but the general wishes no foolhardiness. He is sending a small party, because you can all the more easily escape attention."

"All right, sir," I replied: "I'll do my best to come back safely, and report. May I tell Major Harding I am going?"

"No, I will do that. You must get off quietly. If that old bear, your captain, hears you are chosen instead of him, he will rouse the whole regiment with his grumbling."

"Captain Burch's grumbling means nothing," said I. "He's as brave as a lion."

"Of course he's brave," replied the colonel. "If he wasn't he wouldn't be an officer in my regiment very long. But come, Wilmot, go pick out your men, and be off with you."

I had no difficulty in obtaining the necessary number of volunteers. After getting my men together, and receiving such brief directions as our colonel deemed necessary, I gave the word, and started down the hillside, succeeding, after several tumbles over loosened rocks, in passing quietly through the picket-line, and mustered my little command in the glen.

Moving round the base of the hill, now thickly covered with troops, we entered a road which ran along the bank of a creek. Going on towards the Confederate lines until we could hear voices, I called a halt. Every thing seeming exceedingly quiet, I established a few sentries, and made up my mind for a comfortless bivouac while awaiting developments.

My men, having volunteered for what they expected would be exciting duty, were naturally restless over the apparently barren result of our midnight expedition. In this mood they began poking about the bank of the creek like so many deer-hounds who had lost their scent. Cautioning them not to stray away too far, I wrapped myself in my cape, and, leaning against a massive rock, speculated on the events the coming day would bring with it. Despite these thoughts I had almost fallen asleep, through sheer weariness, when Dennis roused me with an excited whisper.

"Leftinant darlint, thim divils, the Ribs, are up to some mischief beyant."

"Where? What are they doing?"

"Down the road, a bit. Shure, Sergeant Foster and mesilf saw thim, just now."

"Come, come, Dennis, no nonsense now. What did you see, or did you only imagine something?"

"Now, did I ever give ye a false alarrum?"

"Not that I remember, Malone. But why don't you speak to the point?"

"Oh, av coorse! That's the way wid yez all. An Irishman's a fool always."

Finding that Dennis would take his own time in imparting his information, I walked rapidly down the road; at the same time ordering him to get the men together and follow me. Half a dozen rods below I found Foster, the sergeant, crouching at the edge of the creek, intently peering across. Slipping down by his side, I asked Foster what had happened to alarm him.

"I scarcely know, myself," he replied; "though I'm sure something queer is up on the other side there."

I followed his eyes to the opposite bank as he spoke, but could discern nothing. At the same time Dennis came up with the men, who, taking their cue from me, crouched on the grass in silence.

"But you must have seen something, Sam: else why send Dennis to me?" I remarked in a low tone.

"Well, you see, sir, Dennis and I found a cherry-tree just above; and we climbed into it to get some. While we were feeling our way among the limbs, I distinctly heard a voice give the command to halt, and with it the sound of several men dropping the butts of their muskets on the grass. A few minutes after, some order was given, which I did not understand; when something heavy was thrown on the ground. Dennis and I then slipped out of the tree, and I sent him to tell you."

I made no reply to this whispered explanation, contenting myself with listening. A few seconds after, we all heard something fall into the water with a sudden splash. Bidding my men keep quiet, I took Foster with me, and crept cautiously down the creek a few paces.

"See there!" whispered the sergeant, as he excitedly seized my arm.

"Where?"

"Why, there!" he replied, pointing eagerly to the figure of a man dimly seen struggling through the deep water of the narrow creek.

"Hush! Pass the word for our men, and make no noise," said I, watching the fellow in the water.

As my men joined me, we crawled noiselessly towards the spot where the intruder evidently intended landing. When he clambered up the bank, Foster and I caught him by the throat, thus preventing his giving an alarm. The Confederate, completely surprised by our assault, surrendered almost without a struggle; the touch of my revolver to his forehead showing him the folly of such an effort. Tied to his waist was a strong cord, which I divined to be for the purpose of hauling some object across. The men gave it a steady pull, soon having in their possession a stout pole.

I was now satisfied that a reconnoitering party was endeavoring to cross the creek; and, as the end of our bit of timber had another cord fastened to it, I told my men to pull it also, and so landed a second pole.

In the mean time I had mustered the whole of my party, preparatory to receiving whoever might venture across the rude bridge. Scarcely were these arrangements perfected, when a Confederate officer crawled slowly over. He was immediately seized, but made so desperate a resistance I was afraid our presence would be discovered by those left behind.

The affair had now become really exciting, my men being crazy with delight at the fun in prospect. We had not long to wait; for, soon after the officer had been disposed of, they began creeping, one after the other, over their narrow bridge. As each new-comer appeared, he was seized in silence, and hurried to the rear, until we had bagged nearly thirty; Dennis keeping tally in excited whispers, as the captured birds were taken from the trap they had themselves contrived.

Our visitors were evidently astounded at the unexpected turn of affairs; for, as each man came over, he was made a prisoner before he realized the fact. Indeed, I began laughing quietly as the number of our prisoners increased, wondering how long it would last. As Dennis tallied twenty-eight, a second officer was captured. After him no more came, so I concluded that the entire party must have crossed. Sending our prisoners to the pickets for safe keeping, I ordered Dennis and a couple of the men to go over on the logs; a low whistle from the corporal speedily announcing that all was clear. As soon as nearly all my men had followed me across the creek, I left Foster and a squad of four or five men in charge of the bridge; while I started to explore the fields with the remainder, taking the precaution to drop a few men at intervals to keep our trail should a hurried retreat be necessary.

Cautiously leading the detachment over the soft turf, I made my way towards a solitary tree, dimly discernible in the faint starlight. Every sound seemed hushed, yet I felt that our adventure was nearing a crisis.

Leaving my party in a hollow, Dennis and I crawled along on our hands and knees, with a couple of men, until we stumbled on a sentinel, whom we quickly overpowered, and sent to the rear. On reaching the tree, I saw that we were on a picket-line of the enemy, though why it extended in that direction I could not for the moment imagine. The mystery was speedily solved, however; for we soon heard the monotonous rumble of artillery, accompanied by the shuffling tramp of infantry, — sounds which told us that a large force was in active movement on the interior line.

For several minutes the corporal and I lay prostrate under the tree, listening to the movements of the enemy. As the different orders were hoarsely repeated, I was convinced that at least a division was being massed on the plain before me;

the natural inference being that some important demonstration on our flank was contemplated. Surmising that the Confederates were preparing for an assault upon the Round Top at daylight, I decided to return to our lines, and report the facts.

Directing Dennis to take our men quietly back to the creek, I remained for a few seconds to take a final survey of the situation.

A hasty glance towards the columns of troops I fancied I could see moving in the darkness was all I dared venture on: so I reluctantly turned to follow my men. As I did so, one of the neighboring sentries approached the tree in the belief that I was his comrade. Seeing it was too late for a quiet retreat, I hastily picked up the captured man's musket, and assumed his vacant place, determined to risk being taken prisoner in order that my brave little squad might get away in safety.

"How still they 'uns are over thar!" said my unwelcome friend, as he came up, and pointed with his musket towards the creek.

"Yes, they are quiet," I replied in a guarded tone, at the same time keeping a close watch on the man I felt would soon prove a deadly antagonist.

"What mought they be a-doing?"

"I don't know," I replied.

Scarcely had the words been uttered, when the sentinel, who had now come up quite close, suddenly dropped his head as he caught sight of my gold shoulder-strap.

"Why, who be yeou?" he cried, making at the same moment a sudden, instinctive rush upon me.

I was ready for him, however; and, with a desperate sweep of the musket I had clubbed in my hands, dealt the unfortunate sentry a terrific blow on the side of the head, which felled him to the earth like a log. On seeing the man fall, I dropped the musket, and, drawing my revolver from my sword-belt, started on a run towards the rendezvous of my command. The struggle on the picket-line had, however, attracted the attention of the sentinel on the right, who sent a bullet after me as I disappeared in the gloom. The report of his piece at once alarmed the entire line, for they immediately opened a spattering but harmless fire.

When I reached the bridge of poles, I found my men forming to resist the attack they expected, my appearance among them being hailed with evident satisfaction. Hastily re-assuring them, I lost no time in sending the command scrambling over the logs, one or two of the men tumbling into the creek in their eager haste. Once over, we destroyed the bridge by throwing it into the water; and I was glad to find that I had not lost a man, only one of the party being slightly wounded by a random bullet.

We had no time for congratulations, however; for the Confederates were now swarming along the creek. The rapid exchange of musketry brought us reinforcements, and I proceeded to report my discovery at brigade headquarters. The information was deemed of such importance, that the fusillade of the pickets was soon drowned by the roar of our battery on the hill, as a score of shells were hurled in the direction of the massed force of the enemy.

Dennis was in ecstasies over the novelty of our adventure, and always insisted afterwards that it had a decisive influence on the battle of Gettysburg.

CHAPTER XX.

A WONDERFUL CHARGE.

*" One effort — one — to break the circling host!
They form — unite — charge — waver — all is lost! "*

SEVERE as had been the fighting on the first and second days at Gettysburg, it was destined to be surpassed in heroic daring and savage courage on the third day. The two armies had so often tried each other's mettle, they knew that this day would bring the crucial test of strength and valor; that it would not only decide the campaign, but also the duration of the war. Therefore no bugle was needed to wake our men at sunrise, for all anticipated a day of desperate struggle and awful carnage.

It was almost daybreak when I and my reconnoitering party rejoined the regiment. As we climbed up the hill, which was still encumbered by the unburied dead who had fallen the previous day, we found the entire army on the alert. Already the breakfast-fires were shedding a fitful glow over the wide field. Standing, as I was, on the highest ledge of the Round Top, I could distinguish the outlines of our entire position, even at that early hour, as they were betrayed by the bivouac fires of the army. As far as the eye could reach, a belt of flame lay upon the fields. Extending along the ground, in a slightly curved line, for over three miles, it then turned to the left, doubling round like a fish-hook: the shank rested on the Round

Top, the stem lay along Cemetery Ridge, the elbow near the village of Gettysburg, while the barb touched Culp's Hill.

Quietly enjoying my breakfast of biscuit and coffee, I sat and watched the mists and shadows disappear as the hot July sun rose over the South Mountains on our left. Bit by bit the wide landscape lay revealed, and the details of the battle-ground were distinctly visible; enabling me to gain a clear idea of the strategic importance of Meade's line. Along the base of the ridge, and closely following the irregularities of its contour, I could trace the low stone breastworks. Behind this improvised rampart lay a broad bank of dark blue: it was the infantry in position. Nearest us, almost under our feet, lay Griffin's division; and beyond it I saw the banners of the Third and Second Corps, with a part of the Eleventh and Sixth, Sedgwick having come up during the night. In front of the main line of battle, I could pick out the faint ribbon of the skirmish or picket line; while, behind the infantry, the artillery had taken its position on the higher ground in the center. It was a formidable array of guns; for, even at that distance, I could count over sixty pieces standing silent and grim in the early sunlight. The army was indeed stripped and ready for the combat, the deep silence which rested on the battle-field being ominous of the coming strife.

Hour after hour passed, and the day rapidly advanced in all its brightness and warmth; yet not a single musket-shot had been heard since sunrise, no sound occurring to betray the presence of two great armies in deadly antagonism. But this deceitful calm was at length broken; for, as our colonel ordered his officers to examine their men's muskets, a solitary picket-shot was fired in the glen, quickly followed by others. There seemed no occasion for the firing, it being probably started in a spirit of mischief; but once begun, the rattle of musketry ran along the whole front of the army, like the snap of a mighty whip-lash. Then, being expended, it died away, and silence again fell on the field; only a few dropping shots being heard, here and there, among the trees beyond the glen. By and by the extreme right woke up, and I could see that the skirmishers there had some provocation for their activity. The distance was too great for us to hear their fusillade; a thin pencil of white smoke alone betraying the fact, as it slowly drifted in the morning breeze over the rocks forming the ridge.

Thus the two armies rested in the hot sunshine. Noon came, yet there was no movement apparent on either side. Fresh ammunition and rations had been served out to us: every musket was ready. It was a period of suspense, as well as rest; for every man in the ranks experienced a curious feeling of expectation. In the midst of it all I fell asleep, only waking when Dennis announced dinner as ready.

"This waiting for something to do is confoundedly tiresome," said Captain Burch, as he stretched himself listlessly in the shade of the big rock we were sheltered by. "I wish they would move somewhere. Any thing would be better than this."

"You are always impatient, Burch," replied Major Harding. "For my part, I am very glad to have a rest. I should think that you who have had to foot it from the Rappahannock River into Pennsylvania would be quite satisfied to lie still."

"Oh! that's all very well in one way," retorted the captain; "but I wouldn't mind betting that nine out of ten of our men are of the same way of thinking."

"W-w-well, I s-s-sup-pose so," stuttered young Whipple, a tall, raw-boned lieutenant, who was the butt of the regiment; "b-b-but y-you kn-know we had a d-d-dread-f-ful h-hard t-t-time of it y-yes-terday. W-w-what's the use of g-getting ang-ang-anx-ious?"

"Come, come, Whipple, that will do: none of your long speeches," said Captain Burch with a laugh. "If we had to wait for you to give the orders, we would n-n-never get them."

"I don't know about that," remarked the major. "It's odd, but did any one ever hear Whipple stutter in a fight? While we were clambering up this queer-shaped hill yesterday, he encouraged his men, and swore at the enemy, as straight as any of us."

"T-t-that's b-be-because I g-get too excited, and for-forget to st-stut-tutter," exclaimed Whipple.

"Halloa! I say! What's that they're up to, over there?" exclaimed Captain Burch, as he took a survey of the field through Major Harding's glass.

"Where? where?" cried two or three voices.

"Why, there! Over by the edge of those woods, on the other side of the field. Don't you see they are putting a battery in position?"

"So they are," said Major Harding, peering through the glass Captain Burch had handed him. "It's not one battery, but two of them. I can see eight pieces in line already."

As the major spoke, I shaded my eyes with my hands, and distinctly saw that several guns had been unlimbered, almost at the edge of the woods we knew must be occupied by the enemy's center. There was some important movement on foot: that seemed quite certain. These batteries meant mischief.

"See! There's more of them!" cried the major again. "A little farther on. And now there's another. By Jove! Burch, you won't have long to wait for something to do."

"I am devilish glad of it," muttered the captain.

Other eyes besides our own had noticed the enemy's movement; for there was a sudden stir among the rank and file, while the signal-men on the rocks above our heads began waving their flags furiously.

"To your places, gentlemen!" shouted Colonel Lloyd. "Every officer to his post."

Buckling on our swords, we obeyed the order, and hurried to our places along the line.

"They're bringing up a lot of artillery over there, lieutenant, aren't they?" said Sergeant Foster to me, as I reached the company. "We'll be getting some of their shells pretty soon, I expect."

"No doubt," I replied. "Tell the men to your left to keep themselves well covered. You lie down too, Sam: there's no use your exposing yourself."

"Be jabers, there'll be the divil's own row whin thim guns begin barkin'," exclaimed Dennis, gazing at the long line of Confederate guns which had now been placed in position.

"Now, none of your nonsense, corporal. Lie down, sir, and keep that silly head of yours out of danger."

"All right, leftinant. But why don't ye do the same?"

"By and by. Now, men, keep well under cover. This hill is a goòd mark for those fellows."

The men obeyed the order quietly; then Captain Burch and I crouched behind a rock, and watched the assembling batteries. I could see that there were ten or twelve batteries in line by this time, with more steadily moving up, until there were at length fully one hundred guns in the formidable array. Half an hour passed, yet not a shot had been fired: the batteries silently waited for orders to begin the combat. Looking down our own line, I found that the Federal batteries on the ridge were on the *qui vive;* for in the gaps I had noticed in the line during the morning there were now others moving in, until the ledge of irregular rocks was one mass of heavy guns. It was now evident that a terrible and tremendous artillery duel would soon commence.

During the half-hour of painful suspense, the pickets on both sides were strangely silent. They knew that their puny efforts would be thrown away in presence of so much heavier metal, so they waited with the main body for the cannonading soon to begin.

Suddenly a puff of smoke appeared on the extreme left of the Confederate line of guns, and I heard the shrill scream of a shell as it flew over the silent field toward our central position. Then another, and another gun was fired; then the shells came in couples; next by the score. Piece after piece opened fire in regular succession, and battery after battery went into action, until the whole of the one hundred Confederate cannon were pouring a deadly, dreadful storm of bursting iron on our devoted center; while we men of the little Round Top also found the shrieking demons flying over our heads or burying themselves in the loose rubble below our feet.

The bombardment of the enemy had been fully and fairly opened before our batteries deigned any reply, but when their guns did get to work the pieces were rapidly served. The fierce and furious combat was now progressing in dead earnest. Despite the efforts of the officers, our men, becoming excited as the engagement grew hotter and hotter, persisted in rising to their feet to watch its progress. As we shared their feelings, we gave up the effort to keep them down.

The roar of the cannonading now became deafening in its rapidity and intensity. The enemy's batteries were hidden from our view by a great bank of sulphurous smoke which hung over and enveloped them ; the bright flashes of the guns, as they belched forth their iron hail, alone indicating the position of the pieces engaged. On our side the artillery were, however, clearly visible; for the smoke from the guns lay over the lines of infantry, hiding them entirely as they crouched behind their breastworks. We had now fully ninety of our heaviest pieces at work, huddled together on the ridge held by Hancock's corps. The army was held spell-bound by the magnificent spectacle; for the opposing batteries made terrible music, the hills and mountains reverberating with the awful roar of nearly two hundred active cannon.

For two long hours this terrible double ·bombardment continued, and a dense white cloud lay upon the entire field like a hot mist. The fierce, maddening shrieks of the shells, as they flew noisily through the scorching sunshine, or burst over our heads, the groans of wounded men lying all around us, the fragments of ragged iron whistling about our ears, scattering death everywhere, made up a scene never to be effaced from memory.

The smoke prevented my seeing the effect of the Federal fire on the Confederate line of guns; but on our side caisson after caisson exploded, and several guns were either dismantled or drawn off the field as they grew too hot to handle. But the removal of these did not lessen the fury of our fire, for no sooner did a battery go galloping to the rear than its place in the awful line was promptly taken by a fresh one. As the cannonading proceeded, the shells directed at the Round Top increased, and our casualties betrayed the accuracy of the practice. Stretchers were constantly passing to the rear in the fields below, and lines of dead were accumulating as the men carried the bodies of their comrades away from the breastworks. Our men now needed no caution to shelter themselves, for the merciless shells drove them to their breastworks. Poor Whipple would never stutter again: he lay dead near me, his head shattered by the fragment of a shell. Every now and then some poor fellow in the ranks gave a groan of pain, and went crawling over the rocks in search of the surgeon, or after a convulsive shudder lay passive in death.

The monotony of this fearful duel between the Confederate and Federal batteries became at length oppressive; and I longed for it to cease, even though its ending brought to us the more deadly storm of leaden bullets. Then we should at least be active, and could give as well as take: now we were powerless in the presence of the cannon, having to submit to their blows in silence.

At the end of two hours the fire from Lee's guns visibly slackened, an example soon followed by our exhausted artillerists. The Confederates had evidently tired of the fierce Titanic struggle, and the cloud of smoke on their side of the field began slowly to lift as piece after piece grew silent. Still the fusillade of shells was by no means to be despised, for the air continued to be filled with deadly fragments. In half an hour, however, the awful music fell into a monotone, and then it gradually dwindled down to a few sulky guns on either side.

Finally our batteries stopped firing altogether, the enemy after a few spiteful discharges also becoming silent.

The lull that ensued was more appalling than the thunders that had preceded it, and it was with a feeling of awe that we waited to see the next movement of Lee; for, the Confederates having assumed the initiative, we knew that Meade would remain on the defensive.

The sun soon dispelled the heavy clouds of smoke, and the broad expanse of territory occupied by the two armies was once more visible. Then I saw that the Confederate batteries had suffered as well as our own; for several pieces were lying on the ground, helpless and useless. Major Harding, with his glass to his eyes, also announced that the ground occupied by their guns was covered with dead. The terrible account had been duly balanced. Now that the artillery was hushed, our corps pickets began firing rapidly: so we looked for an assault upon our elevated position. But this skirmish musketry came to nothing, the enemy having no doubt made a feint to draw away our attention from the real movement soon to be disclosed.

"I say, Wilmot," exclaimed Captain Burch, "don't you see that man on a white horse?" and he pointed towards the belt of woods occupied by the Confederates.

"Yes. It must be an officer giving orders. I wonder what is coming now."

"Probably an advance by their whole line," replied the captain. "What a dreadful task it will be to come across that big open field!"

I did not reply: so we silently watched the white horse, as he carried his rider swiftly along the lines which were evidently forming under cover of the trees. Now the animal would disappear in a hollow, only to re-appear and be lost to sight again, as the ground rose and fell. On, on, he galloped, without any perceptible check to his speed, until at length both horse and rider melted from our view in the far distance.

Just then I became aware of a sudden bustle among the

loose pile of rocks near the left of our regimental line. Turning round to discover the cause, I saw that General Meade had come up to survey the field. None of his staff, except Warren, were with him. Both officers gazed intently through their glasses along the enemy's lines, for some minutes, being at the same moment joined by several general officers.

"A council of war," whispered Captain Burch in my ear.

A COUNCIL OF WAR ON LITTLE ROUND TOP.

I nodded silently, and continued to watch the group. On the right of General Meade stood Sykes, our corps commander, and with him Sedgwick of the Sixth. Behind these two corps generals, higher up among the rocks, sat Pleasonton of the cavalry, and near him Ayres who now commanded our division. The generals conversed quietly together, seeming to be comparing notes. Warren was, as usual, nervous in his movements, and intense in his watch upon the enemy. Sedgwick stood like a statue, his bearded face giving no sign of his thoughts; while the nattily dressed cavalry commander slapped his long boot with a slender riding-whip, apparently as careless of the result as he would be on a review. Sykes, like Warren, was busy with his glass. In the midst of the distin. guished group of officers sat the gray-haired commander of the army, quiet and steady as of old. His soldierly figure, and impassive, intellectual face, betokened a man fully prepared to do his whole duty, yet conscious of the tremendous responsibility resting upon his shoulders. Calmly listening to the comments and suggestions of his generals, and nodding now and then in answer or acquiescence, Meade watched Warren's face, as his chief engineer eagerly scanned the woods beyond for signs of a movement in the enemy's lines.

"Here's that white horse again!" exclaimed Captain Burch.

Turning my eyes away from the little knot of generals, I saw that the captain was right; for the mysterious horseman was returning as rapidly over the ground as he had gone. There was something new to see this time, however; for as the rider came galloping back, lines of troops appeared at the edge of the woods behind him. As he rode swiftly towards us, these lines lengthened, until we could distinguish whole brigades and divisions forming in line of battle. For over a mile the white horse passed, and the Confederate infantry extended in close array over the entire distance. Then the officer and his horse disappeared behind a clump of trees, and the enemy's troops moved slowly into the field until their entire line became visible. There it halted, and seemed to be aligning itself on the center. As we watched the progress of this portentous movement, with quickening pulses, a second line of battle appeared, and, marching out of the woods, halted a few paces behind the first.

"They are going to charge," said Major Harding, glass again in hand. "I can see the skirmishers forming now in front of the line."

The major was correct; for, as he spoke, we all saw a thin

line of men moving out from the main body. It was quite evident that a general advance in force was contemplated by the Confederates. This cool preparation for a desperate charge was indeed a startling and thrilling spectacle. Thousands upon thousands of veteran soldiers were quietly getting ready to advance over an open field, half a mile wide, for the purpose of attacking an army fully their equal in strength and courage. As I watched those dark-brown lines my blood, already hot with the excitement of the hour, coursed madly through my veins until I felt my cheek flush with suppressed emotion.

At length the preparations seemed complete, for a gun was fired near the center; and as its solitary shell flew towards our line, the colors in the Confederate ranks began waving, and the two compact lines of infantry marched slowly, steadily forward.

" Isn't that magnificent?" cried Captain Burch.

" Positively grand," replied the major.

I looked round for a moment at the group of generals, finding a marked change in their attitudes and demeanor. General Meade stood in the center; but he was as motionless as the stones under him, his eyes intently fixed upon the advancing lines. Not a muscle of his face moved; yet I saw he felt the crisis, for a look of stern determination rested upon his features. Warren was leaning forward, the very picture of eager, hopeful expectation; and there was a restlessness about the man that accorded well with his thin, nervous face. Sedgwick had brought his steel-scabbarded saber round in front of his body; and he stood unconsciously at parade rest as he watched the Confederate movement, his heavy jaw and massive beard giving his entire figure that air of resolute courage so characteristic of the Sixth Corps leader. Pleasonton, though still perched up on his aërial seat, no longer tapped his polished boot; for he, too, was watching with steady, curious eyes the threatening advance. Ayres had disappeared; but behind Pleasonton peeped Kilpatrick, his face the most excited of all, and he was evidently uttering rapid comments on the scene in progress. Suddenly General Warren stepped a pace or two forward, and gave some order to a signal-officer, turning at the same time to his chief, as if asking consent. General Meade nodded affirmatively, and the flags were soon waving in cabalistic fashion to their fellows on the right and center. The commanding general had now grasped the scope of the intended movement, and was preparing his army for the onslaught.

"I say, leftinant, who the divil is that chap?" asked Dennis, pointing to a man dressed in civilian attire.

I was as puzzled as the corporal, for the sight of a citizen in such a place was a novelty to me. He seemed to take matters very coolly; for he stood leaning against a huge bowlder, and gazed through a large field-glass he carried slung over his shoulder. Then he turned, and, walking deliberately towards the assembled generals, asked some question. General Sedgwick gave the answer, when the stranger took a note-book from his pocket, and began writing. I then knew he was a newspaper correspondent, a fact I explained to Dennis.

"An' do thim writin' fellers ever get killed?"

"Sometimes," I replied.

"What is he doin' here, anyway?" continued the corporal.

"They always keep as near the commanding general as possible," said I; "to get the news, I suppose."

"Well, this is a quare world anyhow!" said Dennis. "A fellow with a pencil and a bit of paper helpin' to foight a battle!"

The correspondent was evidently at his ease, for he strolled about as nonchalantly as if there were no such things as shells or bullets. Though his dress was not at all military, still there was something about the man that betrayed his connection with army and campaign life. A suit of navy-blue cloth, the coat cut short for horseback-riding, and closely buttoned across the chest, revealed a symmetrical figure, while his feet and legs were incased in a pair of boots made of tan leather and reaching nearly to the hips. A dark-blue flannel shirt, the collar confined by a black-silk necktie tied in sailor fashion, and a wide-brimmed felt hat, completed his costume. As I stood watching him, he put a hand into his pantaloons-pocket; the action revealing the butt of a revolver, which appeared to be fastened round his waist by a leather belt. Altogether he looked like a man ready and perfectly able to take care of himself.

"Why, there's Charley Osborne," said Major Harding, as the stranger approached us.

"And who may Charley Osborne be, major?" said I.

"He used to be an officer; but now he is a war-correspondent, and a devilish clever one too, I believe."

"How are you, major?" said the new-comer, as he stepped forward. "This is a splendid place to view the ground. No wonder Meade came up."

"I suppose you have been all over the field," remarked Major Harding.

"Pretty much. I had to leave when poor Reynolds was bowled over, in order to send a dispatch. But I got back last night, and have been in the saddle nearly all day."

"What are they doing on the right, Osborne?" asked the major.

"Waiting, just as you are doing here. I tell you what it is, major: there's going to be an awful row here pretty soon, when that line gets fairly moving," said Osborne as he sharpened a pencil.

"Of course: any one can see that," responded Major Harding. "But I think we can beat them back."

"I hope so. But our line is fearfully weak in the center, and Meade knows it. He seems tolerably confident, however."

"I am glad to hear that," said I: "confidence on the part of our general is half the battle."

"Quite right. By the way, isn't your name Wilmot?"

"Yes, sir."

"Excuse me," said Major Harding. "I ought to have introduced you to one another. Please consider it done."

"You were pointed out to me just now, Mr. Wilmot, as the officer who made that reconnoissance last night: so I came to get your story. It will make a capital incident in my description of the battle."

"Oh! it's not worth talking about," said I, surprised to find myself getting famous. "You can surely find something more important and interesting than my adventure to write about."

"I don't know about that," replied Osborne. "People at home want wayside pictures as well as big canvases. Come, lieutenant, just tell me how it was; for we shall all be busy very soon."

At that moment another cannon-shot was fired on the Confederate side of the field: and, as we all turned to look, I saw it was a new signal; for the advancing lines of battle now quickened their motion, and came forward even more rapidly than before. Both Osborne and myself forgot our conversation in watching the coming charge, for at the same instant our artillery opened fire on the Confederate lines of infantry. Once begun, the cannonading soon became general along our whole line, a deadly storm of shells being poured into the ranks marching so gallantly across the open ground. The Confederate batteries replied; and under cover of their stubborn fire their infantry came on, and on, until they won the admiration of their opponents.

As yet no Federal musketry had broken out, our veterans knowing too well the value of every bullet in a crisis like this. Still the assaulting lines continued to march on, until it seemed, from where I was standing, that the leading one touched the breastworks along our center. Then, and only then, a vivid flash sprang from the earth, followed by a sharp rattle as the Federal skirmish-line opened fire. The volley had no apparent effect on the Confederates, who continued to advance steadily, sweeping the skirmishers before them like chaff in the

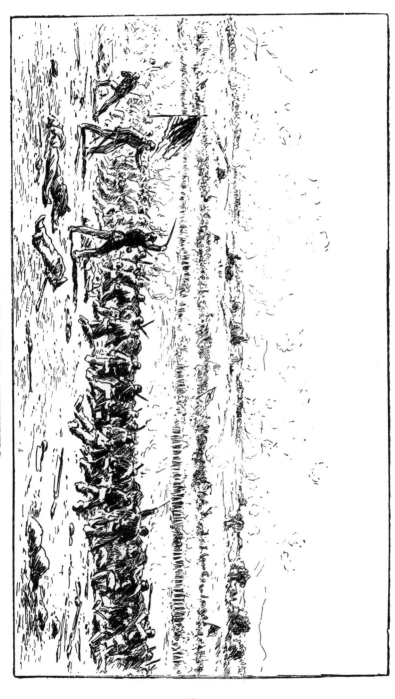

THE FINAL CHARGE AT GETTYSBURG.

wind. A minute later, a deafening crash of musketry broke upon the ear, and we knew that the main line had opened fire. Despite the sunlight, the flame from our men's muskets could be distinguished as it played to and fro along Cemetery Ridge. Then for the first time the Confederate line seemed to waver; but only for an instant, for it soon rallied, and, as if by one common impulse, dashed itself like a mighty wave against the wall of steel, before it. The Federal artillery on the higher ground behind our infantry now tore the enemy's ranks with a storm of iron balls until it seemed that none could stand before them and live. But the troops under Longstreet had gained an impetus which carried them clear up to, and at intervals into, our lines. For twenty minutes the terrible hand-to-hand struggle continued; and I saw, by the sudden movements of Hancock's corps, that his line had been pierced and broken. It was, however, soon reformed; and, although the second line of the Confederates joined and strengthened the first, our defense was too fierce and stubborn to be overcome. Finally the attacking force quivered, and a moment later the entire body was in full retreat.

A tremendous thrilling cheer now rose from the throats of our army, only to be drowned by the renewed broadsides of our batteries as they savagely played on the shattered and retiring divisions.

"That scene is good to me for a couple of columns at least," said Osborne, as we all resumed our places in the line at the call of our colonel. "Halloa! By Jove! Old Meade is off, so I must go too. Good-day, gentlemen: this is the last you will see of me on this field. I shall ride all night for a telegraph-wire."

"Do you consider the battle over, then?" asked Major Harding.

"Sufficiently so for my purpose. You may have plenty of fighting, but I doubt it. Lee can never get his army in shape after such a repulse. No: unless I find a different opinion prevailing at headquarters, I shall gallop off to announce a victory."

"Good-by, Osborne," said the major. "When do you expect to join us again?"

"Oh! I shall ride to Frederick City, and telegraph my story, and overtake you on the other side of South Mountain in time to see another brush, should there be one. Take good care of yourself, old fellow." As he spoke, Osborne ran down the hill, swung himself into his saddle, and disappeared over the road we had advanced the previous afternoon.

By this time the Confederate lines had reached the shelter

RELIEVING THE WOUNDED.

of their own guns, and soon after entered the woods from whence they had emerged to make the desperate charge. We never saw them on the field of Gettysburg again. The bloody plain, over which Longstreet had led his men, was thickly covered with the dead and dying; for, even when the defeated troops had escaped out of musket-range, the shells from our guns mowed them down by scores at every discharge.

Once more comparative silence rested on the battle-field; and we busied ourselves in succoring our wounded, or removing the dead that had fallen on our own line.

CHAPTER XXI.

FACE TO FACE.

"Thou shalt not see me blush,
  Nor change my countenance for this arrest."

 HARLEY OSBORNE had hardly departed when we were surprised to see General Meade and his staff return to the Round Top, where they remained until sunset, as our elevated position afforded a magnificent view of the field. Now that Longstreet's corps had buffeted itself to pieces by its heroic charge, the general held quite a levee of distinguished officers. Generals from the right and center came up, one after the other, to report the results of the engagement, or receive orders for their future movements. Frequently these officers clambered among the rocks that were piled up at the apex of the hill. Their bright shoulder-straps soon attracted the attention of some Confederate sharpshooters ensconced in an out-cropping ridge of rocks on the opposite side of the glen. So annoying did the persistent practice of these marksmen become, that General Fletcher was requested to send a party down into the glen for the purpose of silencing them.

"Lieutenant Wilmot, the general wishes to see you," said the sergeant-major to me as Captain Burch and I were washing down a few crackers with some coffee.

"General Fletcher? What can he want? Do you know?" said I.

"Not exactly, sir. But there's some sort of movement on foot; for I heard General Warren say something about the glen, and Colonel Lloyd mentioned your name."

"Another reconnoissance, Frank, by Jove!" said Captain Burch. "You are in luck again, my boy! Why the devil can't they give a captain a chance?"

"I wish they would. I think I've had enough of extra duty. However, we must obey orders." And I at once proceeded to report to the general, finding him among the assembled corps commanders and their brilliant staffs.

"General, you sent for me, I believe," said I, saluting.

"Yes, Wilmot: you were down in the glen last night, were you not?"

"Yes, sir: down in the sunken road by the edge of the creek."

"Precisely. — General Meade, this is the young officer who captured the party of Confederates so cleverly last night," said the brigadier.

"A very neat affair," replied the general, smiling at me through his spectacles. "I congratulate you, sir."

I bowed, feeling my cheek flush at the old general's praise.

"You see those sharpshooters in that cluster of rocks across the hollow?" said General Fletcher, pointing towards them.

"Yes, sir."

"Well, Wilmot, I want you to volunteer to lead a party down there, and either drive them out, or keep their infernal rifles quiet. What do you say?"

"You might as well order me down there, and be done with it," I replied laughingly. "Of course I'll go if you wish it, general."

"Thank you, Wilmot. I was sure you would be willing, though it will be ugly work. Now go and pick your men: forty will be enough. When you get them together, Colonel Lloyd will give you further instructions."

I touched my cap, and withdrew. Calling Sergeant Foster

and Dennis, we soon had our party organized. There was no
delay in securing sharp, willing fellows; for our men had been
cooped up on the hill so long, that any thing promising excitement was a decided relief. Among them was Sergeant Johnson
from another company, who was accepted at his urgent request.

On reporting to Colonel Lloyd, I received my instructions.
We were to go forward in skirmish order, and once in the glen
I was to act according to circumstances.

"Do nothing rash, Wilmot," said the colonel. "General
Fletcher expressly said so. We don't want to lose you, now
that you are on the road for promotion. Keep cool, my boy,
whatever you do."

"I'll do my best, colonel," I replied, touched by his kindness.

"Good-by, Frank: good luck to you," said Colonel Lloyd,
holding out his hand.

I returned his hearty grasp, and, turning to my men, gave the
word. We were soon going helter-skelter down the precipi-
tous face of the Round Top; the men spreading out to the
right and left like the edge of a fan, as I had directed them to
do.

Scarcely had we begun the descent when the sharpshooters
sent their bullets whistling among us. Two of the men fell
wounded before we got half-way to the bottom; and by the
time our scattered line reached the level ground three more
were down, one of the poor fellows being killed. I had previ-
ously instructed the party to cover themselves as best they
could on reaching the glen, only advancing when I waved my
handkerchief as a signal. Every man was to fire whenever he
saw something to aim at; and, as all their pockets had been
filled with extra cartridges, I knew we could keep up a steady
and constant fusillade for some time.

When I reached the foot of the hill, I dropped behind a
bowlder standing conveniently in my path, and saw that the
men were following my example. The line being thus established, we opened a rapid fire sufficiently accurate to keep

the enemy's riflemen tolerably quiet. From bowlder to bowlder we darted forward at intervals, thus gradually reducing the range; and, looking up, I had the satisfaction of seeing Generals Meade and Warren standing undisturbed on the lookout station. We had made their position a safe one, at all events.

An hour passed in this way; then General Meade retired, and a signal was given for me to return. On attempting to obey, I found it would cost too many lives, so decided to remain for the present. If we must be hit, it was better to fall fighting

"GOING FOR" THE REBEL SHARPSHOOTERS.

instead of retreating. Shaking my head at Colonel Lloyd's mute command, and trying to prove in pantomime the hazards of a retreat, I prepared to advance on the sharpshooters. General Warren, who was still standing on the rock, seemed to be pleased with my decision; for he waved his hand encouragingly, the simple act setting my men to cheering lustily. Their shouts accomplished what the Confederate rifle-bullets had failed to do, for the general immediately disappeared from our sight.

"That's jist loike Gineral Warren," remarked Dennis, who, as usual, was near me. "He'd make a good Irishman, he's so fond of a scrimmage."

" Well," I replied, " I'm glad he approves my plan, for then the colonel can not scold when we get back."

" We'll not get back so aisy, leftinant darlint. But you're in the roight: it's betther to die facin' thim divils beyant, than to be shot runnin' away from thim, loike so many rabbits."

" Pass the word to the sergeants that we are going forward, but that no man must go too far in front of his neighbors," said I, hoping to put a stop to the corporal's loquacity.

" We're a noice lot of naybors, anyhow," muttered Dennis as he repeated the order.

Little by little we crept forward, with the loss of only one man, until the line reached the narrow strip of clear ground in the middle of the glen. Here I knew we should be compelled to charge: yet I hesitated at giving the order, because I had no idea of the real strength of our opponents. The question was, however, settled for me in an unexpected manner. Sergeant Johnson, who commanded the left, had succeeded in adroitly working his way, with half a dozen men, into a clump of bowlders that overlooked the rocky nest in which the Confederate riflemen were hidden. Seeing the importance of his position, the sergeant sent a well-directed volley among them, which, being followed by another from our main line, caused evident confusion.

This was our opportunity, so I waved my handkerchief; and we dashed forward, seizing the ledge in good style, as the enemy retreated, though we missed taking any prisoners beyond three wounded men lying behind the rocks.

As we won our little victory, I heard our brigade cheering us; and, though we knew our party could not well be relieved before morning, the praise of our comrades repaid us for the danger passed through.

Making such disposition of my command as seemed best for holding our new position, I made up my mind to pass another wakeful night. Of course we could have no fires; so I munched a cracker or two by way of supper, Dennis grumbling disconsolately at the meager fare. One of the men offered me some hoe-cake he had found in the haversack of a dead Confederate, but I declined it with a feeling of horror. Dennis was not so squeamish; and, as I watched him munching the dead man's provender, I realized the vicissitudes of war, and how soon men become hardened in the presence of danger and death.

The sun went down, and the night proved a dark one. Already the sulphurous gases engendered by the heavy cannon-ading and musketry during the past three days were gathering vapor in the sky; and I knew, that, as on all great battle-fields, we should soon have rain. The feeling that the enemy's power was broken for the time made our army careless, for numerous fires were blazing all along the main lines. The Little Round Top was clearly defined in outline by these ruddy flames, mak-ing our advanced position appear all the darker by the contrast. Thus the day passed into night.

Midnight came; and I had just seen the sentinels changed, when one on the right fired his musket. I immediately ran over to him.

"Why did you fire, Ferguson?" I asked.

"I think there's somebody down there in front, for I heard the clink of a musket against a stone just before I let drive," was Ferguson's answer, as he finished reloading his musket.

"Well, don't fire again, unless you really see something, until I return. I am going down along the line."

All of the sentinels were excited by Ferguson's shot, so I found them naturally on the alert. Sending one of them for the reserve, I went back to the man causing the alarm; finding him kneeling, and on the lookout for developments. Soon after Dennis came up with ten or fifteen men.

"What's the matter, leftinant?" he whispered: "are we attacked?"

"Not yet," I replied in the same low tone; "but we may be soon, if Ferguson here is right. He thinks he heard some one in the hollow below."

"Look! look!" cried Ferguson eagerly, as he pointed out into the darkness: "don't you see somebody now?"

"No, I don't; but wait a minute, corporal: scatter the men a little, and send Sergeant Johnson word to be ready to resist an assault on the left," said I, as quietly and composedly as I could, though I now began to fear we were in a bad box.

I had scarcely uttered these words, when I distinctly saw three or four men creeping over the ground a few rods in front. Knowing that a bold stroke was best, I changed my tactics, and, instead of acting on the defensive, determined to attack. Dennis and his men had not yet time to move: so, with a sudden impulse, I shouted, —

"Forward, Zouaves! Charge!"

My men followed me willingly, so we went bounding over the rocks like so many deer. Our movement was entirely successful; for the Confederates were in a little bunch, only half-prepared for the assault they contemplated, so found themselves surrounded. Two or three attempted resistance when summoned to surrender; but they were promptly knocked down, our prisoners numbering nearly twenty men.

Sergeant Foster coming up with some of his men, I sent him to the rear with our captives, keeping Dennis with me a few minutes to see if there were signs of any more.

"Begorra! Master Frank," said Dennis, laughing gleefully, "if you kape on at this rate, we'll be after gobblin' the whole of Gineral Lee's army."

At that moment, as if he had sprung through the earth, we were confronted by a man.

"Come, you fellows!" exclaimed the new-comer authoritatively, "we must go back. There's not enough of us to seize those rocks, now that the Yanks are on the watch. Come, fall back, I say, and make no noise."

"You are my prisoner, sir," said I, clutching his arm, and thrusting the muzzle of my revolver into his face. "Surrender, sir, as your men have done."

"Damnation! Trapped? and by a Yankee."

"Yis, trapped loike a burrd," replied Dennis, seizing the prisoner's other arm. "Ye see,.it's a thrap of yer own contrivin', so you can't complain."

"Oh! I know I'm caught, safe enough. You needn't hold me like you would a dog. I surrender. It's the fortune of war." And, as the Confederate spoke, he unbuckled his sword-belt, and handed his weapons to me. As I put out my hand for the belt, the prisoner seized my arm in his turn, hoarsely exclaiming, —

"Is that you, Frank Wilmot? Good God! Am I *your* prisoner?"

"Tom Marshall!" I cried, thoroughly startled and amazed at the recognition.

"Yes, Tom Marshall. Very much at your service, sir," he replied sarcastically. "So we meet again, Mr. Wilmot, do we? But under rather different circumstances from when we parted."

"I wish to God you had fallen into other hands than mine!" I replied, touched to the quick by Tom's sneers.

"An' is this an ould frind of yours, Master Frank?" asked Dennis wonderingly.

"Yes, Dennis; one of my dearest friends."

"And now we are sworn enemies, meeting on the battle-field," interrupted Tom.

"No, Tom," I replied warmly, "not enemies. We can never be that. Remember your last words when we parted, — 'brothers always.'"

"Pooh! we were boys then," retorted Tom.

"Bein' yer frind, av coorse ye'r sorry he's a prisoner?" persisted Dennis.

"I'm sorry the chance fell to me to make him one," said I.

"Thin, why not let him go agin? Shure, there's nobody here but our three selves. None of the b'yes knows we've another prisoner."

The suggestion was a startling one. Could I do it? And I

began weighing my duty against the warm feeling of friendship I still entertained for my prisoner.

"Arrah! an' why don't ye let yer frind go?" said Dennis, in a pitying voice. "Shure, nobody will be the wiser."

"I will!" I cried. "Tom, you are no longer a prisoner. Go in peace, and God bless you, old fellow!"

"Do you really mean it, Frank?" he asked, evidently bewildered by my words.

"Yes. I release you. Here is your sword again. Kate Marshall shall never say I made her brother a prisoner of mine."

"Well, I now believe in the old saying that women rule the world," said Tom with a light laugh, as he took back his sword and revolver.

"Dennis, go back to the line. I'll follow you in a moment," said I.

The corporal took the hint, leaving Tom and me alone together. As he disappeared, Tom seized my hand, and wrung it heartily.

"This is very good of you, Frank. I know how hard it is for you to do this, for I can appreciate your sense of duty to your own side of this miserable quarrel. God bless you, my dear boy, for letting me go! I'll never forget it while I live," and Tom's voice grew tender as we clasped hands once more.

"I'll walk a little way towards your lines: I suppose it's safe?"

"Oh, yes! Our pickets are a good ways off, else you might have been my prisoner instead of my captor."

"How so? I don't understand."

"Why, when that fellow of yours fired off his confounded musket, I saw we were discovered, so I told my men to lay quiet until I got reinforcements; but I changed my mind, and was coming back to withdraw them when you caught me. Do you know, I took you and that Irishman for some of my own men," and Tom laughed carelessly.

"That explains why we captured you so easily. But this is a strange thing, Tom, our meeting here to-night."

"Isn't it! You know I said we would meet again."

"And what a change has come over the country since we last saw each other, three years ago!"

"Ah, yes! Why, Frank, you would scarcely know the old valley now."

"How so?"

"It's a perfect wreck. The fields overrun with weeds, shade-trees cut down, houses and barns destroyed by fire or shattered by shells: even the negroes are gone. My God! what a price we're paying for secession!"

"You are indeed, Tom," I replied. "Of course you now see that that very act of secession has precipitated the evil you so much dreaded. The slaves are now emancipated."

"Yes, — by Lincoln's proclamation; but that only holds good where your armies have trod, or are in possession. We have plenty left yet."

"GOOD-BY, TOM."

"It is only a question of time," said I. "You can not expect, surely, that the South is going to finally win."

"To tell you the truth, Frank, I do not. But we must part here. Yonder fire is my line." And Tom seized my hand in a fervent grasp.

"Good-by, Tom. Let us hope that when we meet again it will be under happier auspices."

"Oh, this war is gone up! The Southern cause is dead. This battle has already turned the scale against us. I suppose we shall be running away from you soon," said Tom bitterly.

"I wish the war *was* over. I am tired of this terrible slaughter," said I.

"So am I. But Bob Lee won't give up just yet. Ah! Frank, I'm cured of my foolish ideas of State and Southern rights and wrongs! There was no need of our going to war."

"Is that the feeling in your army?"

"To some extent, though it is not expressed in words."

"Then, why not say so openly? Peace can be made if your leaders speak the word."

"But the terms, Frank! There's the rub. No, there will be a good deal more fighting before there's peace, more's the pity."

"It's sad business," I replied: "would the end were near!"

"Would it were, indeed! But I must be going. We part now, Frank, dearer friends than ever. Good-by, old fellow!" and as Tom wrung my hand he darted away in the darkness. I was again alone.

CHAPTER XXII.

LOST AMONG THE DEAD.

" With shivered armor strewn, and on a heap
Chariot and charioteer lay overturned."

S Tom was disappearing in the darkness, I
stood listening to his retreating footsteps
until they died away in the distance. Then I
realized that I had parted once more from an
honest heart and true friend. What did it
signify that he wore the Confederate gray, and
I the Federal blue? we were still brothers at
heart. Soldiers on opposite sides of a mighty
struggle, we were still held by the bonds of
our college friendship. I therefore felt rejoiced at our meeting, even though it had led
me to swerve from the strict line of my duty
in releasing him.

When we had parted three years before, it was in the sunshine, and our paths lay among the signs of peace and prosperity. Now Tom had left my side in the gloom of night, on
the battle-field, strewn as it was with the stiffened corpses of
those whose fate it had been to fall. What a contrast!

Putting aside these thoughts with an effort, I at length
turned my steps towards the little picket, whose fortunes were
for the time bound up in my own.

I had proceeded only a short distance, when I became aware
that I was on new ground ; the rocks and bowlders over which
Tom and I had stumbled being no longer in my path. This

was a dilemma for which I had little relish, for I was anxious to reach my command as soon as possible. I knew it was dangerous to shout, for I might draw upon me the fire of my own pickets; and there would be little glory in being shot by Federal bullets.

Impatient and angry at my own stupidity in not having kept the bearings of my position, I took a careful survey of the lights along our main line, hoping by that means to discover the rocks. But the fires on the interior lines were smoldering as the army slept: so I was the more confused, not knowing which way to turn. Walking cautiously towards such lights as I could see, I had not gone far when I suddenly tumbled headlong into a wide ditch. Rising to my feet again, I was startled to find that I had fallen over some corpses. Then the dismal fact dawned upon my mind: I had missed my way, and was lost, — lost among the dead of the battle-field!

The sickening odor that rose from the bodies I had unwittingly disturbed by my fall, proved that they had been dead some time. The men had, no doubt, fallen early in the day when we were hurried from our reserve position to succor the Third Corps. Still, this knowledge gave me no clew to my whereabouts, for I did not remember having seen any ditch during the few minutes my brigade had remained in the glen. The absence of any rocks or outcropping ridges was proof that I had strayed: so I endeavored to find the way back, by turning sharply to the right, hoping soon to find my feet on familiar ground. But this movement, instead of bringing me to the rocks I had left, carried me farther over the field; and I began wandering recklessly about, neither knowing nor caring whither my errant footsteps might lead me.

It was my first experience of a deserted battle-field in the darkness of the night; and, though not easily cowed, I became possessed by a feeling of nameless horror at being thus compelled, as it were, to keep unwilling companionship with the dead. Danger might be faced, — indeed, would have been welcomed as a relief; but the feeling that I could not escape from this labyrinth of death was indeed an awful sensation.

Once I tumbled, at full length, over two bodies, my horror increased at finding my face close to the swollen and bloody features of the dead man who lay uppermost. The corpses seemed to be everywhere, for at times I could not put my foot to the ground without feeling some portion of a man's body beneath it. Turn where I would, I found myself surrounded by these revolting evidences of man's hatred and strife. My head grew dizzy, and a feeling of sickness crept over me, as I staggered over the ground, carpeted, as it was, with the slain of both armies. Here were confused heaps of dead men, Federal and Confederate, lying mingled as they fell fighting one another. Feeling my way among them, I found three or four lying close together, side by side, at their feet another body, at their heads two more. One poor fellow had evidently struggled a moment for life after receiving his mortal wound, then, pillowing his head on the breast of a dead comrade, lay passive as Death swept his dark wings over the plain. Judging from the position of some other bodies I stumbled over a few paces beyond, a fearful shower of grape and canister must have torn the ranks of a regiment into shreds; for fifty or sixty men lay here in a row, some on their faces, others on their backs, while the attitudes of a few betrayed the agony endured before death ended their sufferings. Though these bodies could be but dimly seen in the darkness, I fancied the glazed eyes of the dead were leering at me. Leaving the sleeping battalion, I came across the corpse of a little drummer-boy, who lay with his arms still clasped around his drum, his head shattered by a shell. Brave boy! he had beaten his last rataplan. Now the scabbard of a sword jingled as my uncertain foot struck it, the wearer being in a sitting posture, his legs shattered by a round shot.

Death! death everywhere, in all its horrid, awful forms! The swift bullet and the cruel shell both had been at work; and I realized what a price is paid for victories.

Still, I could not find my picket-post, and was wholly ignorant of my whereabouts; for now I came to the scene of another
desperate, bloody struggle, the bodies rapidly accumulating
under my feet, as they lay in confused masses on the grass.
Tumbling over one of these ghastly mounds of half-rotten
flesh, I was startled at finding a human hand thrust into my
face. For a moment I imagined I had found a living man
amidst the dead, but on closer scrutiny I saw that the hand
was a lifeless one. The soldier's death had been so instanta-
neous, that, as he fell with outstretched arm, the muscles became
rigid, the stiffening fingers remaining poised in death, pointing
to the heavens whither the spirit had taken its flight. The
man's musket lay across his chest; and, putting my hand on the
weapon, I found it still clutched by the dead owner.

Half mad, with a feeling of fear tugging at my heart-strings,
I dashed wildly from the spot, and, stumbling and falling, continued my career over the encumbered field.

Yet I did not escape the presence of the dead; for, as I subsequently discovered, I was going round and round, like a man
entangled in the depths of a forest. Owing to the darkness, I
imagined that I had traveled a mile, though in reality I did
not leave the vicinity of the glen. Besides the bodies, my feet
encountered muskets and knapsacks in extraordinary confusion;
and once I narrowly escaped a fall over the distended carcass
of a horse, killed perhaps while his rider was bravely cheering
on his men, or trying to restore order in a broken line. Next
my knee struck an exploded caisson, and a moment after I ran
full tilt against a dismantled cannon. Round the piece there
had been an awful combat, for the sod was thickly covered with
the dead. Utterly exhausted by my unavailing efforts to
extricate myself from this mass of moldering corpses, I determined to halt where I was.

"I'll go no farther," I cried. "If I must lodge with the slain,
I'll do it here."

Seating myself on the broken field-piece, I waited impatiently for the dawn that was to drive away these wild fancies and restore me to my men. But the darkness still held my senses inthralled; and, as I threw myself on the disabled cannon, I fancied that weird arms were pointing with shriveled fingers at the living, shrinking man in their midst. Try as I would, I could not shake off the feeling that uncanny shapes were abroad; and

LOST ON THE BATTLE-FIELD.

I fell more and more under the influence of these ghostly fears, despite my better reason. The exciting duty I had performed since reaching the field of Gettysburg had so affected my nervous system that these hallucinations seemed dread reality. Thus I watched for the daylight.

Not a shot had been fired since I parted with Tom Marshall. Both armies were exhausted by fatigue, and they slumbered in silence. Nearly two hundred thousand men were sleeping around me, while I was sitting wakeful and alone among the dead.

When I began hoping that the day would soon break, strange lights appeared in the distance, disappearing as soon as seen.

Supposing them to be carried by ambulance-parties in search of wounded, I rose to meet them. But before I had taken many steps, I was surprised to see one of these mysterious lights quite near me, though there were no footsteps, no voices. The flame grew brighter and brighter, and then suddenly expired. Then the truth flashed upon my mind: the light was caused by the mephitic gases escaping from putrefying corpses.

" Help — help — water — water ! "

The words were uttered a little way off, in a moaning voice; and when I heard them I knew some wounded wretch needed succor. With a feeling of relief at the presence of some human life among the dead, I hastened towards the sounds.

"Water—water! — my God! — is there — no help — water — a — little — water! "

" A DRINK OF WATER, FOR GOD'S SAKE! "

The faint and weary cry was now almost at my feet. Dropping on my hands and knees, I crawled cautiously forward.

"Where are you? I bring you water," I cried cheerily, my nerves now as firm as steel.

" Here," said the voice more faintly.

In a moment I was at the man's side, finding him in the midst of a group of the dead.

" Here you are," said I, unslinging my canteen and holding it to his lips. " But don't drink too fast."

The wounded man clutched the vessel, and soon I heard the water gurgling down his throat: when he stopped for breath I took the canteen from him, fearing that if he drank too much it would kill him.

"Ah, that was heavenly! Oh, how thirsty I was! I thought you would never come!"

"I only heard you call a moment ago, and came as quickly as I could. How long have you been lying here?"

"I don't know. I was hit when we first began to fall back, and could not get up again. Then I fainted, I suppose. When I came to again, I found my leg was smashed."

"That must have been the day before yesterday. Do you belong to Sickles's corps?"

"Yes. We got doubled up in the orchard here."

"But how did you contrive to live so long without food or water?" I asked, marveling at the man's tenacity of life.

"I had a little water when I went down, and I managed to get some more from the canteen of the dead man here beside me. I did not care much for food, though I did eat a little yesterday. But I was afraid of those shells. I expected every minute to be hit. One of them burst a little way off, and blew a dead man all to pieces. I thought the same thing would happen to me before they stopped. Oh, it was awful to hear those shells!" and I could feel the poor fellow shudder at the recollection of his fears during that terrible artillery duel.

"Well, you will be all right now," I replied encouragingly. "When daylight comes, I'll see you safely carried to the rear."

"Give me another drink. I feel so thirsty and faint!"

I gave him back the canteen, and he took a long, long draught. But it was to be his last; for the strength gained by imbibing the water set his pulse beating quicker, and the hemorrhage of his wound broke out afresh.

"Say, friend, I feel very weak. Am I going to die? Oh, say I'm not dying!" and the wretched man's voice quivered with agony as he asked the question.

"I hope not, my man. Keep quiet now. It will soon be daylight."

"All right," he replied, resting his head on a corpse behind him.

By this time the first faint streaks of daylight began stealing over the field, enabling me to distinguish objects at a little distance. Still kneeling beside my new-found charge, I watched the trees and rocks reveal their outlines. Next the corpses of men and horses, the broken cannon, the scattered muskets, all the *débris* of the battle, became visible in their rude deformity and confusion. Little by little the light grew stronger, until my whereabouts could be ascertained. I then found, that, on parting with Tom Marshall, I had unwittingly moved to the right of our line, and so wandered in a circle scarcely a thousand yards from my little party.

Looking across the open plain, I could see the ground thickly covered with the dead, the result of the Confederates' mad but heroic charge. In rifts like new-mown grass in the hayfield, lay long lines of slain men; while here and there were confused heaps of corpses, as though Death, the reaper, had already begun to reckon up and garner his harvest. Everywhere, on either hand, before and behind me, was death, — death in all its diversity of form.

Here lay the placid figure of a young man, as though asleep, his head resting on the arm that held his musket. Death had come to him with a light touch, swiftly, mercifully. Before the body had fallen to its mother earth, the spirit had soared aloft above the shock and turmoil of battle. Near this young and apparently sleeping soldier, the shattered and contorted limbs of a gray-haired man betrayed a different fate; for the swollen and blackened face of the corpse bore traces of the suffering endured before death had set its irrevocable seal on the life struggling for supremacy.

Averting my eyes from this broad expanse of slaughtered men, I turned my attention to the wounded one before me. Alas! death had added another victim to the long list to be made upon that bloody field; for he had expired, silently, peace fully, while asleep. If I had been too late to save him, I had at least the consolation of knowing that I had soothed his last hour.

I should never know who he was; and none of those who loved him would know that in the silence of the night, with his head pillowed on a corpse, his life had ebbed away.

"And this is the glory of war!" I exclaimed, rising from my knees to join my command.

CHAPTER XXIII.

MOVING IN PURSUIT.

"The army, like a lion from his den,
Marched forth with nerve and sinews bent to slay."

OON after I had rejoined the regiment with my men, Sedgwick's corps advanced across the field in heavy columns. But how different was the scene! When the Confederates came, they had to face a storm of lead and iron, only to be beaten back after frightful loss. Now the Sixth Corps marched quietly over the plain, heralded by no sound of cannon. Amidst profound silence the three long columns reached the trees where Lee had formed his lines for the charge. When the Federal army saw the corps carry their Roman-cross banners into the woods, it knew that the Confederates had abandoned their position.

"Lee has retreated! See! Sedgwick crosses the line without firing a shot!" exclaimed Major Harding, gazing through his glass.

"You are right," said Colonel Lloyd. "General Warren said yesterday he believed the enemy had fallen back."

"Then, why didn't we have a general advance at once?" grumbled Captain Burch.

"That's a question I have just asked myself," said the colonel; "for I heard Warren urge Meade to send Sedgwick's and our corps over right after that terrible charge of theirs. But Meade preferred to wait a day : he perhaps feared a trap."

"Trap! As if we couldn't charge and fight as well as they," exclaimed the pugnacious captain angrily. "We always lose the fruits of our victories by indecision and cautiousness. I'm sick of it," and the choleric captain began swearing in a frightful way.

"Come, come, Burch," remarked Major Harding in his usual good-natured tone. "You always find fault. Remember the great responsibility resting on Meade's shoulders. A single false step might imperil the whole campaign."

"It's those people in Washington, who are to blame," said Captain Burch.

"Never mind, captain : we have good reason to be grateful for our victory," said Colonel Lloyd. "This battle is the turning-point in the war."

"A good deal to brag about, after losing twenty or thirty thousand men : very satisfactory that, I must say."

"Upon my word, Burch, you are exceedingly difficult to please. Battles can not be fought without somebody being killed," replied the colonel impatiently.

"Oh! never mind him, colonel," said Major Harding. "Burch is never so happy as when he has a fair chance to grumble : it's his way."

"That's right, go ahead : I'm used to being abused."

As the captain spoke, our sergeant-major approached the colonel.

"Orders from brigade headquarters, sir. We are to be ready to move at a moment's notice."

"Of course. Now that the bird has flown, we are to go on an infernal chase until we haven't a leg to stand on," growled Captain Burch, evidently delighted at having a fresh opportunity to vent his spleen.

"Do be quiet, Burch," said Major Harding sharply. "If you don't like campaigning, why don't you resign ?"

"What! go home before the job's over? No: I'll stick it out, and see the end of this confounded war, if it don't put an end to me;" and the captain laughed in a jeering way that grated on my ears.

The sound of our brigade bugle put an end to the conversation, and we busied ourselves in seeing the men into their places. As Captain Burch and I listened to the sergeant's roll-call of our company, we found twenty-one men absent, nine of them reported as killed. There was no time for sorrow, however; for the brigade began moving off the hill immediately after. As we descended into the road, I saw that the whole army was in motion; our batteries were already leaving the crest of Cemetery Ridge, and long lines of infantry were on the march. But, instead of following the Sixth Corps, we were going towards the rear.

Away on our right a column of cavalry appeared on the road, where we had seen the rider of the white horse previous to the Confederate charge; and, as they came galloping up, I knew the pursuit had begun in earnest. An hour later, and the field of Gettysburg was deserted; its unburied dead and sinister rows of new graves alone attesting the recent presence of the contending armies.

"Well, Master Frank, that's the end of the biggest scrimmage we've had yit," said Dennis as we turned into the road.

"Yes, indeed. You and I, Dennis, will remember Gettysburg as long as we live," I replied.

"Begorra, I don't want to forgit it: we had more fun there than ivir before. An' that frind of yours, he'll not forgit it in a hurry, aither."

"We will not talk of him, Dennis. I saw General Fletcher this morning, and told him the whole story."

"An' what did he say?"

"He looked grave at first, but, as I went on, his face brightened, and he seized my hand, and called me a right good fellow."

" The ould brigadier is a thrump, that's what he is," said Dennis enthusiastically.

" He gave me a bit of advice which I shall follow, and I want you to do the same."

" I undherstand. The divil a word more I'll shpake about it," and Dennis dropped away from my side as if to avoid further temptation.

We had marched only a few miles when the threatening rain descended, and soon we were all drenched. So pitiable was our condition that a halt was called near a range of hills; and as the men put up their shelter-tents, and built fires, I heard the dull booming of distant cannonading. I knew by this that the advance had struck Lee's rear-guard, so we would be soon at his heels. The corps broke camp at daylight the following morning, in a pouring rain which continued until noon. Wet to the skin, the troops splashed through the mud merrily, and crossed South Mountain during the afternoon, leaving the rain behind us as we passed over the range. By forced marches we finally reached the Upper Potomac, near Falling Waters, three days after.

As the corps joined the army, we were ordered into line of battle; and at the same moment I was called for picket-duty. We had scarcely reached our post when orders came to advance as skirmishers.

" Troth, and we're in for another scrimmage," said Dennis, examining the nipple of his rifle; " though this skarmishin' is nasty work."

" You need not have volunteered to come."

" I volunteered because we have the divil's own luck together," replied Dennis. " Don't I always have lots of fun along wid ye? "

" There will be precious little fun here," said I, tightening my sword-belt, " but plenty of hot work.'

Just then the bugle sounded, and away went the line through the woods. Cautiously moving from tree to tree, we had gone only a few hundred yards, when bullets began singing in the air, like the buzz of angry bees. At the same moment the men in possession of a road on the right began firing rapidly. The musketry ran rippling along the line as the men advanced, and the woods rang with the reports of our rifles. Judging from the rapidity of our opponents' fusillade, they were in strong force; and, though we gained ground, several of our men were hit.

"Captain Hoyt is killed, sir," said a sergeant from one of the other regiments, as he ran towards me.

"Killed? How?"

"He started from one tree to another near the road, but was picked off directly he showed himself."

"Well, you must go to the left, and tell Captain Judkins he is in command now, and say I have taken the right of our line until he can come up. Look out you don't get hit yourself."

As the sergeant disappeared on his errand, I proceeded cautiously towards a brick schoolhouse that stood by the side of the road. Just as I reached the last tree nearest the building, I heard Dennis's voice.

"For the love of God, don't come any closer, leftenant darlint, or you're a dead man. Shure, they've got the range on us."

Wondering where the corporal could have got to, I looked in every direction, but failed to see his face.

"Where the dickens are you, Dennis?" I shouted.

"Here, sir: here amongst the children's copy-books," cried Dennis, his face peering at me from inside the schoolhouse-door.

"Come out of that, you skulker," I shouted angrily: "what possessed you to go in there?"

"We thought it wud be an illigant place to shoot from, but thim divils in the abbathy beyant have got the dead wood on us, and we durstn't stir a hand or a fut."

"How many are there of you?"

"Foive, besides mesilf; an' thim Ribs are puttin' their bullets in the door-frame as though they were drivin' nails in a man's coffin."

"Well, stay where you are for the present."

Darting from tree to tree until I gathered eight or ten men, we crept into the abatis that blockaded the road. Here we had a clear range of the pits commanding the schoolhouse; our bullets breaking up their fire, and enabling the corporal and his comrades to escape.

"Shure I've heard it said that too much larnin' is a dangerous thing, but I never knew how much thruth there was in the ould sayin' until I got caught in that murdherin' bit of a shkoolhouse," said Dennis, as he and his party joined me among the fallen trees in the road.

"I wonder what the schoolmaster will say when he comes, and sees how they have riddled his door and windows," remarked one of Dennis's companions.

"Troth an' I dunno. But if the leftinant hadn't come up as he did, faix, some of us would have finished our eddication by this toime. As fur the door, it's splintered into kindlin'-wood."

The Federal musketry had now became general all along the skirmish-line of our corps, those belonging to the division on our right succeeding in breaking through the pits occupied by the Confederates, their men falling back sullenly. As we entered the open fields, Captain Judkins came towards me, holding his arm as if in pain.

"I've got it pretty hot, Wilmot," said he, "and must go to the rear, for the wound is a bad one. You are in command now. Remember you are the only officer left, so take care of yourself."

Nodding in reply, I continued to push my men forward in order to straighten the line. The Confederates at the same moment broke away on a run; and off we went with a rush after them, my men loudly cheering. Suddenly the bugle sounded a halt, and we obeyed the call, though we could not

imagine why it was given. Sitting down on a stump, I waited
for further developments.

To my surprise, there was no sign of any strong force of the
enemy, no batteries on the rising points of ground as one might
expect. It was very strange. The stubborn fight made by
their pickets, followed by so hasty a retreat, was so unusual, I
could not understand it.

"An' where the divil have they all gone to?" said Dennis;
"an' why have they stopped us now roight in the middle of the
hunt?"

"I'm sure I don't know," I replied. "It seems like a general
skedaddle, over there."

As I spoke, the corporal's eyes became fixed on some object
in the distance.

"An' what can that be?" he asked.

"It looks like a man," I replied.

"Why, it's a nagur," shouted Dennis, leaping to his feet.

The contraband continued to approach until stopped by one
of the sentinels, who pointed to me. The negro at once came
forward to where I was sitting.

"Is yer de gineral?" he asked with a broad grin on his
ebony features.

"What general do you want?"

"Why, de big gineral, — de biggest of dem all. I just thou't
as tho' yous mou't be a gineral."

"What do you want to see the general for?"

"I wants fur to tell him de inforbation. I golly! I'se a
heap of news fur de old man," and the darky laughed gleefully.

"Tell us what ye mane, ye murdherin' black sarpint," exclaimed Dennis, his eyes blazing with anger. "Out wid it this
minnit, or I'll send ye to kingdom come in a jiffy."

"I'se no brack sarpint, no mor' dan yous be. I'se a cullured
gem'man. Dat's what I is," undauntedly replied our sable
visitor.

"Be quiet, Malone," said I. "Come, my fine fellow: you must tell me first what your news is, before you can see any general."

"Arrah, let's hang the black divil to the tree below. He's a spy," cried Dennis, evidently intending to frighten the poor negro. "Say, boys, shall we do it?"

"Yes, yes. Up with him!" replied two or three of the men, joining in with Dennis's humor.

"O massa, massa! I'se no spy. Don't you go fur to hang

"DEY'S ALL DONE GONE, SAH!"

dis yah nigger. I'se Pete, a rigilar Union man. I'se tells yer all I knows, an' dat's a fac'."

Seeing that the man was thoroughly frightened, I took advantage of Dennis's joke.

"Well, be quick about it, then. What do you know?"

"Well, yer see, massa ossifer, dey's all done gone dis heah four hours."

"All gone! Who has gone?"

"Why, massa Lee and all the Varginny sodgers. Dey's be's clar' gone 'cross de ribber."

" Are you sure of that? Come, my colored friend, be careful what you say."

" Fo' God, massa, it am de trufe. Dey's bin all gone. I'se seen dem go 'cross dis yeah morning wid my own two eyes;" and the negro raised his hand as if taking an oath.

This was indeed news for General Meade; and it explained the activity of the Confederate pickets and their precipitate retreat when we finally entered the open country. Sending the contraband to the reserve, in charge of a file of men, the entire line of pickets soon received orders to advance. The men dashed forward like a pack of schoolboys at play, but we found no trace of Lee's army until we reached a road in the hollow. Then the story of the retreat was easily read. Knee-deep in mud, I saw that one of Lee's columns had pushed through it in great haste: infantry, cavalry, and artillery, all left their traces; while two or three wrecked wagons, half-buried in the mire, showed how urgent had been the haste. Lee had once more out-maneuvered, out-generaled us: we must .now seek him on the old familiar ground along the line of the Rappahannock and the Rapidan. The fox had doubled on the hounds, but we would soon catch the scent again.

While my men were rummaging among the *débris* of a deserted camp in search of trophies, the several corps came advancing towards us in grand lines. But it seemed a foolish show of numbers, now that the foe had so cleverly escaped. Along the river-bank a cloud of cavalry was galloping , and as they rode forward, and were hidden by a belt of trees, some dropping shots told too plainly the fate of the Confederate pickets who had so bravely held us in check while their comrades crossed the Potomac in safety.

That night our army began moving for the fords below Harper's Ferry, in hopes of being able to head off Lee at the gaps in the Blue Ridge Mountains.

CHAPTER XXIV.

AN ADVENTURE ON THE ROAD.

" He that stands upon a slippery place,
Makes nice of no vile hold to stay him up."

E had reached the Pleasant Valley, in the most picturesque part of Maryland, and were already in sight of the South-Mountain range. The movement of the army was very rapid; for the need of haste was urgent, Lee having secured the interior line of operations. The constant and fatiguing marches we had endured ever since leaving Gettysburg had so inflamed my injured foot, the pain became at last unbearable; and I was compelled to ask permission to fall out of the line for rest. I made my application to General Fletcher, when the column halted during the afternoon a few miles after we passed Antietam bridge.

"I'm very sorry you are unable to keep up with us, Wilmot," said the general, as he countersigned my surgeon's pass. "If I had a spare horse, you could serve temporarily on my staff, but unluckily we are short of horse-flesh. You can be of great use, however, even in the rear. It is very necessary that all the stragglers should be hurried forward, for we shall probably cross the Potomac in two or three days. So you will please use all possible diligence, lieutenant, in overtaking us, and I rely on your zeal in bringing up the laggards."

" I'll do my best to do so, sir," I replied, delighted at having a definite duty to perform, though in the rear of my corps.

" I've no doubt of it, Wilmot," said the general kindly, "else I would not ask you. Of course you will find unruly fellows among the stragglers, as well as good, willing ones: so use the latter to discipline the others. Good-by: I see the column is in motion ahead."

It was with strange emotions that I saw the brigade march on, leaving me sitting by the wayside. I almost felt that my comrades had deserted me.

I had been sitting by the stone wall for nearly an hour, watching the fag-ends of the command creep on after the main body, when to my astonishment I perceived Dennis Malone leisurely walking back over the road. As soon as he caught sight of my face, the faithful fellow flourished his fez over his head, and ran towards me.

" Why have you left the regiment, Dennis?" I exclaimed, as he coolly sat down by my side and unslung his knapsack. " You are not sick or wounded?"

" The saints be praised, no! I'm as solid and sound as a six-pound shot. But, master Frank, you mustn't be angry. Though I'm not sick, I felt bad enough whin I found you had fallen out of the ranks becase of yer fut. So I made bould, an' tould the docther I'd take a pass mesilf, and look afther ye." And the simple-hearted corporal turned his beaming eyes to mine.

" And the doctor excused you?" said I incredulously.

" To be shure he did. Why not? Don't iverybody in the rigiment know I'm yer silf-appinted guardeen? Ould Physics laughed whin I tould him, an' sed I'd be no good in the ranks widout ye. so he handed out the pass. Here it is."

" Well, Dennis, I am very grateful to you, though I am often at a loss to understand why you think so much of me."

" That's what ye always say," retorted Dennis. " You forgit the day ye saved me loife in the shwamp, whin we were foightin' our way to the James. But I'll niver forgit it, anyhow."

"Oh! you canceled that debt at Gettysburg, when you thrust your bayonet through that poor fellow's throat, while we were fighting over those guns. But never mind, sergeant: we will be able to overtake the regiment in a few days."

"Sargeant? What d'ye mane by that? Is it a sargeant I am?" exclaimed Dennis eagerly.

"Yes: Captain Burch handed your name to the colonel this morning. Sergeant Foster is a lieutenant now. All the promotions will be announced to-night as soon as the regiment goes into camp."

"Wirra, wirra!" whimpered Dennis. "To be read off a sargeant before the b'yes, an' me a sthraggler!"

"It's all your own fault," I replied, laughing despite my pain at the woful face of my new sergeant. "It's your own fault. You are always putting your foot in it."

"Nivir moind, leftinant, so long as it's not the wrong one," said Dennis, with a grin on his honest, good-humored face. "You and me are together, an' that makes it all roight."

"Thank you, sergeant. To tell you the truth, I am glad enough to have you with me, for I can scarcely walk. Until I get a good rest, I shall not be able to take the road. Let us choose a spot for camping."

Dennis jumped up, climbed the stone fence behind me, and took a survey of the surrounding country with all the gravity of a staff-engineer selecting suitable ground for the encampment of a corps.

"Now, what is it to be?" he asked, descending from his perch of observation. "Is it to be an open camp, or a close one?"

"What in the name of common-sense do you mean?"

"Is it to be in a house, or undher a tree? Ye hev yer choice."

"Under a tree, by all means," I replied, "and near water where I can bathe my foot. It's so long since I slept under a roof, I should suffocate."

" Wid all the pleasure in loife. I'm in favor of an open camp mesilf, an' thare's an illigant spot down in the hollow beyant."

So saying, Dennis picked up my blanket and haversack, and helped me to rise. With some difficulty and intense pain I contrived to reach the wide-spreading tree he had selected, finding it situated near a mill-race. The afternoon was nearly spent by the time we had settled ourselves; and while Dennis went on a foraging expedition, I enjoyed a bath in the swiftly running water, afterwards falling into a delicious sleep.

When I awoke, Dennis was by my side, busy over the fire preparing supper; and at his bidding I remained stretched on my blanket, grateful for my rest and relief from pain.

It was the first time I had fallen so far in the rear of the army, since we had been abandoned on the Rappahannock picket-line; and the novelty of the situation amused and interested me.

Though the evening was fast approaching, I could see that the main road was still full of straggling soldiers, many of them evidently loitering simply for the freedom of action it gave them, though the greater part were suffering from illness and exhaustion. Even horses had succumbed to the fatigues of the march; a section of a battery having fallen out, and gone into bivouac in the fields on the other side of the road.

As the sun began to sink behind the distant range of Tatoctin Mountains, the white tops of a wagon-train could be seen in the distance, as it slowly proceeded in the direction the corps had gone; and I heard the clatter of a cavalry patrol or escort as it trotted over the little wooden bridge that spanned the creek. The voice of a plow-boy shouting to his cattle, the loud barking of a dog at a neighboring house, and the mournful caw of a crow flying overhead, were then the only sounds. All else was quiet; and it was strange to find one's self in the midst of peace so soon after the excitement of battle, and the stirring sights and sounds attending an active campaign.

After supper and a quiet smoke of our pipes, Dennis wrapped a wet handkerchief round my swollen foot, when we went to bed with our weapons safely stowed between us. It was not until the afternoon of the second day that I ventured to take the road; having a double purpose in view, — to rest my foot, and give time for the stragglers to get well on ahead.

We had proceeded only a few miles when we fell in with a party of a dozen who had gone into what seemed a permanent camp. I at once ordered them to pack up and accompany me, which they did after considerable grumbling. In this way I gathered nearly fifty men before sunset, and then halted for the night. The next day we were on the march in good season; and I was fortunate in overtaking another officer, my junior in rank, besides two or three sergeants. As I now had over one hundred men under my command, Lieutenant Beach was a great acquisition.

With his help and that of the sergeants, I managed to keep my ill-assorted battalion in decent soldierly shape; and we were near the South Mountains when the hour for camping arrived, the number of men being now nearly two hundred.

The next morning I roused the men for an early start, as I hoped to reach the lines of the army before nightfall. A few of the stragglers had decamped in the darkness; their absence not being regretted, for they had kept the rest in ill-humor by their mutinous spirit. Dennis had found a stray horse somewhere during the night, and improvised a saddle with his blanket, and one of the men picked up a broken bridle and bit: so I was duly mounted, and presented a tolerably imposing appearance at the head of our little column.

We made a march of five or six miles before the sun was warm, hoping to get to the mountain-gap before noon. In this we were doomed to disappointment; for at a cross-roads we suddenly encountered a force of fifty or sixty cavalrymen, under command of a captain, having in custody some three hundred Confederate prisoners. Halting to let them have the road, I was surprised to see their commanding officer draw rein.

"I'm glad we have met you, sir," said he courteously. "You are to take charge of these prisoners."

"Nonsense!" I replied. "These are a lot of stragglers I've picked up. Why should I take your duty off your hands?"

"Because such are my orders; which were, to turn these men over to the first infantry column I met, and return to my brigade, now on a reconnoissance."

"But this is not an infantry column, I tell you: only a few stragglers I am taking into camp."

"You seem to have got them into pretty good shape," remarked the captain. "From the looks of your command you can't deny you are infantry, and in column."

"But it's a difficult job for infantry, as you are pleased to call this ragged battalion of mine. We can not ride a man down as you can, should he attempt to escape."

"Pshaw! Haven't you your muskets? If any should attempt to run, shoot them down," replied the captain coolly.

Finding that there was no help for it, I called my command to order, and saw that every musket was properly loaded; then, reluctantly signing a receipt for the prisoners, watched the cavalry gleefully gallop away.

"This is a nice piece of business, Beach," said I, looking at the prisoners seated in the road. "It's a bad job, but we must do our best."

"Well, do you know now, I rather like it, Wilmot," replied the lieutenant.

"Begorra! it's the best thing that could have happened. It'll give the b'yes something to think of, an' kape them out of mischief," remarked Dennis.

"I hope so," said I. "Lieutenant, you will take the head of the column, while I ride in the rear. Malone, you stay with me. The other sergeants must keep well out on the flanks."

These directions being obeyed, I gave the order to march.

On mounting my horse I found that Dennis had obtained a spare saddle and bridle from one of the cavalrymen, so I felt more at ease on my steed. The captain had advised me to take the road to the right, as it led direct to Harper's Ferry, distant some twelve miles: therefore I took the new road, and proceeded.

The prisoners seemed quite content, and gave us no trouble. Indeed, one informed me that the cavalry had hurried them greatly, so our more moderate pace was an agreeable relief. I had announced that all who obeyed would be kindly treated, but if any one attempted to run away he would be shot. As these orders were expected by the Confederates, they jogged along very amicably. We marched at a sharp pace for infantry; because I was determined to reach the Ferry before nightfall, and so rid myself of my troublesome charge.

In an hour or two we reached the outlying spurs of the mountains that help to form Pleasant Valley, and by noon were in the midst of the range. Halting my command, I marched into an open bit of ground in the woods to the left of the road, and allowed my prisoners and their guard to rest by the side of a mountain brook which went tumbling noisily over its rocky bed. The Confederates were huddled together in the center, with my men sitting around them, a few files being on guard. Though our halting-place was entirely hidden from the road, I deemed it prudent, as we were going away from the army at every step, to throw out a few pickets among the trees on the side of the road. I gave the command of these pickets to Dennis, instructing him to keep them concealed. Much to the annoyance of both prisoners and escort, I forbade the lighting of fires, as the smoke might betray our presence. This precaution proved to be a wise one.

With my revolver on the grass beside me, I sat apart, nibbling a biscuit or two, thinking of the many adventures I was having, and wondering if this was to be the last one.

Suddenly Dennis came running in.

"Be all the powers! we're in the divil's own scrape now. Shure, there's a lot of Rib cavalry coming down the mountain. Begorra! the boot's on the other leg now; for we'll all be captured, and go to Richmond the wrong way."

"Don't talk so loud!" I exclaimed, thoroughly startled at Dennis's words. "Are you sure that they are Confederates?"

"Shure! Don't ye suppose I know a butthernut coat from a blue wan?" replied Dennis in an indignant tone.

"Go back and reconnoiter. If they discover us, fire off your piece, and take to the trees. We will do the same at your signal. Cavalry can not pursue us in these woods. Meanwhile I must keep these fellows quiet."

As Dennis saluted, and darted into the woods again, I called to my men, and ordered them to cover the group of prisoners with their muskets, and at the same time telling the Confederates that any outcry on their part would be the signal for a volley into their midst.

It was a dreadful moment. Here I was prepared to slaughter unarmed men, purely at the instinct of self-preservation; for I had no desire to be made a prisoner, and marched to the Confederate capital. The prisoners failed at first to understand our alarm and sudden change of demeanor, but the sight of two hundred muskets sternly leveled at their breasts taught them we were in danger. Still the love of life was too strong for them to make any effort for liberty, so they cowered down and remained silent, motionless. Then the sharp clatter of horses' hoofs sounded in the stony road, and I felt as if my heart had stopped beating during those few moments of terrible suspense. Our only danger was that my horse might neigh at the near presence of the cavalry, and I uncharitably wished the animal dead.

To my delight, the intelligent creature remained quiet, only pricking up his ears at the sounds in the road. In a few minutes, which seemed hours to me, the column passed on: still Dennis's musket remained mute. I began to breathe again,

when Dennis came back, waving his hat, a sign that the danger was over.

"Hurroo! They're gone, the saints be praised! They're in
a hurry, as though the divil was afther 'em. We're all safe,
b'yes."

"That was a narrow escape, Wilmot," said Lieutenant Beach.
"I've not had so close a squeak of it since I've been in the
army. Thank Heaven, they didn't molest us! for I hated
the alternative of shooting down these poor devils."

"We would not have had much time to do it, even if I had
given the word," I replied.

As I spoke, we were again startled by the sound of more
horsemen. Dennis disappeared under the trees, but soon returned shouting out that it was a force of Federal cavalry.

I ran out to the road, bidding Lieutenant Beach to bring our
column after me. On reaching the road, I found myself in the
midst of one of Kilpatrick's regiments.

"Are you in pursuit of that Confederate cavalry that has
just passed?" I asked of an officer, as he drew rein in astonishment at my unexpected appearance.

"Yes. Are they long gone?"

"They can not be more than a mile or two ahead."

"All right. But who are you? and what is this you have
with you?" asked the officer as my command began filing into
the road.

"A lot of prisoners bound for Harper's Ferry," said I. "We
had fortunately halted in the woods, or we might have been
captured in our turn."

"Oh, no! They knew we were too close after them for that,
I fancy. Though they might have split a few heads open.
But this won't do for me: I must be off."

"One moment, sir. Is the road to Harper's Ferry quite clear?
It's ticklish business, this guarding prisoners on foot."

"Oh! it's quite safe," was his response: "you can move
ahead without fear. Good-by, and good luck to you!" and

then, putting spurs to his steed, the speaker dashed off after the rear of his column.

We had not gone far when we heard rapid shots being exchanged among the hills; and, on looking back, I could see that our cavalry had overtaken their quarry, and were pushing them hard.

If my men had been willing to do. duty before, they were now enthusiastic. Their narrow escape from capture had shown them the danger of straggling, and the value of discipline and organization. True, we were taking a longer march than if we had kept straight on after the army; but the novelty of our situation and the comparative freedom of our movements delighted them. The Confederates were naturally depressed by the fact that they had been so near freedom, but they accepted the situation without a murmur.

We reached Point of Rocks, a few miles below Harper's Ferry, by sunset; and, as my command descended the steep road to the river-bank, I heard my name uttered by some one in the rear. Turning in my saddle, I recognized Osborne, the correspondent.

"What in the world have you there, lieutenant?" he cried on overtaking me.

"A lot of prisoners taken by our cavalry with a train they destroyed over in the valley."

"Where did you find them?"

"I didn't find them," I replied with a laugh: "they found me."

"I never was any hand at guessing riddles," said Osborne rather impatiently. "How did you come by the Confeds?"

Briefly explaining, I halted the column under the towering cliffs of stone which give the place its name, and announced my intention of proceeding to the Ferry.

"You had better stop here for the night," remarked the correspondent. "It will be quite night before you can reach the Ferry, and may lose some of your prisoners in the darkness. I would advise you to go down the river instead of up. They won't thank you for your prisoners there."

"Why? Is the place threatened?" I asked.

"Not yet. But there's no telling what Lee may do. A part of his army is still at Martinsburg."

"I am disposed to follow your advice, but where am I to stow away these bothersome prisoners?"

"Why, right here in the sheds. They're all empty. The quartermaster can have no objection."

"Speaking of quartermasters, reminds me that we have no rations. Perhaps, after all, I had best go to the Ferry."

"Nonsense! I'll introduce you to Marston. He's a crusty old chap, and may make a fuss at first; but he'll come round in time."

"Oh! if I'm to beg for supplies, I prefer going to the Ferry. The general in command will, of course, see that I am taken care of."

"You're almost as crotchety as old Marston," said Osborne. "Come along and see him."

"You correspondents take matters very easy, Osborne."

"Why shouldn't we? Independence is our motto."

"So I judge, by your way of doing things," I replied. "Where is this paragon of quartermasters to be found?"

"There are his quarters," said Osborne, pointing to a house near the railroad-sheds.

Requesting Lieutenant Beach to keep the men together, I followed the correspondent.

"Major Marston," said he, accosting an elderly officer we found seated on the veranda, "allow me to introduce Lieutenant Wilmot. He's got a lot of prisoners, and wants rations."

"Haven't any to spare," replied the quartermaster ungraciously. "How many men are there?"

"About five hundred in all," I replied. "We have not a mouthful to eat."

"Where are you going?"

"I did intend going to the Ferry, but Mr. Osborne tells me they are expecting an attack up there : so I think I'll stay here over night, and start down the river in the morning."

"You had better," replied the quartermaster. "They would give you a blessing up at the Ferry, and send you kiting back."

"Well, major, if you will let me put the prisoners in the sheds, and give us a day's rations, I shall be all right."

"Oh! I'm not going to issue any thing : most of our stores were sent away days ago."

"Come, major, let Mr. Wilmot have the grub for his party. I'm going to write a dispatch to-morrow, and shall mention the arrival of the prisoners : it will look well to say that Major Marston supplied them," said Osborne coaxingly.

"Well, if you intend that, I don't mind doing something," replied the quartermaster, evidently mollified by the prospect of a little newspaper fame. "Bring up your party, lieutenant."

"Didn't I tell you we would manage it?" said Osborne, as we rode back to my command. "There's nothing these quartermasters like more than being mentioned in the newspapers."

"What earthly use can it be to them?"

"Oh! you see, they are always in the rear, and are seldom thought of. Why, I know one fellow who keeps a scrap-book ; and he is always doing correspondents favors, just for such chances."

A few minutes after, I marched my nondescript battalion to the sheds, and had the gratification of seeing both prisoners and guards bountifully supplied with food. Declining the quartermaster's invitation to supper, Lieutenant Beach and myself quartered ourselves in a corner of the shed, and watched Dennis prepare our supper. He had managed to buy some bacon and eggs, and was in his element.

"By George!" said Osborne, sniffing at the odor of the broiling bacon, "I guess I'll bunk in with you myself, if you have no objection."

" None in the least. You forget what service you have been to us," said I.

" Fudge! old Marston was bound to help you. I only hastened his decision."

" Well, sit down. What's the news?"

" Meade is pushing rapidly for the gaps in the Blue Ridge. His advance is already past Leesburg, and the main body will cross the river to-morrow or the next day. Your corps is at Berlin. I suppose you heard of Vicksburg?"

" Vicksburg? no: we've heard nothing. What has happened? not a defeat?"

" Defeat! I should say not. Why, don't you know that Pemberton has surrendered, bag and baggage?" said Osborne wonderingly.

" Surrendered! you don't say so!" exclaimed Lieutenant Beach. " Of course we haven't heard any thing: you forget it's nearly a week since we saw the army."

" Well, it does seem odd to find anybody who don't know of Grant's victory."

" When did it occur?" said I.

" On the fourth of July, the same day we beat Longstreet back at Gettysburg. I tell you what it is, that fellow Grant's going to make his mark before this war is over."

" Well, Meade has given Lee the hardest blow he's got yet," remarked Lieutenant Beach.

"·That's so," said Osborne : " he won't make any more invasions. Do you know, I begin to see the beginning of the end?"

" I'm not so sure of that," I replied. " The Confederates will fight as long as they have a leg to stand upon."

" Of course they will," retorted Osborne; " but hang it, man, they can't fight for ever."

" No, but they'll not give up until every resource is exhausted."

" Sure enough," said the correspondent. " All the more glory in whipping them."

"Well, Osborne, you won't have much share in it. Why did you leave the army?"

"My wound was a pretty bad one, — I got it at Antietam, — and they mustered me out: so I went back to the pencil and note-book. It's more exciting and pleasant, besides being better paid."

"Supper's ready," cried Dennis, dishing up the bacon and eggs.

The night passed quietly; and, after breakfast the next morning, I bade Osborne and the quartermaster good-by, taking the road for Berlin, a little straggling village on the river-bank, arriving there during the afternoon. Marching up to our corps headquarters, I made my report to General Sykes, who seemed astonished at my arrival.

"Upon my word, sir, you deserve great credit for your success. Bringing up so many stragglers in such shape was a good thing, but to escort a lot of prisoners with such a command was a greater feat."

"Thank you, general; but Lieutenant Beach deserves as much credit as I do."

"You both did well. I am proud to have two such officers in my command," replied the general warmly. "The provost-marshal will relieve you of your prisoners; then you and your men can return to your respective regiments."

The transfer was soon made, when, after saluting the general, I dismissed my battalion, and soon after was among my brothor officers, relating my adventures.

CHAPTER XXV.

FENCING FOR AN OPENING.

"Leading on land his bravely toiling men,
  Sought a possession he could safely hold."

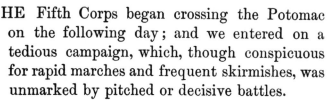

HE Fifth Corps began crossing the Potomac on the following day; and we entered on a tedious campaign, which, though conspicuous for rapid marches and frequent skirmishes, was unmarked by pitched or decisive battles.

But, though Meade failed to do more than occupy Lee's attention in the Virginia Valley, events in the West and South-west moved rapidly. The battle of Gettysburg and the fall of Vicksburg were followed closely by the capture of Port Hudson, so the Mississippi was practically free its entire length. Then came news of the battle of Chickamauga, with its terrible losses and partial defeat. The crippled condition of the forces under Rosecrans and Thomas took from us the Eleventh and Twelfth Corps, while the draft-riots in New York further weakened our strength. Lee sent Longstreet and his corps to Tennessee, consequently our antagonistic operations fell naturally to the second rank in their relative importance.

Preventing the Confederate army passing through the lower gaps, we rested a few weeks along the line of the Rappahannock, only to fall back on Centerville before a threatening movement by Lee, finally regaining possession of the valley and the line of the Rapidan. Meanwhile Burnside's escape by the rais-

THE WINTER CAMP.

ing of the siege of Knoxville, in Tennessee, was followed by the desperate battles at Chattanooga, Lookout Mountain, and Missionary Ridge. During the winter Meade made an effort to get a foot-hold on the southern bank of the Rapidan; but we were checked by the intense cold at Mine Run, so fell back to Culpepper to await in winter camp our spring campaign and the coming of Grant, the new lieutenant-general.

The frost and snow had disappeared, the grass in the fields was again green, and the buds on the trees were beginning to burst, when signs of preparation for a movement multiplied. Besides the drafts of recruits, and the convalescents from the hospitals, a large number of new regiments from the Washington forts made their appearance. General Grant came and re-organized the army. By the end of April, 1864, the several corps gathered near Culpepper; and a few days after I was again on my favorite duty, in command of a picket-post holding a ford on the Rapidan River, being now a captain.

Though the nights were still quite cool, I enjoyed the change from hut-life; for there was a feeling of exhilaration at being once more on active duty in the extreme front. We found the enemy strongly posted along the opposite side of the river, but as yet there had been very little firing to harass the sentinels. Standing on the bank by the side of the road that led to the ford, late in the afternoon of the second day, I noticed a Confederate officer lying on the grass on the other side, coolly taking a survey of the river and our line. He apparently feared no danger from our muskets, owing to the *quasi* peace that had prevailed so far; but I expected every moment to hear the report of a gun, knowing that my men were easily excited.

The officer was quite young, and it seemed foolhardy for him thus to expose himself. A chance shot by some indiscreet sentry would set the whole line of pickets in a blaze; and, as my orders were to remain quiet unless a movement took place, I determined to warn the reckless and exposed officer.

Stepping out from under the trees, I lifted my cap as a friend-

ly salute, which was promptly answered by the Confederate as
he hastily leaped to his feet.

"You had better keep under cover," I shouted, "unless you
really want to be shot."

"Thank you for the warning," he replied. "I thought we
were not fighting just now."

"No, not at present. But you ought not to show yourself
so openly. Get under cover, sir, or my men will be sure to
fire."

"All right. I've no desire to be made a target of just
yet."

As he uttered the words, the young officer waved his hat
courteously, and turned on his heel. He had scarcely done so
when one of the men a few rods below me sent a bullet whistling over his head. Sharply reproving the sentinel for his
unprovoked attack, I soon quieted the remainder of the line;
and the silent river continued to flow between the armies
undisturbed by any warlike sounds. The incident was, however, a pleasant one; and I was glad that the Confederate lieutenant had escaped. To kill him under such circumstances
seemed like murder; and it was pleasant to know that by my
courtesy I had probably saved several lives, for scarcely had
the echoes of the sentinel's musket ceased reverberating
through the woods than I saw that the pickets on the opposite
bank were on the alert. Another indiscreet shot, and we
should have had warm work on our hands.

The evening darkened into night; and I was quietly making
the rounds of my line after supper, with Sergeant Malone, as
usual, at my side, when we were both startled by several shots
fired rapidly on the right of the post. Anxious to know what
had happened, I was soon among the men, finding them reloading their pieces.

"Hadley, what was this firing for?" said I to the man nearest
me.

"Well, I don't exactly know, captain," he replied: "Tom

Bowles over there fired at something in the water, so I did the same."

" You had no business to fire just because Bowles did, unless you really saw some one to fire at," said I sharply. " We shall have the enemy blazing away next, and all for nothing."

" I don't think it will be about nothing, sir," said Bowles, who as yet remained silent. " I fired at a man, or something like one; and then all the other fellows began banging away like a lot of fools."

Knowing that Bowles was a cool, cautious soldier, I began questioning him; at the same time giving directions that there must be no more firing unless I ordered it.

" Are you quite sure it was a man you fired at?" I asked Bowles.

" As sure as one can be in the dark, sir. You see, I was standing here, quiet enough, not thinking of any thing in particular, when all of a sudden I saw something moving in the water. It was too big for a muskrat, and I knew it wasn't a cow; so I up with my musket, and let drive at it."

" Well, what happened then?"

" Why, nothing as I could see. The boys began making such a racket, I lost sight of the fellow: so I reloaded and waited, knowing you would come up."

" Maybe the divils are thryin' to get across the river unbeknownst to us," sagely remarked Dennis.

" Oh, nonsense!" I replied. " If it had been any one but you, Bowles, who began the firing, I should be apt to think you had been half asleep."

" No, captain, I was wide awake. I am sure I saw something like a man's head, but perhaps it was a log."

" Very likely. But keep a sharp lookout," said I, turning to go towards the left of our line. " If any of you see or hear any thing, wait until you are sure what you are about. Then fire if you must."

"An' what do ye think it was, captain?" queried Dennis, as we retraced our steps.

"I can not imagine what Bowles could have seen. I hope it was not a man; though it is likely, for the scouts are always busy just before a move."

"Bedad, it's a reckless way of risking yer loife. Shure, it's death to be caught. Don't they always hang spoies?"

"In most cases. But spies are necessary in war."

"Whisht! Begorra, I seen something just thin," whispered Dennis, stepping to the edge of the bank and listening.

"Where?"

"Right here, just undher yer fut."

I knelt down, and, creeping to the edge, peered cautiously over into the water. I could not discern any thing at first, and was beginning to believe Dennis had simply imagined something, when he clasped my hand, whispering excitedly,—

"That's him!"

I gazed intently through the darkness, and saw the figure of a man sitting on the exposed roots of a tree, his legs dangling idly in the stream. The bank was fully twelve feet high just there, and the swift current had washed away the soil below so that the roots of the tree projected over the river. It was evident that the unknown wished to gain an entrance through our lines. Was he a deserter, or a spy? We must capture him alive if possible. But how? That was a problem we must solve by cool action.

We continued to watch the intruder, who seemed to be taking his ease very unconcernedly; and I found it difficult to keep the sergeant quiet.

All at once the man climbed upon the big root he had been using as a seat, and began edging his way towards a spot a few feet below, where a jutting bit of rock would give him a lift up the bank. Silently nudging Dennis, I crept along the bank above his head, the sergeant taking a position below the rock.

It was an exciting moment, for the fellow began making his

way up the bank as Dennis and I faced each other. He would be soon at the top, and find himself a prisoner. Though Dennis was even more excited than I was, he behaved admirably. We were sure of our game.

The man's head appeared over the edge of the bank, as he silently and slowly pulled himself up, until he finally lay prostrate between us.

"Don't move, or you're a dead man," I cried in a hoarse

ARREST OF THE SPY.

voice, as I seized him by the wrist, Dennis at the same instant flinging himself bodily on top of our prisoner.

"All right," quietly responded the captive. "I surrender. Don't shoot me."

Surprised at the cool audacity of the man, I permitted him to rise, but keeping a close hold of his arm. Dennis called two or three of the nearest sentries, who were greatly astonished to find that we had a prisoner. The Confederate quietly submitted to have his hands pinioned behind his back with a blanket-strap, and we started for my bivouac fire.

"This pays us up for the scout we lost on the ould Rappahannock last summer," said Dennis to me as we were thread-ing the narrow path through the woods.

"Yes," I replied, "if he isn't a deserter."

"Divil of a desarter is he. Shure, an' if he was desartin' he'd have tould us so long ago."

Dennis was right. My prisoner was no deserter. Men like him do not desert their cause at the opening of a campaign, however hopeless it may be.

On reaching my reserve, one of the men threw some dry sticks on the fire, which, breaking into a blaze, gave me an opportunity to survey the Confederate.

Dressed in a handsome Virginian uniform, and carrying a pair of revolvers in his belt, the man's face was shadowed by the broad-brimmed hat he wore; yet there was an air of the dare-devil about him that indicated a man of no common cour-age.

"Well, sir, what are you going to do with me?" he asked in a clear, steady voice.

"I shall keep you here under guard until morning, and then send you to headquarters," was my reply.

"Very well; but surely you don't expect me to sleep with my hands tied behind my back."

As the man spoke, Dennis Malone leaned forward, and peered inquisitively into the scout's face.

"Captain darlint! don't ye see who he is?" exclaimed the sergeant excitedly.

"Who do you mean?" said I.

"Why, the prisoner: who else?"

"No, I don't: do you?"

"Shure, an' I do; and so do you, Master Frank. It's Bob Haines, the missin' sargeant, an' nobody else."

"Sergeant Haines!" said I incredulously, for I remembered the name very well.

"Halloa, Dennis! so you are a sergeant now, eh? I congratu-late you. — Well, captain, as you have recognized me at last, suppose you undo this infernal strap;" and Haines — for it was indeed he — began laughing.

"How is this, Haines? Why are you playing Confederate?" I asked.

"Oh! I'm a scout now, — on the Federal side of course, — and I was trying to slip through the lines when you nabbed me. Upon my word, captain, you did it nicely."

"Untie his hands, Dennis: there's no further need of that precaution. — You must stay here, though, Haines, until daylight," said I, giving the fire a kick to make it burn brighter.

"Of course. I expect to, and you may as well put a guard over me," he replied cheerfully. "But I wish you would give me something to eat: I'm awfully hungry."

Dennis soon provided the necessary food; and, as Haines ate his supper with the zest born of long fasting, I lay before the fire conjecturing how he came to be a scout. I remembered that he had disappeared from the regiment while we were maneuvering at Aldie Gap, a few days after I had rejoined the army from our abandoned picket-line. I also recalled the remarkable indifference manifested by both General Fletcher and Colonel Lloyd at his mysterious absence. I had neither seen nor heard of him since, and in fact had almost forgotten him.

Haines, having satisfied his appetite, produced a corn-cob pipe, and joined me in a quiet smoke. The men had all withdrawn from our fire to their own, only Dennis being near us.

"Well, Haines, this is a singular meeting," said I at length.

"Isn't it?" replied the sergeant scout. "I didn't know my old corps had moved up from the railroad line. When did you come up to the river?"

"Only three days ago. The whole army is concentrating for a move," was my answer.

"So! I'm glad I've got here in time."

"Shure, an' it must hev bin ticklish work to get through the Ribs' lines," said Dennis.

" Yes, indeed ! though I managed it easy enough after all,"
replied the scout.

" How did you do it ? " I asked.

" Well, you see, I walked down to the river this afternoon,
and began asking questions of the Reb pickets, at the same
time keeping my eyes open. I soon discovered that there was
a gap in their line, owing to a small creek that enters the
Rapidan half a mile above; and by making a circuit through the
woods, I struck the river at the mouth of the creek. The current was pretty swift, so I just launched out and swam silently
down stream."

" Some of our men fired at you," I remarked. " It's a wonder you were not hit."

" Not at all. Only one of the men saw me; and, when I
heard him cock his rifle, I just dove under the bank, and was
soon under cover."

" You ran a regular gauntlet, in fact ? "

" Just so. The only danger was, that the fellows on the
other side might see me and fire also."

" You were confoundedly self-possessed, Haines, when we
laid hands on you," said I.

" Why not ? " replied the scout with a low laugh. " I could
scarcely expect to get through our lines unnoticed. All I was
afraid of was, that you might use your revolver, — shoot first
and ask questions afterwards, you know. It was only necessary to surrender quietly to be safe."

" Suppose we had not recognized you : what would you have
done ? "

" Simply played my part as a Confederate, and asked to be
sent to headquarters under guard. Once with the general, I
was all right." And Haines re-filled his pipe.

" Upon my word, Haines, you are a cool hand ! " said I
admiringly.

" One needs to be cool in my business. A scout has to
have his wits about him."

" How came you to turn scout? " I asked, my curiosity now fully aroused.

" It was a very simple matter, and all an accident. I don't mind telling you and Dennis the story, if you care to hear it."

" Be jabers, we're just dyin' to hear it! " exclaimed the sergeant.

" Well, here goes. But it's a pretty long yarn."

And Haines at once proceeded to tell his story, which must serve as another chapter.

CHAPTER XXVI.

THE SCOUT'S STORY.

" Away, then, — work with boldness and with speed,
On greatest actions greatest dangers feed."

IRST you must remember how the old Fifth Corps started for Gettysburg, and our brigade went through Aldie Gap into the Loudon Valley to support Pleasonton's cavalry during their skirmish with Stuart's troopers. I need not remind you of the dance they led us. What I have to tell happened after that.

The brigade had gone into bivouac on the slope of the hills; and as the sun began to sink behind the western range of the Blue Ridge, on the other side of the valley, I congratulated myself on the prospect of a quiet night's rest, after the hard day's service we had passed through. I was busily engaged in preparing supper, when all my expectations disappeared by a summons for picket-duty. Excessively annoyed, I slung my knapsack and rifle over my shoulder, and in a few minutes after was moving with the detail into the valley toward the outposts.

When I bade my comrades the usual careless farewell of a soldier, I little anticipated the adventure in store for me; and as my old friend and tent-mate, Tom Burroughs, looked up from his hardtack and coffee, grumbling in no amiable mood at my departure, neither he nor I imagined that it was our last sight of each other on earth. Two years of constant service, and plenty of hard knocks successfully encountered together, had given Tom and me confidence in the future; and we had already exchanged many a thought on the day our regiment would return home. Tom, however, was never to see home again, poor fellow! for he met a soldier's death in the charge you fellows made so gallantly at Gettysburg, before the Little Round Top.

The picket billets had all been told off as the sun went down in a blaze of color; and I was placed in command of a small picket-post towards the left of our line, my position lying directly across an old by-road which skirted the mountain range at our back, and led to the village beyond. The evening was clear and warm; and as I passed along my chain of sentinels, and gave the countersign, I found the scene a very lovely and refreshing one, making me lose my regret at leaving camp. The birds were flitting in the trees above my head, seeking their nests; while the soft and busy hum of the summer insects made the stillness more marked by the contrast. The massive outlines of the mountains were fast becoming lost in the shades of night; and I almost forgot that I trod the soil of Virginia, so like did the scene appear to that of my own Northern home.

Cautioning my men to keep a sharp lookout for any movement on the part of the enemy, and, above all, not permit any lurking guerilla to assail them, I retraced my steps to the rendezvous of my guard, finding their fire deftly hidden by a huge bowlder.

The evening deepened into night, and the second relief of sentries had been duly posted, when I suddenly heard the one stationed in the road give a hurried challenge. No response was made to his summons, however; and I was settling myself in my snug corner once more when the same sentry uttered another and more excited call of " Who comes there? "

Fearing that he might use his rifle without due provocation, and so needlessly alarm the entire line, I stepped down to his post to reconnoiter; finding Weaver, the sentinel, standing in the middle of the wagon-track, on the alert, and peering intently into the shrubbery which skirted either side of the road.

Uttering a low word or two to apprise him of my coming, I approached, and asked what had alarmed him.

"I don't know exactly, sergeant," said he; "but I'll swear that I saw a man run across the road just now, down by that pine-tree."

"You challenged twice, Joe," I remarked. "What did you see the first time?"

"Nothing; but I heard a twig crack a moment before, and I thought I saw the tree move a little."

I glanced down the road as he spoke, but could discern nothing, despite the moonlight; and, supposing it was a squirrel that had caused the alarm, I uttered my thoughts aloud.

"I tell you, sergeant, it was a man, if any thing," exclaimed Weaver doggedly: "I guess I know a man from a squirrel when I see one."

"Very likely," I replied soothingly. "Just you stand here on the lookout while I go down the road a bit."

Gently drawing back the hammer of my rifle, ready for use, I crept cautiously down the road until I reached the tree, but, as I expected, discovered nothing. With a quiet laugh at Joe and his fears, I cautioned him against any more needless alarms, and passed through the line again. I had proceeded scarcely a dozen paces, however, when I distinctly saw the crouching form of a man hurry across the road a few rods below.

The thought flashed upon me in an instant, that this must be Joe's friend, and up to no good, that was evident. Ashamed of my sneer at the sentinel's watchfulness, I ran towards the spot where the intruder had disappeared in the bushes. But I was too late, for no trace whatever could I find of the skulker. Indeed, I began to doubt my own sense of sight, so strange did the whole affair appear. Determined, however, to sift the matter thoroughly, I searched in every direction, yet could find nothing that would give me a clew to the mystery.

Chagrined at my failure, but fully satisfied that some mischief was afoot, I returned to Weaver, and told him what had háppened.

Joe at first seemed only relieved to learn that he had not been mistaken in his challenge, but soon joined in my annoyance at our having been so cleverly outwitted. We fully agreed that the fellow was a spy, and that he had managed to slip past Joe while the latter was watching my movements down the road in front.

As Weaver had seen no more men, I left him with a caution to be silent regarding the occurrence, and at once made a tour of my line; finding all of the men very quiet and unconcerned, none of them dreaming that our chain of sentries had actually been penetrated in so bold a manner. In due time, and in no amiable mood, I reported the facts to the commissioned officer in command of the brigade pickets; and he immediately notified headquarters, at the same time sending me back to my guard with a sharp reprimand for what he was pleased to term *my* negligence.

The remainder of the night was passing off very quietly, and I was nodding over the fire after midnight, when an order came for me to report forthwith at our brigade headquarters, another sergeant relieving me of my command. Fully expecting a sound lecture from General Fletcher, I stumbled off in the dark to report as ordered. Upon my arrival I was at once ushered into the general's tent; where, instead of our brigadier, I found myself confronted by a tall and dashing fellow, fully equipped in a Confederate lieutenant's uniform.

"Are you the sergeant who so nearly captured me to-night on the picket-line?" said the stranger in a pleasant voice.

"I suppose I am," I replied, "if you are the man who crossed my line of sentries by the old dirt-road. But how under the sun did you come here?"

"Oh! that was easy enough, after I succeeded in eluding you. As for my being here, I need only say I am a Federal scout."

At this moment General Fletcher entered the tent in a hurried manner, and said, —

"Sergeant Haines, I am very glad that you did not create any alarm over the entrance of our friend, the scout here, into our lines; for it so happens he does not wish his presence known, as we are on the eve of a general movement. My object in sending for you is to make an arrangement by which he may proceed to General Hooker's headquarters. You and he must change clothes."

"General!" I exclaimed, quite taken aback by the novel proposition.

"You must, I tell you; and not only must you take his uniform, but his character also, and contrive to slip through our lines to-night on a special scout."

"But, general, you forget that I am not prepared, nor fitted by experience, for such hazardous duty. I must really decline the latter part of your programme."

"Of course I know very well I can not compel you to go, sergeant," replied General Fletcher; "but I'm sure you won't refuse when I explain the matter a little."

"Tell him the whole story, general," said the unknown : "I can see that he'll go, after all."

"The fact is, Haines," pursued the brigadier, "our friend here, who is known inside the Confederate lines as Lieutenant Fred Watson, is in possession of very important information which must be transmitted to General Hooker at once. He managed to come this way from General Lee's headquarters, while carrying orders to General Ewell, who commands the enemy's advance; and it is imperative that these orders be delivered in due time, else Watson's future plans for usefulness are entirely upset."

"But," said I, "why can't his information be sent to General

Hooker by some one else, and he take the orders to General Ewell himself? I will undertake to get him through the picket-line again without any trouble."

"No, no!" exclaimed Watson: "that won't do at all, for I have to sketch routes on a map at headquarters. You don't suppose I'm fool enough to carry plans and marked maps on my person, do you?"

"Come now, sergeant, volunteer like a man, and make no more bother," said the brigadier, rather testily at my stubbornness.

"Well, I suppose I must do as you say, sir, now that I understand the case so clearly," I reluctantly replied. "But I don't see how I am to overtake General Ewell without a mount."

"Oh! that's easily managed," said the scout eagerly, "if you only make haste and get through the lines before daybreak. Go a hundred yards or so down the road beyond your picket-line, where the sentinel challenged me, and you will find my horse there all ready for you."

Making no further objection, I at once began to strip; and soon found myself metamorphosed into a Confederate officer of the most approved type, the scout's uniform fortunately proving a decided fit. Watson then handed me his Confederate passes, a pair of revolvers in excellent order, and a small packet of soft tissue-paper wrapped in a sheet of tinfoil such as they put tobacco in. This packet contained the orders and secret instructions for General Ewell from General Lee, the text of which formed a part of Watson's information.

While the scout and I were exchanging uniforms, he informed me that I would have no difficulty in personating him, as he was not known except at the general headquarters of the Confederate army; and he took occasion to give me a few hurried hints as to my conduct while inside the enemy's lines. Watson confessed, however, that circumstances and the exercise of my own wits would be the best guide; so he only insisted that I should, after delivering the packet to General Ewell, leave him as soon as possible, and return to our own army, in order that he himself might go again on scout duty.

Bidding the general and the scout a hasty farewell, I slipped out of the tent, and plunged into the bush near by. I had looked at my watch while stowing away a big roll of Confederate scrip given me by Watson, and noticed that it was after the hour for my second relief to go on post again. I would therefore find Weaver on duty; and, as I made my way toward the road, I determined to take him into my confidence, and so pass through the picket-line.

Cautiously creeping past my reserve guard, who were fortunately nearly all asleep, I managed to gain Weaver's post without much difficulty. Joe was standing in the road, quietly leaning on his musket, no doubt thinking of the spy and my supposed disgrace. A word from me placed him on the alert; and, taking care not to be seen by the neighboring sentinels, I hurriedly told Joe my errand and orders.

Satisfying himself of my identity, Weaver permitted me to pass, with a low whistle of surprise, faithfully promising to keep my secret; being much amused, as I afterward learned, at the idle rumors in circulation the next day, explanatory of my disappearance.

Bidding Joe good-night, I walked rapidly down the road beyond the pine-tree, and was gratified to find Watson's horse all right, just as he had left it; so sprang nimbly into the saddle, and cantered off. I had already made up my mind as to my route, and intended making a wide detour until I could with safety strike into the main road for Snicker's Gap.

It was then almost daylight, and I had made good progress across the valley before the sun began to redden the horizon. As my horse cantered gayly forward, my spirits rose with the novelty of the occasion; and I enjoyed the sudden change in my fortunes all the more because it came unexpected. I knew that my disguise was perfect; and I felt quite proud of my new sleeve-embroidered jacket, decorated as it was with a set of handsome Virginia State buttons, worth a mint of money in Confederate currency: I naturally had, therefore, no great fears as to my ultimate success. Having ridden across the valley without hindrance, I was congratulating myself on an easy entrance into the lines of the enemy, when my ear caught the sound of horses' hoofs. Failing to discover any one either ahead or behind me on the road, and noticing a cross-road a few rods farther on, I urged my horse forward to reconnoiter.

Scarcely had I reached this cross-road, than a wild halloo on my right showed me I had encountered a Federal cavalry patrol. As it was no part of my plan to be captured by our own side, I made a choice of necessity, and dashed madly up the road towards the mountains in order to escape. When the patrol came thunder-

THE CHASE.

ing along after me in hopes of securing a prisoner, I found my mare equal to the emergency; for she rapidly gained ground in the race. This fact only added to my danger, however: for every few seconds a bullet came whistling past my ear, my pursuers making a regular target of me; though their fusillade fortunately proved ineffectual, owing to the necessary unevenness of their aim.

Expecting each moment to be hit, I galloped doggedly on,

hoping that I might be lucky enough to reach some Confederate outpost before either myself or my horse was wounded. The scouting-party at my heels evidently divined my intention, ere we had galloped half a mile; for I could see they were already repenting of their rashness. It only needed, therefore, the appearance of a few Confederate cavalrymen at a sudden turn in the road, to rid me of my troublesome pursuers. The chase, however, proved of decided service; for as I checked my mare, and halted near the *vidette*, I was not suspected, the corporal in command merely saying, —

"Well, lieutenant, you had a narrow escape from going North the wrong way, hadn't you?"

"Yes, sir: it was indeed a close shave," I replied, "though I don't think I should ever have seen a Northern prison if they had caught me."

"Why not?" exclaimed two or three voices.

"Well, you see, gentlemen, I've ridden hard all night from General Lee's headquarters; and I have papers on my person that might make the Yanks believe I was something like a scout."

"Oh! that's it, is it?" said the corporal. "Well, I'm glad we happened so close when you rode up. I suppose you want to go to the rear."

"By all means; and I would thank you to send an escort with me to the nearest general officer, for my business is pressing."

"All right, sir: we won't keep you. — Here, Graves, you go with the lieutenant," added the corporal, nodding to the nearest trooper.

With a brief salute to the corporal, I followed my guide up the rapidly rising road; for we were then entering the gorge of the mountains leading into the Gap.

Like most soldiers, Graves proved talkative, — a trait I encouraged, for I wished to post myself a little before I was brought in contact with the general, whoever he might be.

"How came you outside our lines, sir?" asked Graves as he hitched his saber-belt into an easier position.

"I took the shortest cut through the Loudon, not knowing the Yanks had got into it. I only discovered the fact by the dead horses lying in the roads below."

"You were mighty lucky to run across us as you did," said Graves. "It's a wonder you didn't fall in with any more Yanks: the valley is full of them."

"How came you fellows to fall back after whipping the Yanks, as you evidently did?" I inquired, affecting ignorance of the true state of affairs.

"We fell back to encourage them to come down again to-day," replied Graves, evidently gratified at my words. "We thrashed them pretty bad yesterday, that's a fact; though their cursed infantry bothered us a good deal."

Much amused at the fellow's conceit, I continued the conversation; ascertaining that General Fitz Hugh Lee's brigade of cavalry held the Gap, and that I was being taken to his headquarters. Graves also informed me that General Ewell had already crossed the Potomac; and Longstreet's corps had passed through Winchester the day before, and would probably cross the river before morning of the following day. General Hill had relieved General Longstreet, and was now supporting the operations of the Confederate cavalry under Stuart in holding the Gaps. The Confederates evidently anticipated a sharp engagement that day, a scout having reported an entire Federal corps in motion through Aldie Gap, — a pure fiction on his part, as I had good reason to know.

After proceeding a mile up the Gap, my guide suddenly abandoned the road, and escorted me to a clump of trees on the right, where I found the Confederate brigadier at breakfast, — a fact that told me he anticipated an early move.

"What's this?" queried the general as he turned sharply round at the sound of our approach.

"I am the bearer of dispatches from General Lee to Lieutenant-General Ewell, sir," said I, dismounting, and showing him my pass. " I am desirous of proceeding as far as Winchester immediately."

The brigadier glanced at the pass, and, finding it genuine, replied, "Very well, sir, you can go; though I don't see how you are to reach General Ewell on that beast."

" I have an order for a fresh horse for use at Winchester, sir, unless I can get one nearer at hand," said I with the air of a man accustomed to such favors.

BEFORE THE CONFEDERATE GENERAL.

" I would give you a mount, lieutenant, with pleasure," said the general, noticing my hint; "but you are better off now than two-thirds of my men. You will have to wait for another horse until you reach Winchester."

" Much obliged to you, sir, all the same. I will do my best. I have the honor to bid you good-day, general."

" Perhaps you would like some breakfast before proceeding," said one of the staff-officers courteously.

" I am much obliged to you," I replied; "but I must decline any thing more than a cup of coffee, if you have such a luxury at hand."

" Fortunately we can do that much for you. But how came you to ride through the Loudon Valley? You ran great risk of capture," he continued as a contraband produced some coffee and a plate of corn-cakes.

"You may well say that, for I was hotly pursued under the foot-hills just now. My reason for striking through the Loudon was, that I intended crossing the Potomac below Harper's Ferry; but your unexpected maneuvers yesterday prevented my doing so."

"We had to fight to keep Hooker from moving too rapidly," replied the aide; "but the engagement had no important result."

"Well," remarked the general, "we are likely to have hot work to-day, for one of my scouts reports their infantry in motion through the Aldie Gap."

"He is mistaken," I said in a confident tone; "for I ascertained last night from a citizen, that the main force of the Yanks were still in camp on the other side."

"Is that so?" exclaimed the brigadier: "I hope it is, upon my soul, for we are not prepared for a decided stand."

"You forget, general, that our entire army is now past Front Royal," said I, sipping my coffee with the air of a man confident of his information.

"I'm glad to hear you say so, lieutenant, for it proves that this infernal race will soon be over," said the general.

"I consider it over now, in fact," said I, springing into my saddle again. "I must make haste and overtake the advance. So good-day, gentlemen."

My progress through Snicker's Gap was an uneventful one, and I fully enjoyed the ride over the mountains. By eight o'clock I had commenced the descent into the Valley of the Shenandoah; and, as I struck the open road, my eye was insensibly attracted by the novelty of the scene spread out at my feet. Every thing was in seeming confusion. The main roads leading to the River Potomac were marked by clouds of dust, evidence of the movements of large bodies of troops and trains. The plain to the right was dark with moving masses of troops, and my pulse quickened with the thought that I was now a spy inside the lines of the enemy.

When fairly across the Shenandoah River, I gave my steed the rein, and by noon was cantering over the neglected pavements of Winchester. I found the town full of troops and wagon-trains; and with some difficulty wended my way to the railroad-depot, which I learned was the quartermaster's storehouse. On my arrival, I presented my order for a fresh horse to the officer on duty. He glanced at the document, and with an oath threw it contemptuously aside, saying as he did so, —

"Beg your pardon, lieutenant, for my apparent rudeness. But those people at general headquarters seem to think we can furnish any thing. Here you bring an order for a horse, and I haven't one even for myself."

"Oh! never mind, quartermaster; though I am sorry I can not get a fresh horse, for I am in urgent need of haste. I'll do the best I can, if you will give me some short forage to take with me."

"Come, now, that's reasonable talk. We have, luckily, a lot of oats on hand just now. One of General Ewell's trains came in this morning from Maryland, with all sorts of stuff."

In such good-humor did the quartermaster become, in consequence of my unaccustomed complaisance, that he invited me to dinner at a house hard by, kindly permitting me to pay sixty-five dollars for it in Confederate scrip. He informed me that General Ewell had crossed the Potomac near Williamsport, and was pushing rapidly across Maryland for Pennsylvania. I accordingly made up my mind to strike one of the fords above Martinsburg, and endeavor to overtake the column near the border-line.

"Do you know whether the Yanks have any troops in Maryland?" I asked as we discussed our frugal meal of rye-coffee, eggs, ham, and wheat-cakes.

"Why, bless you!" he replied, "they haven't got over the surprise we gave them by turning their flank so neatly, after

MARCH OF THE CONFEDERATE ARMY INTO PENNSYLVANIA.

that infernal fight at Brandy, which so crippled us in horse-flesh."

As I trotted out of the town, I found the Berryville pike-road completely choked by General Longstreet's wagon and ammunition trains; accordingly turned into the Smithfield road toward Mount Summit, finding the infantry in possession.

Fresh as I was from the midst of our own well-appointed and disciplined army, the contrast afforded by these Confederate troops was a striking one. Marching pell-mell, with no heed to order or formation, the infantry scuttled along at a terrific rate of speed. The men were but lightly clad, very few had a knap-sack, nor were they much burdened with blankets or shelter-tents; betokening great suffering and hardship in wet and tempestuous weather. The day being then a warm and pleasant one, the troops seemed in great spirits, laughing and joking over the prospect of going over into "Maryland, my Maryland." None of the men had, however, that rugged, healthy look so noticeable in our own army.

I had very little difficulty in making good progress past these ragged but brave-looking troops; as they nearly all avoided the road, preferring the turf on either side, to lessen the dust. When I reached the fork of the Mount-Summit road, I over-took General Longstreet and his staff, as they sat on their horses watching the progress of the corps. Determined not to fight shy of any one, I rode boldly up to the general, whom I recognized by his abundant beard and flowing hair. Inquiring if he could give me any advice regarding my route toward General Ewell's column, I stated I carried dispatches from General Lee for that officer.

"I don't know exactly where General Ewell is pushing for, myself, lieutenant," said the general courteously. "I only know that I am to cross above Martinsburg, and then press across the country until I connect with him."

"I understood that was your route," I replied, as though I

knew all about it. "I presume General Stuart's cavalry will cover your flank."

"Yes: I rely on his co-operation to some extent, now that General Ewell has taken Imboden and Jenkins with him."

"My own idea, general, was, to strike across the river right ahead, and endeavor to overtake General Ewell near Hagerstown, by the Sharpsburg road. I believe those roads are all open."

"That would be your best route," replied General Longstreet. "Do you know the purport of your orders, or have you duplicates for me?"

"General Ewell is to make a rapid movement on Chambersburg, and at the same time collect supplies."

"Well, if that is all," exclaimed General Longstreet with a genial laugh; "he seems to have anticipated his instructions pretty well; for I saw two immense trains coming from him yesterday."

"Indeed! I am glad of that. But I must beg your permission to ride forward. Here are my passes, sir."

General Longstreet merely glanced at my papers, saying, "All right, sir: I trust you will have good success. Please tell General Ewell for me, that I expect to open communication with him to-morrow or the next day. Do you know whether General Lee is coming up?"

"His headquarters were to be at Cedar Creek this morning, I believe; and he will probably reach the river to-night. Good-day, sir."

Lifting my hat in salute, I rode off, reaching Martinsburg before sunset, and soon after forded the Potomac just above the town. I had a lonely ride for several hours, when, my faithful mare showing signs of fatigue, I decided to rest for the night, which I did in a deserted barn; being quite refreshed in the morning.

At daylight I was again in the saddle, somewhat stiff from my unaccustomed horseback-exercise; but I persevered, and kept the road all day, meeting a citizen now and then as I pushed forward. As the evening drew on, I found myself near Hagerstown, where I expected to find General Ewell. Riding on for a mile or two farther, I was rewarded by the sight of a camp, which I rightly judged to be that of Ewell's corps. The pickets soon had me in charge, and I was immediately escorted to the general's headquarters, situated in a house on the other side of the town. As soon as my arrival was announced, I was ushered into his presence.

"Well, sir!" said the general sharply, "what is your business with me?"

"I have ridden from army headquarters, sir, since the day before yesterday, and bring you these dispatches," said I, handing him the tinfoil packet I had received from Watson.

General Ewell hurriedly opened the packet, and, walking over to a lamp, soon mastered their contents, saying as he did so, —

"You have arrived in good time, lieutenant; for I was finding myself at the end of the brief instructions given me by General Lee before crossing the Potomac."

"I was told to make haste, sir, and would have reached you some hours ago, had I not been disappointed in obtaining a fresh horse at Winchester."

"That was unfortunate, and I thank you for your perseverance. Where do you intend going next?"

"I am directed to strike the Potomac below Harper's Ferry, join General Stuart, and report your progress; but I shall never reach him with my mare, as she is completely used up."

"You shall have another from a batch of fat Yankee horses we captured to-day," replied General Ewell.

"I passed General Longstreet's corps near Martinsburg yesterday, general," said I: "he told me to say that he expects to overtake you to-morrow."

"Glad to hear it: we need him very much," said the general, leading me to the veranda, and introducing me to his staff.

One of these young gentlemen, finding that I had ridden hard all day, suggested supper, which meal I soon discussed. Finding my blankets and saddle on the veranda, I made up my bed there, the night being a sultry one; and I soon fell asleep, despite the dangers by which I was surrounded.

The sun was well up when I awoke. The troops were already in rapid motion, and I had scarcely achieved my toilet before a summons to breakfast came from the staff. An hour after, we were galloping hard after General Ewell as he rode forward to gain the advance of the corps, I having been furnished with a powerful horse wrested from the possession of some Maryland farmer.

I had intended leaving General Ewell at Hagerstown, under pretense of taking the road for Berlin; but my plan was upset by a report that the Federals were in possession of the lower fords. I was therefore compelled, in order to avoid suspicion, to remain with the general until a more favorable opportunity offered; and accompanied the column until it reached Chambersburg. The scenes I witnessed were both novel and interesting, so much so, indeed, that for a time I forgot my danger in the possible arrival of some new carrier from General Lee, who would readily expose my imposture, and doom me to meet the fate of a spy.

As we progressed, I was astonished at the celerity with which the Confederate cavalry gathered immense droves of valuable cattle, besides accumulating other stores. The entire country seemed panic-stricken by the devastation going on.

When our column reached Chambersburg, one of the divisions was sent to Carlisle and a second towards York, the intention being to force the passage of the Susquehanna River; the Confederates being in high glee at the apparent hesitation of the Federals in pursuing them. While I was casting about for a plausible excuse to leave, news arrived that the Northern militia had destroyed several bridges on the Susquehanna; and I ascertained that a retrograde movement had already been commenced by the advanced divisions of the Confederate army.

General Lee being reported to be at Hagerstown, I bade adieu to General Ewell, ostensibly to join general head-quarters.

On riding out of Chambersburg, I found every thing in confusion; and it was easy to see that the programme of operations had been suddenly changed, — the effect, evidently, of some bold maneuver of the Federal army. Both Longstreet and Hill had been checked in their movement on Harrisburg; and, when I reached the vicinity of the South Mountain range, I was surprised to see both of their corps moving rapidly for the upper Gaps, preparing to cross.

Near midnight I overtook the main body of General Long-street's corps as it passed through the Gap, and experienced no difficulty in ascertaining that General Lee intended concentrating his forces the next day.

While I sat on my horse by the roadside, vainly endeavoring to discover the destination of the troops as they pressed forward, the clew was unexpectedly placed in my hands. A staff-officer suddenly accosted me, and asked if I knew the road or the distance to Gettysburg. The name fell flatly on my ear, though I saw in an instant that a clever stratagem might aid me in getting the information I sought.

"You are fortunate, sir, in your question," I replied: "I have just come from there."

"Indeed! Then General Ewell is in possession?" he exclaimed eagerly.

"He must be by this time," said I at hap-hazard, endeavoring to discover his meaning.

"But how came you here?"

"Oh! I was sent up to communicate with General Longstreet, and I am now waiting for a chance to get through to General Hill with orders for him," said I, getting a little frightened at the necessity for so much invention.

" Well, my errand is a more important one, sir: so I must request your aid to set me on the right road."

" With pleasure, sir," I replied: " I'll ride back into the val-ley with you, as far as the cross-roads."

Without another word, we both rode on as fast as the moving column would permit, until we reached the open country. On taking up the conversation again, I inquired of my companion if he did not believe we would have a battle soon. He ex-pressed the opinion that a collision could not be deferred many days; also informing me that the entire Confederate army would be concentrated near Gettysburg before the close of an-other day, as the Federals were reported to be moving rapidly up from Frederick City.

" But why make a stand at Gettysburg?" I asked. " My impression was, that General Lee intended to first strike Harrisburg."

" So he did, yesterday: but General Hooker has been suc-ceeded by General Meade in the command of the Federal army, and he evidently means to force a fight wherever he can meet us; so we will not balk him."

" No doubt of that," I replied, " unless the Yanks succeed in outflanking us."

" That may be General Meade's notion, though he'll find himself mightily mistaken by to-morrow night."

Here was news in earnest, and I saw I had mastered the Confederate situation completely. Lee intended to surprise my old corps-commander, by a forced march which would gather his whole army and enable it to fall upon the scattered columns of the dear old Army of the Potomac. By defeating one or two, he would demoralize Meade's troops, and gain another victory. The time for leaving the Confederate lines had at length arrived, and I was now in an excellent position to effect my escape.

Having now left the column, and entered a side road, osten-sibly to show my companion a short cut, but really to avoid

General Longstreet and his staff, who were, of course, ahead, I galloped on for a mile or two until we reached another crossing, when I drew rein, and, pointing to the left, audaciously informed the Confederate there was his road, and prepared to leave him.

"I am a thousand times obliged to you, sir, for your kindness," said he politely. "May I know whom I have to thank for this service?"

"Certainly, sir: I'm Lieutenant Watson, of General Lee's staff, at your service."

" Who did you say?" he exclaimed in an excited voice.

"Lieutenant Fred Watson, special and confidential scout," I replied, feeling quite uneasy at his manner.

"No, I'll be hanged if you are!" shouted my troublesome friend, suddenly drawing his revolver. "You are an infernal Yankee spy! that's what *you* are."

In less time than I can tell you, Wilmot, I had fathomed the depth of my peril. I had unluckily encountered one of Lee's personal staff, and knew, that, if he was permitted to discharge his pistol, the report would increase my danger, even if I escaped a wound. But the human mind acts rapidly: so I formed my plan in a second.

Deigning no reply to the fierce denunciation of my opponent, I plunged both spurs savagely into the quivering flanks of my horse, causing him to plunge in terror and sudden force against the shoulder of my accuser's steed. As the two animals came in collision, I seized one of my revolvers from my belt, and dashed the hand thus weighted full into the face of the Confederate. So terrific was the blow, aided by the impetus given it by the horse's plunge, that the aide reeled in his saddle, and finally tumbled head over heels into the road, bleeding, blinded, and half-stunned by the fall.

As the officer struck the ground, without a moment's hesitation I turned and dashed wildly down the road, revolver in hand, determined to escape, or sell my life dearly.

On, on, I galloped in the uncertain light of an approaching day; but as I grimly sat in my saddle, and urged the horse forward, I felt equal to the perils by which I seemed surrounded. I had ridden nearly a mile from the scene of the struggle, when my horse checked his headlong speed to cross a small stream. As his feet touched the water, my attentive ear caught the sound of another horse in the road behind me, evidently in pursuit.

Supposing that the discomfited aide had recovered himself, and was endeavoring to overtake me, I determined to give him a long, stern chase. My horse also heard the pursuer, and apparently entered into my feelings, for he stretched out into a long, hard gallop that soon gave me the advantage I sought. An hour passed in this way, and yet I could hear my pursuer at my heels, until, becoming tired of the chase, I decided to put an end to it. Drawing my horse to one side, under the shadow of a convenient tree, I awaited the advent of my foe.

Nearer and nearer came the sound of the horse's feet, until he suddenly came in sight. Tightly grasping my reins with one hand, I held a revolver in the other, prepared to open the duel I believed to be inevitable. As the animal passed me I was astonished to find him riderless; and, his quick instinct causing him to check his pace at the scent of my steed, I saw that I had been running away from a horse and not a man. When I had unhorsed my antagonist, the animal had taken fright and naturally galloped after his equine companion, thus doing me an inestimable service.

Laughing heartily over the oddity of the adventure, I took possession of the horse, and more leisurely proceeded on my journey.

Daylight came soon after; when I examined the saddle-bags of the unfortunate aide, who was no doubt in a sad plight. Besides a few biscuits and an under-shirt, I found a map which proved to be of great value; for upon it were traced the projected movements of General Lee's three infantry corps, with some brief comments and directions for General Ewell written on the margin.

Overjoyed at this bit of unexpected good luck, I was busily examining the map, when a bright flash followed by a sudden explosion on my right told me quite clearly that a train of some kind had been captured and destroyed. A short distance ahead I came to another of the cross-roads, so numerous in that section; and a moment later was brought into collision with a mounted Confederate, who ran right between my two horses. Both he and I were dismounted by the shock, and before we could recover ourselves were made prisoners by a portion of General Kilpatrick's cavalry.

Making myself known to the officer in command of the detachment, I was sent under escort to the cavalry general, whom I found a few miles farther on. Exhibiting Watson's secret Federal pass, which he had cleverly concealed in one of the jacket-buttons, I soon convinced Kilpatrick I had need of haste to reach the commanding general; being promptly given an escort and a guide.

We found General Meade near a village called Two Taverns, on the line of Pipe Creek. When I rode up he was nervously pacing up and down under a tree. Catching sight of my Confederate uniform, the general stopped abruptly, and demanded my errand.

"I have just arrived from General Lee's army, sir," said I, "and know something about his plans."

"Where is Lee now, and how is he moving?" asked General Meade, eying me sharply through his glasses.

"Ewell had abandoned his movement on the Susquehanna, sir, when I left the Confederate lines this morning; and he is heading this way. Generals Hill and Longstreet are both moving across the South Mountains to join him."

"I know Ewell has fallen back, but are you sure about the other corps?" said General Meade.

"Quite so," I replied. "I struck both their corps on the

other side of the range last night, and came over with General Longstreet's column. You were reported to be moving in full force to attack Ewell, hence this sudden change in Lee's maneuvers."

"I believe we *are* all here," remarked the general in a sardonic tone; "and I'm glad the beggars are concentrating. Where do you suppose their rendezvous to be?"

"Somewhere near a place called Gettysburg, sir, and I could see last night that haste had been insisted upon."

As I spoke, a staff-officer rode up, when, suddenly catching my eye, he exclaimed, —

"Hullo, sergeant! so you've got back, eh? I was afraid you had got into some trouble."

I had no difficulty in recognizing in the speaker the scout I had been personating while inside the Confederate lines; but, before I could reply to his salutation, General Meade demanded an explanation. Watson briefly related the facts attending an exchange of characters; which statement elicited a few words of compliment from the general, who expressed himself as much pleased with my success, and spoke of promotion as a reward. It was then that I triumphantly produced the Confederate map I had captured in so singular a manner, and was gratified to find its value properly appreciated.

So you see, captain, that was how I became a scout; and I have since learned to like the life for its many excitements as well as perils.

CHAPTER XXVII.

A CHANGE IN FORTUNE.

"Therewith they gan, both furious and fell,
To thunder blowes, and fiercely to assail."

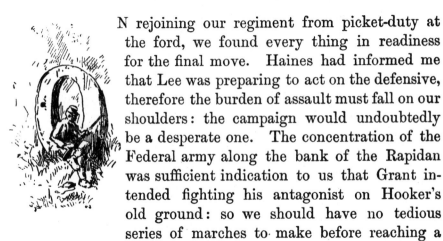

N rejoining our regiment from picket-duty at the ford, we found every thing in readiness for the final move. Haines had informed me that Lee was preparing to act on the defensive, therefore the burden of assault must fall on our shoulders: the campaign would undoubtedly be a desperate one. The concentration of the Federal army along the bank of the Rapidan was sufficient indication to us that Grant intended fighting his antagonist on Hooker's old ground: so we should have no tedious series of marches to make before reaching a battle-field. The *morale* of the army was excellent; and as it had been strengthened by the arrival of the Washington garrisons, and the Ninth Corps under Burnside, there was a feeling of confidence in the ranks.

On the 3d of May the long-expected orders came; and, before nightfall, the entire army was in motion. The Fifth and Sixth Corps, under Warren and Sedgwick, were to cross at Germanna Ford, and form the right and center; while Hancock was to take the Second Corps to Ely's Ford, and, advancing towards Chancellorsville, occupy the left of the formidable line. Burnside's command, having made a straight march from Alexandria along the line of the railroad, was held in reserve. A division of cavalry led each of the infantry columns, and were to uncover the enemy's position.

We marched to within striking distance of the fords, halting at midnight. Being again afoot at daybreak, we reached the river soon after sunrise. As we passed through the woods, our pontoon-train clattered by; and, when we arrived at the top of the steep and winding road that led to the ford, we found Wilson's cavalry division halted among the trees, waiting for the engineers to build the bridge.

It was a picturesque scene, full of that pomp and excitement attending important and serious movements of an army. The sun shone bright and warm through the budding trees, and its rays played in lazy dalliance on many a musket-barrel and saber-hilt. Here and there among the undergrowth, an early shrub was clothed with fresh green leaves, a visible token that spring-time had come; and there was a delicious perfume pervading the forest, that made me think of home and my boyhood pleasures. The colors of the regiments, brigades, or divisions, though torn and tattered by previous campaigns, lost their faded look, as they idly waved in the morning air, or were caught by the gleam of sunshine that streamed through the fairy network of limbs and branches over our heads.

The men were in high spirits, and many a merry jest was passed along the ranks as we slowly descended the hill. It was indeed an exhilarating moment; and as I listened to the murmur of many voices, the sound of hurrying feet, or the monotonous rumble of cannon and caisson, I felt my heart beat high with pride and expectation.

Our bridge was soon finished; there being no opposition offered by the enemy, beyond a few scattered shots from the pickets as they precipitately retired before our imposing numbers. As the last plank fell into its place, the cavalry clattered across, and were soon out of sight. We followed; and by sunset the entire corps had reached the vicinity of Old Wilderness Tavern, at the intersection of the plank-road with the Orange

Court House turnpike. Sedgwick and his men reached the
southern bank of the river before nightfall, bivouacking near
the ford; and I learned from a staff-officer that Hancock had
also reached his position on the Chancellorsville road. The
passage of the river had been successfully accomplished: three
strong corps, comprising nearly one hundred thousand men,
over one hundred pieces of artillery, and fifteen thousand

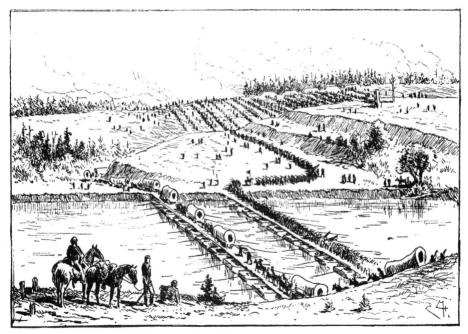

CROSSING THE RAPIDAN.

horsemen, had crossed a swollen and turbulent stream, and
plunged boldly into the wilderness beyond. The reserve corps
and our immense train of four thousand wagons were waiting
on the other side for the result of the impending collision
between the two opposing armies.

"Well, Wilmot," said Major Harding, as we sat eating supper
together, "we are fairly embarked on another campaign. I
wonder who of us will see the end of it?"

"Ah! that is a question time alone can solve," I replied.

"Our regiment will not have the luck of our last campaign," said Captain Burch, who, as usual, was in a querulous mood.

"Perhaps not," responded the major: "we were very fortunate last summer, considering the service we did. Fitzgerald, Dunne, and poor stuttering Whipple were the only officers killed, you know; and we lost very few men at Gettysburg, compared with other regiments."

"We'll pay up for it now," said Captain Burch. "I hate this bush-fighting: you never know exactly where you are."

"Come, come, Burch, there's no use finding fault," I exclaimed, fairly out of patience; for the captain's habit sorely tried my temper at all times.

"I know it, and that's why I do it," said Burch whimsically: "it's the only comfort I have."

"Precious queer comfort it must be," remarked the major. "If I did not know you, Burch, to be as brave an officer as any in the regiment, I should be tempted at times to think you were afraid."

"That's just what provokes me," said I. "He is always grumbling until we go into action: then he is as cool as a cucumber, and as jolly as one could wish."

"Well, well, boys, don't mind me. I know I'm a queer specimen; but you two ought to know Ned Burch by this time," and the captain held out a hand to each of us.

"God bless you, old fellow," said the major: "your heart is in the right place, wherever your tongue may be."

"I suppose you will both laugh at me, but somehow I feel that Ned won't grumble much longer," said the captain.

"Nonsense, man!" exclaimed Major Harding. "Why, you haven't had a scratch since we first came out."

"All the more reason for my going under now. No, I don't expect to escape this time."

"Upon my word, Burch, you are a trifle more disagreeable

than usual to-night," said I. "What in the world put such gloomy forebodings into your head?"

"I'll tell you;" and here the captain's voice unconsciously grew soft and tender: "you must know that I was not always the carping wretch that I now am. When I was younger, and the world seemed as bright as it no doubt appears to you, Frank, I loved a beautiful girl, and rejoiced in the knowledge that my love was reciprocated. We were to be married, Nelly and I; and I was as happy as is possible for us poor weak mortals. Then she fell ill, and died in my arms, her soft eyes full of love for me until death closed them forever. When they lowered my girl's body into the grave, I felt myself a changed man, and became the moody creature I am. Then this war came, and I volunteered, reckless as to my fate. At times I fancy my Nelly is near me, when my heart grows as soft as a woman's. Last night while we were sleeping over there among the trees, I dreamed that she came and told me the end was near. As she spoke, I saw a field in some woods, near a road, and found myself charging across it with the regiment. We reached the edge of the field, and I saw a low breastwork in the brush beyond. Just at that moment a sheet of flame sprang from the breastwork, and I knew I was hit. An intense pain shot through my body, and I awoke to find it all a dream. Depend upon it, though, it was a warning."

"What! frightened by a dream?" exclaimed Major Harding.

"No," said the captain: "I have no fear."

Both Harding and myself were depressed by Burch's forebodings: so we wrapped ourselves in our blankets, leaving our friend gazing into the fire in moody silence.

The sun was already up, when a touch from Dennis woke me from my slumbers, the men being busy over their breakfasts. A cup of steaming coffee and a biscuit sufficed me; for the excitement of the movement took away my appetite, and I was glad when orders came for us to go forward. We passed down the road for about half a mile, until the ground became uneven; finding Generals Grant and Meade waiting for us in a nook in the woods by the wayside. Behind these two officers lounged their brilliant staffs, carelessly watching our corps as it passed. General Meade was standing on the bank that overlooked the road, his soldierly figure contrasting strangely with that of the lieutenant-general, who was seated on a decaying stump, apparently more interested in the toe of his boot than our movements. An unlighted cigar was between Grant's teeth, and he chewed the weed viciously. When our regiment came in front of the two generals, I caught a glimpse of General Grant's eyes, as he lifted them for a moment. Clear and steady, calm and confident, this great leader seemed in that single glance to take in the face of every man within his range; and I was impressed by the strong will betokened by the square chin and the firm mouth of the man who was planning and conducting our campaign. The tall, courtly figure of Meade, his trim gray hair, and neat regulation cap, gave him a martial look, as he leaned on his saber; while the heavy frame of Grant, who wore no sword, seemed the very opposite of my preconceived ideas of our new commander. The wide-brimmed hat, pulled down over his eyes, and the closely clipped beard, made the renowned chieftain appear so unlike a soldier that it needed the uniform and the broad shoulder-strap, with its row of triple stars, to remind one that here was a warrior already famous.

In a moment we had passed, and it was long before I again saw either of these generals.

"An' was that Grant?" said Dennis to me as soon as we were out of sight of the distinguished group.

"Yes. What do you think of him?" I asked.

"He's a quare-looking gineral," responded the sergeant. "But he's a foighter: his eye tells that."

"Do you like his looks, Dennis?"

"Faix, an' I do. Whin he makes up his mind to do a thing he'll hang on like a tarrier."

The line now began breaking off from the road into the

PASSING GRANT AND MEADE.

woods on our right; and, as my regiment followed in its turn, I saw our corps commander, General Warren, standing on some rising ground in front, apparently watching for signs of the enemy we all knew must be quite near. Behind the general, coolly sitting on a log by the side of the road, was Osborne the correspondent, whom we had not seen or heard of since Christmas. Seeing me, he rose and joined us.

"Halloa, Wilmot! so you are going in, eh?" said he as we shook hands. "This promises to be a desperate fight."

"It does indeed," was my reply. "Where have you been to all this winter?"

"You would never guess."

"I suppose not. Is it a secret?"

"Not now. I went down to Nassau, New Providence."

"What for, pray?" I asked in some surprise.

"Oh! our chief thought a few hints about the blockade-runners would be useful and interesting: and, happening to be in New York, he packed me off by the first steamer. But it didn't pay. The blockade business has gone to pieces: so, after roasting a few weeks among the coral-reefs, I pulled up sticks and came home, just in time to join you fellows here among the trees and vines."

"Is the enemy in force here, Osborne?" asked Major Harding.

"That's just what Warren is trying to discover. As yet there are no signs, but they can not be far off."

"Why?"

"Well, you see," replied Osborne, "Lee can not afford to let us pass these dense woods — well named the Wilderness — without a fight, for then we could have him in comparatively open country."

"You talk very learnedly, Osborne," said I, laughing at his confident tone. "You ought to be a lieutenant-general."

"I suppose it does seem odd to you to hear me speak as I do," remarked Osborne; "but we correspondents have to study military problems, as well as the generals, or we couldn't describe campaigns and battles intelligently."

"What do you expect the result will be?" asked Captain Burch.

"Hard to say. But one thing you may be certain of: we're not going across the Rapidan again. Grant has come here to stay."

"I'm devilish glad of it," said Burch. "We must be nearly two to one; and, if we can't hold our ground with these odds, we had better give up and be done with it."

"It's not a question of holding ground, captain," sagely remarked the correspondent. "Grant will fight all round Lee if necessary. He means to turn his flank if possible."

"Hooker tried that, and succeeded for a time," replied the captain with a harsh laugh. "Yet we got the worst licking at Chancellorsville since the war began."

"You mustn't compare Grant to Hooker," exclaimed Osborne warmly. "Besides, Grant has more power: Washington interference is cut off now."

"By the flank, march!" cried our colonel; and away we went crashing through the trees, leaving the correspondent to his own devices.

Our brigade formed the left of the division; and, as we lay in line of battle, I could see that the others were taking up position on the left of the wood. At the same time orders came for skirmishers, Lieutenant Foster being selected to command our regimental detail.

As yet a deep silence reigned in the woods, and one unaccustomed to campaign-life would scarcely believe that a desperate and bloody battle was so soon to commence.

I had begun to ponder on the probabilities of the future, when word was passed down the line that Colonel Lloyd wished to see his officers.

"Gentlemen," said the colonel as we gathered round him, "we are to go forward soon and engage. I learn from General

Fletcher that Lee is believed to be in strong force on our immediate front: so we must be prepared to bear the brunt of this fight. Are the men in good spirits?"

"Couldn't be better," said Lieutenant-Colonel Purcell: "I've just passed along the line, and found them cool and quiet."

"That's well. Now, gentlemen, to your stations."

As the colonel spoke, he held out his hands: we clasped them in turn, and then silently separated to our companies. It was a soldierly farewell and a brave one. Of the nineteen officers present, seven were to die before the sun set.

"Take care of yourself, Frank," said Major Harding, as he shook my hand before walking over to his place in the line.

"I'll try to," I replied briefly but cheerily.

"Zouaves, move forward!" shouted our colonel.

Steadily, silently, the line advanced through the tangled undergrowth for a few hundred yards, when the order came to halt. As yet we had discovered no signs of the enemy, and the pickets remained silent. Finding that we were not to move immediately, the men sat down in ranks and patiently waited. Seeing the major lying on the ground near me, I went over to him.

"Well, Wilmot," said he, as I sat down beside him, "this looks like business: crossing a river one day, and going into an engagement the next, is quick work."

"Yes, indeed," I replied. "It's not what we are accustomed to; but, do you know, I rather like it. Those long marches tire one out so!"

"So do I like it. Though I agree with Burch about fighting in the woods: our artillery is positively useless here."

"But I saw a section of a battery pass up the road only a few minutes ago," said I.

"I know it," replied Major Harding; "but it's only a section. What can a couple of guns do? We ought to be able to use half a dozen whole batteries. No: we must depend on the musket and bullet to-day."

"Where's Colonel Lloyd?" suddenly exclaimed young Jenkins, our brigadier's aide, as his horse came tumbling through the bushes.

"Here," replied the colonel, rising from the ground near by. "What is it, Jenkins?"

"You are to move forward, sir, to the edge of a field in front," said the aide; "and when you get there, have your men fix bayonets, and lie down until the bugle sounds the advance."

"All right, Jenkins: I understand. Attention, battalion!"

Away we went, headlong, through the young timber. Scarcely had the line begun moving when our pickets opened merrily. The battle had fairly begun.

In a few moments we came up to the pickets, and passed through their line. Now the bullets began to spatter among the trees, and I saw one or two men fall. Going on for a few yards farther, I noticed Hyde, one of my men, standing still, the regiment leaving him behind. Angry at the thought that the fellow was endeavoring to slip to the rear, I rushed at him with my sword. But the undergrowth of vines hindered me, and it was with difficulty that I reached the seeming skulker.

"Go forward, sir! what are you standing there for?" I shouted.

As I roughly seized the man's arm, his body swayed for an instant, and, the next, fell heavily to the ground. He was dead. A ball had passed through his brain, while the dense undergrowth had held his lifeless body erect as if alive.

Shocked by the discovery, I dashed on after the regiment, and lay down with the men at the edge of the field. It was a mere patch of cleared ground in the midst of the forest, and had evidently been abandoned before the war began; for several young pines had taken root here and there in the center. We were still in doubt as to the precise position of the enemy; though we knew they were now quite close, by the increased showers of bullets that were clipping the branches over our heads.

Captain Burch crept to my side, his face brighter than I had ever noticed it before.

"We're going in soon, Wilmot," said he in a strange voice. "My dream is coming true."

"Nonsense, man! Confound your dream!" I retorted.

"Ah! but here's the field, and yonder we shall find the breastworks," replied the captain, quietly pointing across the opening before us.

A feeling of awe began to overpower me at Burch's strange words and manner; but it was at once dispelled by the shrill notes of our general's bugle, ordering the charge. The men heard, and understood it also; for, without waiting for our colonel to give the word of command, away they went, pell-mell, over the open ground.

A perfect hailstorm of bullets saluted us as we emerged from the shelter of the trees, and men were soon dropping in every direction. On we went, however; but scarcely three-fourths of the regiment crossed the field, and entered the woods on the other side.

I had stumbled over a wounded man, who fell in front of me when half-way across the field; and, while picking myself up again to follow the regiment, I saw Dennis stoop and seize the colors, as their bearer turned over on his side and expired. Dennis waved the flag exultantly, and rushed to the front. He gained the edge of the woods, when the colors went down once more. I ran towards the spot, seeing the flag rise again as I did so; but Dennis no longer carried them, for I found him stretched on the ground, his face bathed in blood.

"Where are you hit, Dennis?" said I, bending over him.

He smiled faintly, and put his hand under his arm.

"Somewhere in me side," said he. "Bedad, it felt like a cannon-ball."

"Try and get to the rear, Dennis, while you have strength."

"I suppose I'd betther, but I hate to leave ye, captain dear.

Shure, you might get killed without me," said Dennis, half-whimpering at the thought of our parting.

"Come, Dennis, you have your legs: go at once to the rear. Good-by, old fellow."

"Good-by, and God bless and presarve ye!" cried Dennis, as I once more ran after the regiment.

IN THE WILDERNESS.

I had not far to go; for our men, having discovered the opposing line, began pouring in a fierce and destructive return volley. As I joined my company, the musketry grew fiercer and fiercer; and the row of dead and dying lying about our feet rapidly thickened. Our regiment was melting away in the intense heat of the battle.

Then a lull came, and our voices were audible. Looking round, I saw that Major Harding was by my side.

"My God!" he exclaimed, "this is dreadful. We won't

have a man standing if this continues. Why don't they bring up our supports?"

"Where is the colonel?" I asked.

"Over on the right," replied the major. "But Lieutenant-Colonel Purcell is killed. Where's Burch?"

"Here!" answered the captain. "I'm not hit yet, but" —

As he uttered the words, Burch suddenly reeled, clapped his hand to his heart, and then, turning swiftly round like a top, fell dead between the major and myself. His dream had indeed been fulfilled.

Major Harding's face wore a ghastly look, as he gazed, horror-stricken, at the body of his friend.

"Major," said a sergeant belonging to one of the right companies, "Colonel Lloyd has just been killed. The adjutant sent me to say that you are now in command."

"How did it happen?" said I, seeing that the major could not speak for the moment.

"A ball clean through his head," replied the sergeant laconically.

"Come, Harding!" I exclaimed, laying my hand on his arm, "rouse yourself. What are we to do next?"

"We'll go to the rear," replied the major, drawing his hand over his eyes as if in pain. "It's madness to stay here any longer, for they are not supporting us."

While speaking, Major Harding touched two or three of the men nearest him, and told them to go back. They obeyed, and the remainder followed. The whole line wavered for an instant, then the remnant of our shattered and bleeding regiment began retreating in tolerably fair order. Our movement was the signal for a withering volley from the enemy's breastworks. At that moment I felt a sharp, stinging pain flash through my body: the ground seemed to rise up under my feet, and I fell at full length across the body of my dead captain. I tried to rise, but my strength had suddenly left me. I felt the blood gush from my wound, then I knew no more.

CHAPTER XXVIII.

CROSSING THE LINE.

"A confused report passed through my ears;
But full of hurry, like a morning dream."

HEN I recovered consciousness, I saw that the Confederates had advanced their line to the edge of the woods. The musketry had lost its intensity, but the air was filled with the groans of wounded and dying men. Disengaging myself from Captain Burch's corpse, I made an effort to regain my feet; but was too weak from the loss of blood, so fell back to the earth with a sigh of disappointment.

"I say, sergeant, this 'ere Yankee officer ain't dead, after all. Let's pick him up, and git to the r'ar."

As the man spoke, I felt myself lifted up; and my bearers moved rapidly through the trees. I was a prisoner!

The men who carried me were tender in their handling, and I experienced but little pain. Then I saw that we were in a road; and by and by the men laid me down by the side of a creek, among a lot of their own wounded.

"Why, it's Captain Wilmot!" exclaimed a voice.

Looking round, I saw the speaker was a sergeant belonging to the company next my own.

"Are you wounded too?" said I.

"No, I didn't get hit; but a good many of us were gobbled by a flanking-party," replied the sergeant.

"Is Major Harding a prisoner?" was my next question.

"Oh, no! He got off safe. But there's not more than a hundred of the regiment to answer roll-call. I say, captain, they're going to send the prisoners to the rear soon; and I hear there's a Confederate hospital somewhere down the road. Shall we carry you there?" and the sergeant bent over me anxiously, forgetting his own trouble for the moment.

"I don't care: if you like," was my somewhat ungracious reply; for I had lost all interest as to my fate.

Sergeant Hughes said something to a Confederate officer near him, when the latter replied, —

"It's the best thing you can do for him: we have no surgeons here."

In a few minutes every thing was ready for the prisoners to start; when the sergeant and some more men belonging to my regiment lifted me in a blanket, and followed the rest. The easy motion of being carried soothed my pain; and, as my bearers were constantly changed by willing hands, our progress was rapid. I learned, as we went, that the hospital was at Locust Grove, a place I remembered having seen during the Mine-run movement.

The sun was sinking behind the trees, near a cluster of negro-huts, when I was tenderly laid on the sward by the roadside. Looking up, I saw we had reached my destination.

"Good-by, captain," said Sergeant Hughes, as he wrung my hand earnestly. Then the column of prisoners moved on down the road. I was alone.

A curious crowd of men gathered round me; and as I lay on the grass, making a sling for my arm which had been struck by a bullet, I gleaned from their talk that they belonged to General Ewell's artillery reserve. Like us, the Confederates had found their cannon practically useless in these dense forests. Then the group suddenly separated as a mounted officer rode up: one of the men helped me to my feet at his command.

"What part of your army do you belong to, sir?" he asked.

"The Fifth Corps," I replied.

"Who commands it now?"

"General Warren."

"How many men has he?" was the next question.

"Forty or fifty thousand," said I, purposely exaggerating the number.

"Indeed! so many as that? How many, then, have you in the whole army?"

GENERAL LEE AND THE PRISONER.

"Two or three hundred thousand," I replied with a laugh.

"Now you are simply joking," said the stranger quietly. "Tell me, is it true that General Grant is in command of your forces?"

"He is with the army, sir; but we understand General Meade commands it."

"That amounts to the same thing," remarked the officer in a musing tone. "But tell me, sir, how many men have you really, this side of the River Rapidan?"

"Excuse me, sir," I replied: "I know I am a prisoner in your hands, wounded and helpless; but that fact gives you no right to question me as you are doing. I have already answered more of your questions than my duty to my flag permits. You can not expect me to give you any information regarding our army or its strength."

"You are quite right, sir," replied the officer sadly. "I beg your pardon: good-night."

As the speaker uttered the last words, he bowed gravely, and, putting spurs to his horse, was soon out of sight.

"Who was that?" I exclaimed, as the artillerists gathered about me once more.

"General Robert E. Lee, who commands the Army of Northern Virginia," replied a fine-looking sergeant leaning against the trunk of the locust-tree behind me.

General Lee! the famous Confederate leader! So I had really spoken to that brave and gallant soldier.

The night was now falling fast, and I began to feel very stiff and cold. No one had, as yet, been near me to see if I needed surgical assistance. The artillery had meanwhile moved away with their guns, and there seemed to be no large bodies of troops near. Groans came to my ears; but I heeded them not, my own trouble and pain making me selfish. Then I heard the sound of horses' hoofs, and, rising on my elbows, saw a column of cavalry move slowly down the road until they were a few hundred yards away, when they passed off on a side-path towards the right of their line. They were evidently moving towards our left, in anticipation of the battle of the morrow. The force was a strong one, probably four thousand men; and, as it passed, I noticed several leading riderless horses, showing that they had recently been in action.

Though my disabled arm was quite troublesome, there was a sharper pain somewhere in my thigh; and I knew by it that I had there sustained the most serious wound. I noticed that one of the tassels of my silken sash was hanging by a few threads, and putting my hand down, found that the cloth of my pantaloons was stiff with dried blood. I then essayed to rise, and succeeded in getting on my feet for a moment; but I was still very weak, so was glad to lie down again.

The night air grew colder and colder; and I began to shiver and tremble, for I had no blanket. Seeing an open shed near by, I decided to try and reach it: I might get away from the wind that was rising. Unable to walk, I crawled slowly along on my hands and knees, and finally succeeded in reaching the shed. As I crept over the ground, the odd notion came into my head that I must be cutting a funny figure; and I began laughing at the idea. In the shed I found eight or ten other wounded men, all Federals.

"I wish we had a fire," remarked one of the men, as I crawled in among them.

"Don't you wish you were safe at home with your·mother?" replied another mockingly.

"I've some matches," said I. "Can we get any wood?"

"Yes, here's a lot of old barrels," said the first speaker.

"Break up one of them, and we will soon have a fire;" and, as I spoke, I struck a light.

The order was promptly obeyed; for the men saw my shoulder-strap in the blaze of my match, and the habit of discipline was still strong upon them. In a few moments the fire was lighted, and we all huddled round the cheerful blaze. No one seemed to be noticing us, and I began to think we had been forgotten or abandoned by our captors. The light of our fire attracted more wounded Federals, and they made a second one near by. Most of the men had their haversacks, and munched crackers contentedly as they reclined before the burning barrels: but one poor fellow near me had no food; and though his head was bloody, and his face matted with dirt, I could see he was hungrily watching those who were eating. Drawing three or four biscuits from my own haversack, I quietly put them into his hand. He took them greedily, apparently too hungry to think of thanking me.

We were a rather grewsome lot of fellows; for there was not a sound man among us, and our wounds were becoming stiff and sore. Opposite me sat a tall sergeant, the chevrons on his right sleeve being half ripped off by the bullet which had shattered his arm. Beside him sat a stunted specimen of humanity, with an enormous beard spread all over his face, as if nature had sought to make him some recompense for his abbreviated stature; but though the beard ordinarily hid his face to the eyes, it was now parted on one cheek by a gleaming cicatrice, like the mark of a tornado I had once seen on the mountains near Aldie Gap. One had his temples bound up with a dirty handkerchief; which did not prevent the blood trickling down his face to the corner of his mouth, from which he wiped it with his cuff the better to masticate his food. Another poor fellow had been wounded in both arms; and it was painful to see him try to get a cracker to his mouth, only succeeding when a companion, noticing his plight, held it up for him to bite.

I sat in this way for some time watching my neighbors, content to be awake and enjoy the warmth of the fire; but I felt lonely and sorrowful, for I missed the companionship of Dennis, of whose fate I was ignorant. I could only hope he had escaped to the rear of our lines without further wounds; and, as I thought of the ample means provided by the Sanitary Commission for the care of our wounded, I envied the lot of those lucky enough to fall into its hands. The death of poor Ned Burch also depressed me, for I could not forget that his body was lying on the field unburied where he had fallen. I was stunned by the sudden reverse in my fortunes, for it seemed terrible that one short day could bring about such changes. Hitherto I had mostly seen the brighter aspect of military life: now I was to experience the darker and more painful side.

The main body of the Confederate army was evidently changing front towards their right; for every few minutes a staff-officer or mounted orderly would go galloping past, following the road the cavalry column had taken. Now and again a sullen volley of musketry, with the occasional shriek of a shell, came to my attentive ear from that direction.

I had looked at my watch, and saw it was after nine o'clock, when a cavalryman leaped off his horse and approached our fire.

" Well, you-uns, we-uns hev licked you-uns agin," said he, rudely shoving his way among the men nearest him.

" What do you mean ? " said I.

" Why, the Yanks be all running away."

" I don't believe it: if they were, you wouldn't be here," I replied.

" Never mind him, captain: he only says that to annoy us," remarked the sergeant with the torn chevrons.

" Waal, I s'pose you won't b'lieve me, but yer hull army hev gone 'cross the river," said the man as he lighted his corn-cob pipe and stalked away to his horse.

" Do you think our army has really retreated ? " said one of our men, after the Confederate had ridden away in the darkness.

" No," I replied; " but the engagement has probably gone against us to-day."

Early in the evening I had been informed by the artillery-men, that they thought our army had fallen back; but I did not believe it possible. Could it be that Grant had retired his right wing, and extended his line towards the left, in hopes of turning Lee's flank? the ominous mutterings in that direction seemed to warrant such an idea. I tried to piece out the puzzle, but could not. One of the men sitting at our fire belonged to the Sixth Corps; and he told us of their heavy losses, and several of the other men had seen two of the Fifth Corps brigadiers among the prisoners. We had therefore suffered very heavily all along the line, and my poor regiment was reduced to a mere fragment. If Sergeant Hughes was correct, fully three-fourths of the six hundred men who began that fatal charge were dead, wounded, or prisoners.

" I say, captain," said my hungry friend, " I've got a blanket: suppose you and me turn in together."

Accepting the offer with gladness, we rolled ourselves in the blanket, and, despite our hurts, were soon fast asleep.

Soon after daylight we were roused by the provost-guard, who had at length come to look after us. As I sat up, and gave my name and rank to the sergeant, I could distinguish the sound of distant musketry, showing that fighting had again begun. Then the sullen boom of a field-piece, followed by heavier musketry, gave token that Grant was still at Lee's heels.

As it was evident that we were all severely wounded, the provost-sergeant, himself a cripple from an old shell-wound, contented himself with taking our names, at the same time good-naturedly pointing out the location of a spring. A few who could walk volunteered to fill the canteens of those that were helpless; and George Michel, my bedfellow, shared my few remaining biscuits.

Our scanty breakfast over, I stretched myself in the warm sunshine, and watched the progress of events. There were thirty or forty tents standing in the field; while the wounded present, both Confederate and Federal, numbered probably three or four thousand. We Yankees (and I thought of Tom Marshall whenever the word was uttered) were given possession of all the sheds; and we managed to make ourselves tolerably comfortable, there being a small quantity of straw. The ambulances, having been sent to the abandoned battle-field, brought back loads of knapsacks, blankets, and overcoats from our dead. The provost-sergeant brought me an entire kit, so I felt rich in my possessions. In the knapsack were a few letters written by a woman, from which I learned that a Confederate bullet had widowed the writer while she was yet a maid. Her photograph was tied up with the letters, all of which I put away to be returned if fate so willed. After bringing up the knapsacks, the ambulances proceeded to collect muskets and side-arms, and the guns were thrown in an indiscriminate heap near our sheds. This part of the plunder had no interest for us, however; though the time was to come when its presence could not be ignored.

The musketry on the right of the Confederate lines grew louder and fiercer, as the hour of noon approached; but I could learn nothing as to the scope of this new movement or its probable result, so lay listening to the repeated volleys, as they rose and fell in regular cadence, vaguely imagining the

AMONG THE WOUNDED, — CONFEDERATE HOSPITAL.

scene of conflict in progress. Unlike the battle of the previous day, the cannonading was stronger and more continuous; the rolling artillery-fire being at times monotonous in its intensity and vigor, showing that the struggle was a savage one, and hotly contested. It seemed curious to be so near a battle-field, yet unable to participate in it; and the bitter thought was forced upon me that I was a helpless prisoner inside the Confederate lines. During the afternoon I began to feel very hungry, but learned, to my dismay, that there was no food, not even for the Confederate wounded: so Michel and I fasted.

The wound in my thigh pained me a good deal; but the ball came out, and the bleeding ceased. As yet no one had attempted to dress our wounds, the medical resources of the Confederates being remarkably slender.

"How are you getting along, gentlemen?" said the provost-sergeant politely, as he limped along the line of our sheds.

"Pretty well," said one of the men. "But we are awfully hungry: can't you give us something to eat?"

"We expect supplies to-night from Gordonsville," replied the sergeant. "You are not worse off than our own wounded."

"How is the battle going, sergeant?" I asked.

"I dunno. We thought last night your army had gone back over the river, as the line in front of Germanna Ford was gone; but it appears that they went off to the left of their line, and now General Lee is fighting Grant — that Western general of yours — at Spottsylvania."

So this was the key to the situation. Grant intended to force his way towards Richmond, and, if baffled in driving Lee back by direct assault, would push out his left.

No food coming that evening, we went to bed supperless; and I slept a little, despite the soreness of my thigh. Many of the men near me were beginning to feel the severity of their hurts, and a good deal of groaning occurred through the night.

We were not disturbed until long after the sun had risen, when word came that corn-meal and bacon would be served out. The ration turned out to be a very small one, judged by Federal standards; but it was better than nothing. We made a thick gruel of the meal in our coffee-cups; the bacon — a mere slice — serving as salt. But we missed our coffee, and I thought of Dennis and his culinary zeal with feelings of regret.

All sounds of the contending armies had now died away: the air was undisturbed by musket or cannon. This silence, however, only lasted until about noon; when it was broken by sounds of a furious battle, evidently near the scene of the previous day's engagement. It lasted until after sunset, when the firing suddenly ceased; and after that we heard nothing from either army. We were forgotten.

During the afternoon we were gladdened by the appearance of Surgeon Donovan of the Pennsylvania Reserves, he having voluntarily come through the lines under a flag of truce to look after us. The doctor was a character. Short in stature, his red hair cropped close to his head while his fiery beard was allowed to grow luxuriantly, he looked like any thing but a skillful surgeon. His uniform consisted of a velvet pea-jacket, and a pair of corduroy pantaloons which fitted tightly to his well-formed legs, and permitted his wearing a huge pair of tan-colored boots reaching to his waist. Making his rounds in a cheerful way that was very engaging, the doctor soon ascertained our condition, and selected those who must undergo immediate amputation. To my unspeakable gratification, I learned that the wound in my thigh, though severe, was only in the flesh, the bones being uninjured.

"Wash it well, and you will be all right in time," said the surgeon to me, as he passed on to the next man.

The ambulance-trains were now removing the Confederate wounded to Gordonsville, and we received a better ration of meal and bacon. During the next four or five days, all of Lee's men had been carried away; and our men were given the tents, but a few of us clung to the huts. Several barrels of flour came: when some of our men pulled down an old chimney, and built a rude oven in the side of a bank; and another, who was a baker, made us some palatable bread. Death now appeared in our midst, and a little graveyard was begun on a hill behind the dilapidated tavern. The saw and the knife were busy, and Surgeon Donovan's arms were for hours bathed in blood. Then came a new horror; for the wind, changing, brought with it the terrible odor of putrefying flesh from the battle-field, where we knew thousands of our dead comrades were still unburied.

That night, while Michel and I were lying with our companions in the shed, the pile of muskets caught fire in some mysterious way; and a scattering, indiscriminate volley began, as the guns became heated, and discharged their contents. Expecting to be hit every moment, for the bullets were flying in every conceivable direction, yet afraid to move away lest we fall into greater danger, we cowered beneath our blankets until the woodwork on the weapons had been consumed. A man lying near me was killed outright by one of these stray balls, and I heard the next day that two or three others had received fresh wounds. The pile of muskets were, however, useless to the enemy: so we took some comfort in that.

Thus the time passed for three long weeks. The graveyard grew in size; and the men around me were weaker, owing to the scarcity of succulent food and the lack of stimulants. Doctor Donovan labored manfully, and won our love and admiration by his tenderness and devotion.

We heard that our army had pushed on towards Richmond, though our guards were very reticent regarding the results or progress of the campaign. I inferred from this that the Confederates were losing ground; but I soon ceased to take any interest in the movements of Grant or Lee, my whole mind being fixed on plans for escaping. One day poor Michel, who I had ascertained was a Canadian, grew worse; and it was evident that death was near him.

"Oh, my God! Am I going to die?" he exclaimed in a voice of terror.

"I hope not, George," said I. "But you are very weak."

"Oh, don't let me die! I've got a mother who's waiting for me. — My mother! shall I never see you again?"

"Come, come, my man," said Surgeon Donovan. "Don't go on in that way. We can not save you, but don't grieve so."

"But I won't die," cried Michel: "I want to live. My mother wants me. My God! what will she do without me? I must go over the river to meet her."

"Poor fellow! he's going over the river, sure enough," said the surgeon pityingly.

Michel lay quiet for a moment: then his throat began to rattle, and with a sudden spasm all was over.

The death of my quondam comrade affected me greatly; and I limped out of the shed, anxious only to get away from the dead. I had not gone many steps when I was confronted by a tall Confederate officer. On my looking up our eyes met, and once more Tom Marshall and I stood before each other.

CHAPTER XXIX.

THE ACCOUNTS BALANCED.

"I would bring balm, and pour it in your wound,
Cure your distempered mind, and heal your fortunes."

KNEW you were here, Frank," said Tom quietly as we shook hands. "I saw your name on the hospital-register, so was looking for you."

"Yes, Tom, I'm here safe enough. The tables are turned now. I am the prisoner, not you," I replied sadly.

"By heavens! you won't be a prisoner long, if I can help it," exclaimed Tom.

"But you can not help it," said I somewhat bitterly. "We are not on the picket-line in the darkness now."

"Frank Wilmot! I owe you a debt of gratitude, and I'm going to pay it," cried Tom in an impetuous way that reminded me of our college days.

"I don't doubt your willingness to cancel the obligation, but how can you do it?"

"You shall see," he replied confidently.

"How came you in this out-of-the-way place?" said I as we sat down together under one of the locust-trees that fringed the main road. "Why are you away from the army?"

"I've been over in our valley," responded Tom. "I don't mind telling you, Frank, that we are hard pressed for men just now. Grant, that new general of yours, fights like a bulldog.

He never lets go his hold. So I was sent to the Valley to order back some reinforcements, and am now returning to Richmond. Sutherland, the hospital-steward here, belongs in the Valley too: so I have stopped over for the night. He showed me the list of prisoners just now, and your name was almost the first one I read."

"Are they all well at the homestead?" I asked.

Tom's face changed for a moment, and he dug the grass with his spurs as if my question had caused him pain.

"Mother is dead," he said at last, in a low voice. "We lost her last winter."

I clasped Tom's hand in silence; and, as our fingers tightened, the old bond of friendship was strengthened.

"Yes, mother died just before Christmas," continued Tom, when he had recovered from his emotion. "You know she was never very strong, and this cruel war tried her sorely. Constantly changing in military ownership, the Valley has been by no means a peaceful spot; and poor mother felt the strain very much. When winter began to set in, she just pined away and left us."

"And your sister?" said I.

"Oh! Kate is all right, though not the saucy, wayward girl as you no doubt remember her. She seldom smiles now. Ah, Frank! this war has borne heavily on the women of the South;" and Tom shook his head sadly as he spoke.

"The women on both sides have suffered greatly," I replied: "the struggle has been so bitter. But I can readily believe that the Southern women have had the hardest trials."

"But now about your escape. I must manage it somehow," said Tom, changing the subject, at the same time looking about him to see that we were out of hearing.

"I can not see how it is to be done," said I. "Your men here on guard tell me that the Rapidan is carefully watched by your cavalry, and that they hold all the fords."

Tom laughed loudly, evidently amused at my words.

"Bless your heart, boy! Do you imagine we could spare as many men as that would imply? Of course there are a few cavalry scouts along the river, but there are plenty of fords where you could cross unseen."

"I am glad to hear you say so," said I; "for I am still too weak for a swim. Had I known the true state of affairs, I would have attempted an escape long before this. But it is too late now. They talk of sending us farther South in a few days."

"You will not go a mile farther South than you are at present, if I can do any thing to prevent it," cried Tom passionately. "Why, Frank, Kate would never forgive me if I permitted you to remain a prisoner, after the service you rendered me at Gettysburg."

"Does she know?"

"To be sure she does. You don't suppose I would keep that event a secret from those at home?"

"What rank do you hold now?" said I, turning over his embroidered sleeve to change the conversation. "I never could make out your Confederate insignia."

"I am a lieutenant-colonel now," replied Tom rather proudly. "If this war lasts much longer, I may yet be a general: who knows?"

"And I'm only a captain."

"Promotion comes more quickly with us," said he. "Why, my regiment has lost three colonels this campaign. But that has nothing to do with your escape. You must start this very night, so we have no time to lose."

Tom Marshall had evidently learned one thing by his army experience, — the necessity of decisive action. Rapidly and clearly he began sketching out a plan of operations. Sutherland, the steward, would furnish a pass, he having in his possession a few signed in blank by General Ewell; and Tom would get him to promise not to report my disappearance until two or three days had elapsed. Tom also announced that he had procured a spare uniform which would serve as a disguise; for, after crossing the Rapidan, I was to proceed along the foot of the mountains, in the character of a wounded Confederate soldier going home on furlough. This would enable me to pass unhindered, and be a claim for assistance; all of the people in that section being naturally in warm sympathy with the Southern cause. Tom laughingly assigned me to his own regiment, the Third Virginia; and wrote down the names of the officers, as well as a few enlisted men, with some other pertinent details, for me to learn, and repeat in case I was troubled with curious questions. He also gave me some Confederate money, and mapped out my route as far as Warrenton.

"When you get that far," said he, "you know the country as well as I do; and can then make your way to Centerville by the Aldie road. But I must go and see Sutherland now. We have no time to lose, as every thing must be in readiness by dusk."

"Are you sure of Sutherland's co-operation?"

"Quite certain. He already understands my plans, and fully enters into them."

I remained seated at the foot of the tree, after Tom had left me; feeling rejoiced at the prospect of escaping a prison, and reflecting on the many ties that were binding Tom and me together. The glimpse I gained of Kate's sentiments towards me, from Tom's words, brought a sense of exquisite pleasure to my heart; and I was indeed very happy. Hearing a step behind me, I turned, and saw the tremendous boots of our surgeon approaching.

"What are you dreaming about, Wilmot?" said he. "You seem to be basking in the sun like a cat."

"I was thinking of home, doctor," I replied.

"I'm sorry to disturb such thoughts, but I've come to tell you that the ambulances will be here before morning. To-morrow all but the amputation cases are to go South."

"Doctor, can you keep a secret?" I asked.

"If it's worth keeping," he replied.

"Then you need not be astonished if I am missing to-morrow."

The surgeon gave a low whistle of surprise.

"I'm mighty glad of it," said he. "But I'm afraid you won't be able to cross the fords: you know they are all guarded."

"Never fear, I'll get through," said I. "Just forget to report my absence, for I want to get a good start."

"Report you? Do you think I'd bother myself about that? Why, if half the men ran away, I'd pretend not to notice their absence! Report you, indeed!" he repeated, his face as red as his beard with indignation.

"All right, doctor: then I'm safe."

"But do you expect that the Confederates won't miss you? They're sure to do so."

"Oh! I've got friends, and have no fears on that score," I replied.

"Ah, ha! that's the way the land lies, does it? Then I tell you what: when you get to Washington, let them know I'm here with the boys. Maybe they will send out after us. I wish you luck, Wilmot, with all my soul;" and the surgeon, after warmly shaking my hand, stumped away in his preposterous boots to arrange for poor Michel's burial.

The hospital-steward entered heartily into Tom's scheme, though he was prudent enough to keep away from me. Indeed, even Tom and I did not meet again until after nightfall, our rendezvous being the locust-tree.

"Come!" said he in a whisper, as soon as I appeared.

Keeping Tom in sight, I followed him down a side-road that ran to the rear of the tavern, and entered the woods a few hundred yards beyond. Once in the shadow of the trees, Tom slackened his pace, and waited for me to come up.

"Here are your things," said he, thrusting a bundle into my hands. "Dress as quickly as you can."

Hastily donning the Confederate uniform, Tom and I then walked on through the forest in silence. At length we entered a road, and soon after came to a low wooden bridge over a small brook, where Tom halted.

"Well, Frank, we must say good-by once more. Here is a haversack and a loaf of your bread;" and, as he spoke, Tom stooped down under the bridge, and produced the haversack, evidently left there by preconcerted arrangement.

"Good-by, Tom!" I exclaimed. "I hope that when we meet again it will not be to part."

"I echo that hope with all my heart," replied Tom. "But you must not linger here, Frank; for by daylight you should be miles away on the other side the river."

I held out my hand, and felt Tom's strong grasp in mine; then with a full heart I broke away, and started on my lonely, dangerous journey.

Tom had thought it would be best for me to cross the Rapidan just above Germanna Ford; so I followed the road we were on, as he said it led direct to the river. The moon was beginning to show herself above the tops of the trees by the time I had gone a mile, and I had plenty of light on my path. But my progress was somewhat slow; for, though my wound was rapidly healing, I was still quite lame. I struggled manfully, however, for every step I took brought me nearer to liberty.

About midnight I began to see signs of the battle-field. A broken wagon lying on one side of the road was the first thing that attracted my attention; and then the indications multiplied, until at length I came to the Confederate breastworks. The road I was on had evidently been the one used by Ewell when he advanced to meet Sedgwick and Warren. The moon had now risen almost to the zenith, and the ground lay bathed in light. Going on a little farther, I discovered a path leading towards my right; and, knowing that the field over which my regiment had charged could not be far distant, I determined to visit it.

Following the narrow path for a short distance, I encountered more breastworks, and soon after saw an opening in the woods.

It was our field. Clambering over the rude bank of logs and earth that had formed the defensive line of our antagonists, I found myself at last on the well-remembered ground. But what a sight met my eye! In the bright moonlight lay nearly two hundred bodies of my comrades, their picturesque zouave uniforms now blackened by contact with corruption. In rows and in groups, just as they had fallen on that fatal day, these unburied corpses had become wind and sun dried skeletons.

REVISITING THE WILDERNESS BATTLE-FIELD.

The faces that were upturned to the silvery rays of the moon had lost all semblance to humanity, and were now simply hideous masks, the eyeless sockets of which seemed to mock me as I stood among them. But I was not alone; for at my feet writhed countless swarms of the repulsive Virginia tumble-bugs, all struggling for a share in the awful banquet the god of war had provided for them.

Horror-stricken and heart-sick, I gazed over the field and along the line we had held, seeing bodies in every direction and in every possible attitude. Here one poor fellow had crawled to the foot of a tree, and died as he sat. His fez was still on his head, the gibbering skull beneath it seeming to laugh at me, as the jaws had relaxed and fallen apart. On the sleeves were the chevrons of a sergeant. Beyond were the bodies of five or six men lying one over the other; but now they seemed like a design on a carpet, having become flattened to one level. Near these was the body of a man lying apart from his fellows. Falling on his back, the dead man had flung his arms far apart, and one leg was drawn up as if in agony. Now the hands were bare of flesh, and peeped hideously out of the sleeves; while the elevated knee had become shrunken, a wide rent in the cloth permitting the skin-covered bone to protrude. Everywhere about me, these ghastly specters met my gaze. A few feet from where I stood, lay the body of an officer; and, on going towards it, I saw a captain's strap on the shoulder. It was poor Ned Burch, no doubt; for I recognized the tree near by as the one we were standing under when he died. Here was where I had fallen; and by what a narrow chance it was, that my body was not lying there, slowly moldering on the surface of the earth!

"And this is the glory of war that poets rave about!" I exclaimed. "Where are its pomp and circumstance now?"

An owl began hooting dismally over my head, as though answering my words. I listened to the night-bird's hoarse, unearthly cry for a moment, then, turning away, staggered back to the path.

Entering the wagon-road again, I kept on towards the river, seeing more of the unburied Federal dead, where Sedgwick had led his men, until at last I reached the ford. It wanted scarcely two hours of daylight; and, as I knew I must be across and away before that, I boldly waded into the stream, finding it quite shallow. Clambering painfully up the opposite bank, I struck into a deer-path in the woods for a few minutes, and then plunged into the depths of the forest. I had crossed the river unseen, unchallenged: now for rest and sleep. My arm was almost sound again; my leg, though still painful, was fairly fit for use, weak as it was. My camping-ground was formed in a hollow caused by the upheaval of a tree by some storm; and, after gathering a bed of withered leaves, I flung myself on the ground, and dreamed of my mother and my home.

CHAPTER XXX.

RUNNING THE GAUNTLET.

"Herein Fortune shows herself more kind
Than is her custom."

IX days after my crossing the River Rapidan, I drew near the pretty little town of Warrenton, where two summers before I had joined my regiment from the hospital, rejoicing in promotion and the right to wear and wield a sword. Full of ardor and pride in my new rank, when last I had entered the town I gloried in all the martial signs and symbols visible everywhere about me. Then I was going to meet my comrades, and the army in all its glory and strength lay before me. Now how changed was the scene, how different my circumstances! Wounded and sore, alone and in disguise, I was in constant danger. Weary with pain, — for the wound in my thigh had re-opened under the strain lately put upon it, — I dreaded discovery, and started at every sound. The cracking of a twig in the forest, or the sudden dart of a frightened squirrel on the roadside, startled me; and I grew sick with fear at every turn in my path. My dear old regiment was far away, bravely fighting; the bones of my grumbling friend were bleaching in the dense thickets of the Wilderness, and I was ignorant of Dennis's fate.

Fortune had indeed changed with me, and I was tasting of the bitterness of war.

Thanks to Tom Marshall's careful instructions, I had found it tolerable easy to maintain my assumed character of a Confederate soldier. Avoiding the town of Culpepper by a circuitous route, I crossed the plains of Brandy without hinderance, and forded the Robertson and Rappahannock rivers, a few miles above their junction at Beverly Dam. So far my journey had been an uneventful one, for by leaving the main roads I had escaped the attention of the patrols still kept moving by the enemy in that neighborhood. My disguise proved sufficiently perfect to deceive the lonely women I found in the houses on my route, but I knew that at Warrenton I ran great risk of being detected. The danger must be faced, however: so I nerved myself for the trial.

Musing thus, I saw the roofs and steeples of Warrenton near at hand, and in an hour's time I was in its streets; finding them, as I expected, entirely deserted by either army. Boldly marching on, I made my way to the tavern not far from the railroad-depot, finding four or five men lounging on the veranda.

"Good-evening, gentlemen," said I, coolly ascending the rickety wooden steps. "It's very hot to-day."

"Not too hot for June," replied one of the group, an elderly man, the others gazing curiously at me in silence. "But who be you?"

"A poor devil who got hit over by the Rapidan, when we licked the Yanks in the Wilderness," I replied.

"That war over a month ago. Whar hev you bin sence?" asked the old man suspiciously.

"In hospital, to be sure, down by the river. I left thar a week ago."

"It must hev bin a tough march," remarked my interlocutor.

"I'm pretty good on the tramp, sir," said I. "Though I've only a leg and a half left, as you might say."

"Bin wounded, eh? Whar 'bout?"

"In the thigh: the bullet went cl'ar through," I replied,

beginning to feel annoyed at the old man's questioning. But
he had not yet done with me.

"An' whar 'bout might the battle hev bin?"

"Down in the Wilderness, near Locust Grove, t'other side
the Rapidan," I answered, imitating his drawl to the best of
my ability.

"That was a right smart fight, I've hearn," he continued.

AT THE WARRENTON HOTEL.

"Deed it was; one of the hottest I've ever bin in," said
I, amused by the conversation.

"So I've hearn! What mou't yer name be, mister?" and the
inquisitive old fellow eyed me suspiciously as he deliberately
knocked the ashes out of his home-made pipe on the veranda
railing.

"Sconnes, sir; George Sconnes," said I, using the name Tom
had bestowed on me when we parted. "I b'long to the Third
Virginny."

At this moment a young man rode up, a carbine being slung

at his saddle-bow. Quickly dismounting, he fastened his horse to the hitching-post, and approached the veranda.

"Why, thar's my Martin!" exclaimed my troublesome old friend. "Sa-ay, Martin, here's one of yer comrades, I reckon. He's one of the Third Virginny. Bin wounded, too, in the big fight on the Rapidan."

The new-comer eyed me even more suspiciously than his father had done.

"What rigiment did yer say?" he asked in a somewhat surly tone of voice.

"Third Virginny, sir, as this gentleman has told you. What's yours?"

"Don't b'long to no rigiment," he replied with a queer laugh, in which all the others joined.

"Oh! wun of them home-guards I've hearn tell of," I drawled; getting out of temper, for the fellow's manner galled me.

"No, I'm no home-guard. I'm as good as you, tho' I don't b'long to no rigiment. I've fou't for the cause same as you fellows that wears the uniform. Did yer never hear of Colonel Mosby?" and the young fellow laughed mischievously.

"Mosby! Are you one of his men? That must be dangerous kind of work."

"Yes, it's sorter dangerous," he replied, evidently mollified by my implied compliment. "We runs more risks than you fellows in the army, but we've more fun."

"I say, mister," exclaimed another of the men, "I've my 'spicions along of yer. I sort o' s'pect yer isn't no Southerner. I don't b'lieve yer b'long to our side at all."

"Indeed! and what do yer take me to be? Not a Yank?" said I in as bold a tone as I could muster, though my heart was thumping at the danger I was facing.

"Yes, a Yank, an' nothin' else."

"I'm a Varginian, sir," I replied: "why shouldn't you b'lieve me?"

" 'Cause yer don't look like one, and yer don't talk like one nuther."

"Say, mister," interrupted the old man, "part of that thar rigiment, the Third Virginny, war raised right 'bout yeah. Who do you know among 'em?"

Now was the crucial test. Could I pass through it successfully?

"Who do I know? Waal, I don't know the hull rigiment no better than you do; but our present colonel is Hector Randolph, who lives in the Loudon over thar; and thar's Major Crawford, who" —

"He's all right: young Henry Crawford was born and raised right yeah in Warrenton," exclaimed the old man: " wasn't he, Martin?"

"Yes, I 'spose so," replied the son. "But yer said he was yer major: since when?"

"Why, he got it over in Richmond, since the battle of the North Anna. Him and young Tom Marshall got promoted together. Now look yeah, gentlemen, I've stood this yeah kat-akisin 'bout long enough. If yer don't b'lieve me, why don't yer arrest me?" and I frowned and struck the railing with my fist in affected indignation.

"Now, don't yer be gitting mad, comrade," said the young bushwhacker. "Thar's my hand: sorry to have doubted yer, but's best to be keerful these yeah war times."

"That's all right," said I, taking the proffered hand. "I don't object to be questioned; but it's being taken for a Yank, after having one of thar plaguy bullets punch a hole in yer, that made me angry."

"Whar 'bouts du yer b'long?" asked one of the men, who had hitherto been a silent spectator to the colloquy.

"Over to Martinsburg."

"Yer hev a long journey before yer," remarked the old man. "How are yer to git over the mountains with that thar leg? Yer ain't scurcely able to walk, let alone climb."

"Oh! I'll manage somehow. If I can get a bed to-night, I'll start in the morning for Aldie, and go through the Gap. I ought to git thar in two days."

"Don't yer go near Aldie, if yer don't want to be gobbled by the Yanks," exclaimed the guerrilla: "they be in toler'ble strong force thar jist now."

This was good news, for if I could only get near our lines I was safe.

"Sorry to hear it," I replied; "for it's an easier road to travel than thro' old Thoroughfare."

"Tell yer what, ole man," said Martin: "we'll give him supper and a bed, and in the mornin' yer hitch up the ole mar', and take him over the mountains."

"That's a good idee of yourn, Martin. We're bound to help those who hev fou't for the cause."

"No, no," I said hurriedly, for it was no part of my plan to be carried over the mountains: "I am much obliged to you, sir. I can't put you to so much trouble."

"'Tain't any trouble. I'm out of meal, and mou't as well go for it to-morrer as next day."

The old man rose as he spoke, and descended from the veranda. I saw that I must submit to the proposition, else I might again arouse suspicions already so fortunately allayed. Having given Martinsburg as my destination, I did not dare object, though the hospitable offer sadly upset all my plans. I might, however, make my way down the Loudon Valley, and so reach the River Potomac. There was no use fretting: I must follow the path Dame Fortune selected for me.

CHAPTER XXXI.

TO THE RESCUE.

"In this
You satisfy your anger and revenge."

URING our early breakfast the next morning, I learned that young Martin Farquhar had decided to take his father's place in our proposed jaunt over the mountains; he having received instructions during the night to communicate certain orders to the men belonging to Mosby's command who lived in the Loudon Valley. As it was a matter of indifference to me which of them went, I acquiesced, though I felt chagrined at being thus carried so far out of my way. Bidding old Mr. Farquhar a cordial good-by, and making the absurd promise to call when I rejoined Lee's army, I clambered into the dilapidated old chaise; and we were soon on the road through the Gaps.

It was late in the afternoon when we descended into the valley of the Loudon, young Farquhar to my dismay driving straight across. It was nightfall when he halted at a house, where we learned that the Federals were in force at Harper's Ferry and Charlestown. As my bushwhacking friend had defeated my purpose of passing down the valley, I was compelled to remain with his entertainers over night; Martin carrying me in the buggy as far as the foot of the hills, soon after sunrise the following morning.

" I'm much obliged to you, sir," said I, " for your kindness. Some day I hope to be able to pay the debt."

" Look heah ! " cried Martin indignantly, " yer b'long to the ole Third Virginny, and thar's no debt 'bout it."

I shook the young man's hand in silence, for I felt ashamed of having profited by his loyalty to his side of the great national quarrel. Leaving him to go his rounds, I trudged painfully through the Gap.

It was with strange emotions that I passed over the road I had traveled four years before. Then I was in a land of peace and plenty, and my footsteps were free to go where I listed : now war, with its angry front, had ravaged the land, and armed hosts were seeking to destroy each other. Then I was leaving the valley a happy boy : now I was returning to the scene bronzed, disguised, and facing hidden dangers.

Coming at length to the ledge where I had taken my farewell view of the smiling, peaceful valley, on that never-to-be-forgotten summer's morning, I stood and gazed once more at the picture, fairly amazed at the change that had come over the landscape.

Though many of the fields stretched at my feet were full of ripening wheat, the valley no longer wore that air of busy industry as when last I saw it. Now all was hushed and silent. Here and there I could detect wide gaps in the stone fences, and long lines of trenches, showing where the opposing armies had struggled against each other for the mastery. Even the frequent bits of woodland had been touched by the withering hand of war ; for broad swaths of trees had been cut for abatis and defense, their lifeless trunks and branches glistening in the hot June sunshine in vivid contrast with the surrounding foliage. To the right a blackened patch lay like a blot on the landscape, the outlines telling of a home destroyed for ever. Sitting on the ledge, and noting all these changes, my eyes strayed at length to the familiar clump of walnut-trees, under the shade of which I had passed so many careless, happy hours with Tom and Kate. The Marshall homestead was but little changed; though there was an air of neglect about the place, which, even at that distance, struck me painfully. A few of the negro-huts in the hollow only remained, and the neat palings near the house were thrown down or broken. In the roof of the old mansion I could discern an ugly rent, the misshapen outlines of which revealed the path of a shell. Like the rest of the blighted valley, every thing about the house seemed silent and deserted; and I wondered if it were indeed empty. Thus gazing and musing, a sudden impulse seized me to visit the house; though it had been my intention to keep to the river-bank, and endeavor to reach Harper's Ferry.

The sun had set when I crossed the bridge where Tom and I had parted; for my pace was slow and painful, and the night had fallen as I entered the lawn. On approaching the house, I noticed a horse, ready saddled, and tethered to the railing of the veranda. In the old days a horse would not have been permitted on the lawn, and my finding one there was another evidence of the change that had come over the valley. Though in disguise as a Confederate soldier, I knew the need of caution: so stealing up the steps, I peeped through a lighted window.

In the room stood Kate Marshall, her face towards me. But how changed was the girl! Though still beautiful, the faded dress of mourning and her pale cheeks told of sorrow. Just then the figure of a man came between us. He turned; and, to my amazement, I saw the face of Ned Charlton.

"What is he doing here? Does the girl really love the fellow?" With these unuttered words on my tongue, I leaned against the sash, and listened.

"Come, come! Kate Marshall, don't be a fool," exclaimed Charlton. "You know how I love you."

"I care not. When you first told me of it, I rejected you gently, as a woman should. But now you persecute me," was her reply.

"Persecute you, Miss Marshall! I'm a gentleman," said Charlton in his lofty manner.

"Gentleman! You are a pretty gentleman! to steal into my house during my father's absence, because you know you dare not do it in his presence. A fine gentleman! Sir, you insult the word in using it."

"We lose time, Miss Kate. I offer you my love, my honest love."

"Your love is not honest, Ned Charlton, and you are not an honest man," replied Kate with flashing eyes.

"By heaven, girl! what do you mean?"

"Just what I say, sir. You pretend to be a defender of our cause; but I believe you to be, at heart, a miserable traitor."

"Do you? Look you now, my proud beauty, take care how you badger me!" cried Charlton, his dark face distorted with rage.

"Oh! I am not afraid of you, Mr. Charlton. You dare not harm me."

"Dare not? By heaven! you tempt me to show you my power."

"Your power? what could you do?" asked the girl in a curious tone.

"Do? Why, as you have said, you are all alone here: there's not a nigger on the plantation. Ah! you see, I know all. If you don't change your tune, my pretty one, I'll clap you on my saddle, and carry you to the mountains. Once there, you will be glad enough to be my wife."

"Cowardly miscreant! my brother shall pay you dearly for these threats, this insult," exclaimed Kate passionately.

"The devil take your brother! Come, we'll have no more of this. To the mountains you go this very night."

As he uttered the words, the scoundrel advanced to seize the shrinking girl. Before he could do so, I had dashed through the window, and, with a chair, stretched him senseless at her feet.

"Frank!" exclaimed Kate, springing into my arms, "thank God! I'm safe."

"Yes," I replied tenderly, "safe enough, I trust."

"But, Frank, how came you here? and in that dress? That is not a Yankee uniform."

"No. Tom lent it to me to escape with."

"Escape? then you were a prisoner?"

"Yes; but never mind that now, Kate. Thank Heaven! chance brought me here to save you from that villain."

"I say, good people, perhaps you will explain the meaning of all this," cried a voice at my elbow.

Startled at the unexpected interruption, Kate and I turned, only to find that the speaker was Mr. Marshall.

"Frank Wilmot!" he exclaimed, surprised in his turn, "and in Confederate uniform! What does this mean?"

"Yes, sir; Frank Wilmot," I replied, "and in disguise. I was a prisoner, and your son helped me to escape. I shall be quite safe before morning."

"O father!" said Kate, "Frank has saved me from a dreadful fate."

"What on earth do you mean, girl?"

"She means, that, finding her in the power of a villain, I naturally came to her rescue. There he lies," said I, pointing to the floor where Charlton had fallen.

"Why, he's gone!" exclaimed Kate.

It was indeed true. There were no traces of the fellow: he had escaped.

"Come, no more of this mystery," exclaimed the old gentleman impatiently. "What has happened? Who is a villain? Who has disappeared?"

As briefly as possible I related what had occurred. At the mention of Charlton's name, Mr. Marshall's face darkened with passion.

"Ned Charlton? He dare to do this! He shall pay dearly for this outrage! Mr. Wilmot, how shall I thank you?"

" Indeed, sir, I ask no thanks for what I did."

" You no doubt consider my daughter's thanks quite sufficient," remarked the old gentleman significantly. "But depend upon it, Frank, that scoundrel Charlton means to do
you some mischief. As I rode up to the house I heard some
one ride away towards the huts: it must have been he. He
has no doubt recognized you; and, if you are captured in that
Confederate uniform, you will be hanged as a spy. You must
leave this house at once. There is no time to be lost."

" Yes, Frank, father is right. You must go before it is too
late," said Kate.

" Perhaps so," was my reply; "but it seems cowardly to
leave in this way."

" But you are in danger. It is not cowardly to avoid it,"
pleaded Kate.

" There is short shrift accorded spies in this valley," said Mr.
Marshall; "and you would be denounced as such by Charlton.
Have you any arms, Mr. Wilmot?"

" None. If I only had a revolver now!"

" Take mine, and there's my horse at the door."

" No, no! to take your horse would only place you under
suspicion. Besides, I shall be best on foot, for Charlton is too
fond of horse-flesh to trust himself out of the saddle."

As I spoke, I took the revolver, and thrust it into my bosom.

" Hark! I heard horses," exclaimed Kate. " They are coming in search of you, Frank."

" You're right, my girl," said her father, going to the window.
" There's a troop of horsemen in the road. Kate, take Mr.
Wilmot through the house and down past the barn. — You
know the path, Frank. Come, you have no time to lose."

The galloping of several horses now sounded in our ears, and
I did not need any urging to accompany Kate. To stay was to
brave death: to escape would balk Charlton of his contemplated revenge. Kate and I rapidly crossed the open ground
in rear of the house until we came to a path. Here we paused.

The horsemen came thundering along the road, and over the lawn, up to the very door of the house; and I could hear confused voices in angry altercation. It was quite evident that Charlton had returned. Should I slip away like a thief, and leave this brave girl unprotected, and exposed to the insults of a scoundrel like him? The idea seemed detestable. Giving expression to these feelings in words, Kate interrupted me: —

"Have no fear for me. My father is too well known in the valley for Charlton to attempt us any harm. But you we can not save. As my father says, the uniform you wear would be your death-warrant. Go now, and may God bless and protect you!"

She was right. I must go. Taking her in my arms for a moment, I tore myself away, and, with her kiss on my lips, plunged down the narrow path in the darkness.

CHAPTER XXXII.

IN FRESH TOILS.

"You make me strange
Even to the disposition that I owe."

THE distance to the river was so short that I soon reached the bank, and entered the path used by field-hands when peace reigned in the valley. I knew that if I met with no hinderance I could reach the Federal picket-lines by daylight; plodding on to the best of my ability, for I remembered enough of the topography of that part of the valley to know that if our forces were in possession of Charlestown I should find their pickets along the line of Opequan Creek, some miles this side of Harper's Ferry. In the excitement induced by my discovery of Kate's danger, I had forgotten the pain of my wound, nor did I feel it for over an hour after parting from her. But at length my poor thigh grew restive, the pain increased, and I felt the blood running down my leg into the shoe: it was with difficulty, therefore, that I kept moving. Faint and weary as I was, I realized, however, the fact that halting was impossible; for with the dawn Charlton and his followers would be galloping over every field in search of me. To escape, I must keep on my feet, no matter at what cost of pain and suffering. Better to endure that now, and live to enjoy Kate's love, than run the risk of capture, and a miserable death at the end of a rope.

Stumbling along as best I could, but at an uneven pace, I followed the course of the river, as it wound about under the mountains. My progress was, however, so slow and tedious that when the first faint streaks of daylight appeared in the sky I feared I had not yet placed all danger behind. An hour later, and objects around me became distinguishable; but though I saw no signs of being pursued, neither did I perceive any indication of the Federal line. Still, I felt confident they were not far distant.

While thus calculating the chances and changes of fortune, a turn in the path suddenly brought me to a deserted breastwork; and as I slowly clambered over it, two men rushed forward, and made me their prisoner. A glance was sufficient to tell me that they were Federal cavalrymen. At last I was in the hands of friends.

"Mine Gott in Himmel! ver you gome from, eh?" ejaculated one of the men, the yellow chevrons on his sleeve showing him to be a corporal.

"Why, from the other side of the breastwork, to be sure," said I, amused at the stupid question.

"Vell, I see dot meinself. But what for you gome over? Dot's what I vant to know."

"What regiment do you belong to?" I asked, ignoring the corporal's inquiry.

"Dird Neuw Jersey," replied the corporal. "For why you ask, eh?"

"Just to find out. Now send me to the rear: I want to see the officer in command."

"Yaw, dot is all righd. Hans vill dake yer to de major," said the corporal, evidently mystified by my unexpected appearance and confident manner.

"Yous bee mein brisoner," said Hans, laying his big paw on my shoulder; "an' ef you blays me any dricks I shoots you mit de head, preddy quick righd avay."

"Go ahead, my Dutch friend," said I.

" I bees not a Dietchman, I bees von Gherman ! " exclaimed Hans indignantly.

" All right, old fellow. It would take a big bullet to go through that thick skull of yours."

Hans seemed disposed at first to resent my badinage, for he rattled his saber menacingly ; but finally abandoned all belligerent intent, and led the way to the picket-reserve. We proceeded down the path for a few minutes, when I found myself in the presence of the picket-officer. Major Rosenburg listened to my statements very courteously, and expressed his belief in their truth.

" But I must send you down to the Ferry under guard, captain," said he apologetically : " you see, I have only your personal word that you are an officer in the Federal army."

" Of course, sir. That is what I should do under similar circumstances. But please send me at once, for my wound needs attention."

" The man who brought you in here will be your escort," said the major, indicating Hans with a gesture. " Rosenbaum, get your horse, and take the prisoner to headquarters."

" Is there a large force of Federals in the valley at present ? " said I as Hans disappeared.

" Excuse me, sir," replied Major Rosenburg rather stiffly : " I can not give you any information. If you satisfy the general as to your true character, you will then learn all you wish."

" I beg your pardon, major. I forgot I was in Confederate uniform. You are quite right. I bid you good-day, sir, with many thanks for your kindness."

" Good-day, sir," replied Major Rosenburg.

Following Hans to a clump of trees, he soon mounted, and led me into a road. We had proceeded scarcely a dozen rods when my guard caught a glimpse of the revolver I carried in the breast of my coat.

" Donner and blitzen ! You bees hev a peestol ! " he exclaimed.

" So I have. I had forgotten all about it," said I.

" So! What for you dakes me? a dommed fool, eh?"

" You're not far from being one," was my reply, surprised at the man's angry tone. " But I don't understand you, my friend. What do you mean by all this?"

" Mein Gott! You dakes your obbertunity, and shoots me thru mein head ven I vas not looking. Yous shust gib me dot peestol."

" Certainly, if you wish it. Here it is!"

Scarcely had the fellow got possession of the revolver than he cocked it, and poked the muzzle in my face.

" What the devil are you doing?" I exclaimed, leaping back to avoid the weapon.

" Vot I means? Vhy, to shoot you now, righd avay."

" Shoot me!" said I. " Why, you were ordered to take me to the general at the Ferry, you blundering fool. Did you not hear me tell your major just now, that I was a Union officer? Do your duty. I am sorry now I gave you that revolver."

" Oh! yous bees sorry. Vell, I shoots you anyvay."

" Look here, my fine fellow. If I am to be shot, don't you think it will be well to wait until your general gives the order? If you shoot me now, you may have to face half a dozen car-bines yourself."

" I tells yous shust vot I does. I ties yous to mein saddle, dot's vot I does!" exclaimed Hans, as if the thought was a brilliant one.

" I don't care what you do, so you take me to the Ferry," I replied, thankful that the fellow's mood had changed.

Hans immediately made a slip-noose on one end of his lariat, and passed it over my wrist, making the other end of the cord fast to a ring in his saddle.

Finding resistance to be worse than useless, I submitted to my fate, and did my best to keep pace with the horse; but I could not avoid the frequent jerks of the cord on my wrist.

It was fully four miles to the Ferry; and in that distance I suffered greatly, the ignorant brute on horseback seeming to have no compassion. I bore the pain and fatigue with such philosophy as I could muster, hoping to turn the tables on my escort when I saw the general.

At length we entered the little straggling village of Harper's Ferry, shut in as it is by towering mountains on every side. The Shenandoah River now lost its peaceful, placid character; for, finding its passage to the Potomac narrowed by the gorge through which it poured, the stream boiled and foamed in angry mood, carrying its bluster into the waters of the more majestic river beyond. Passing down Shenandoah Street on our way to headquarters, we met a staff-officer on horseback.

"What have you there?" he inquired of my guard.

"He bees von rebel, vot dried to run avay, so I ties him to mein saddle," was Hans's mendacious reply.

UNDER GUARD.

"I beg your pardon, sir," I began: "I am not a Confederate, but a " —

"Oh! never mind what or who you are now," interrupted the aide impatiently: "you can settle that question by and by. — Take him to the guard-house, my man."

"But I want to see the general!" I exclaimed. "It's all a mistake. I *must* see the general."

"Confound your impudence! The general has something else to attend to. The provost-guard will look after you;" and the speaker galloped on out of sight.

Before many minutes I was in an old half-ruined house, on the river-bank, surrounded by some twenty or thirty Confederate soldiers. They informed me that they had been taken on a picket-line a few nights before, and were expecting to be sent to the prison-camp at Elmira. They were astonished to learn that I was not an officer in the Southern army; and I was compelled to explain the circumstances which brought me among them. But I was at a loss how to extricate myself from this absurd predicament.

The guard over these Confederate prisoners was commanded by an Irish sergeant, who reminded me of Dennis by his odd speeches. Being evidently good-natured, I decided to appeal to him. During my forced march to the Ferry, at the heels of Hans's horse, I had lost my hat; the stubborn wretch refusing to stop until I could pick it up. This would be sufficient excuse for my purpose.

"An' is it a hat ye want? Shure, I don't blame ye for wantin' one," said the sergeant; "but how can I get one to fit ye?"

"Ask the officer of the day to let me go to the store, under guard, and pick one out for myself."

"'Deed, an' I will, this blessed minnit."

Half an hour after, one of the corporals called me out, and escorted me to the store, not far distant. As we entered, a group of officers who were lounging near the counter stared at me as if I were some strange animal. To my delight, in the middle of the group I recognized Charles Osborne, the correspondent.

"Good-day, Osborne. What are you doing up here?" was my quiet salutation, as I walked up to him and held out my hand.

"Excuse me, sir, but I don't remember you," replied Osborne, evidently surprised.

"Perhaps not, seeing me in this confounded dress. Don't you remember Captain Wilmot of the Zouaves? we met at Gettysburg, and since very often."

"What! Frank Wilmot, who had all the prisoners at Point of Rocks last summer?"

"The same."

"Why, man, you were reported killed at the Wilderness, and I wrote your obituary. Colonel Harding hasn't been the same man since. How comes it that you are alive?" said Osborne.

"Simply because I wasn't killed, that's all. When I recovered my senses after being wounded, the Confederates had me a prisoner."

"How did you escape?"

"That's a pretty long story: I can't tell it now, for I want you to help me, Osborne."

"All right, old fellow: what is it I am to do?"

"Why, nobody here will believe me when I say that I am not a Confederate, and I can not get audience with the general. You know me: go and tell him."

"What! haven't you seen General Stahl? Why is that corporal with you?" exclaimed one of the officers.

"They have put me among some other Confederate prisoners, and will pack me off to Elmira, I suppose, if some one does not interfere."

"You have been shamefully treated, Wilmot," said Osborne. "I propose, gentlemen, to see this thing out. Let us all go with him to the general."

"Just what I was going to propose," remarked one of the officers: "won't the old man be mad, though, when he hears of this!"

"I came here to buy a hat," said I, laughing; for I was of course delighted at the happy turn affairs had taken.

"Bother your hat!" cried Osborne: "you are more pictur-esque as you are. Besides, when the general releases you we'll have to fit you out in a new rig."

On arriving at the general's quarters I was at once ushered into his presence. The sight of a man in Confederate uniform in the midst of so many of his officers amazed General Stahl; but when Osborne explained who I was, how I had escaped through the Confederate lines, and how outrageously I had been treated, his indignation knew no bounds.

"What!" shouted the angry general: "a Union officer comes through the lines, and is crammed into the guard-house without my knowledge! By heaven! I'll make an example of some one for this. — Orderly, call the officer of the day."

"I beg your pardon, general; but the officer of the day had nothing to do with it. We met a staff-officer on the road just outside the town. It was he who ordered me to be taken to the guard-house."

"His name?" asked the general.

"That I do not know."

"Did you tell him you were a Federal officer in disguise?" demanded General Stahl.

"I attempted to do so; but he would not listen, and, when I asked to see you, said that you had something else to attend to."

"I wish I knew who he was," remarked the brigadier wrathfully.

"Well, sir, though I do not know the aide's name, I can fortunately point him out, for here he comes."

"Lieutenant Forsyth, did you meet this gentleman on the road this morning?" asked the general in a freezing tone, as the officer entered the room and paused in surprise.

"I believe I did," stammered the lieutenant.

"Well, sir, you insulted a brave officer of your own army, and, if you had had a spark of feeling in your heart you would have listened to him even if he had proved to be what he appears, — a Confederate soldier. Lieutenant Forsyth, you will report at once to your regiment for duty: you can no longer serve on my staff."

" But, general " —

" Enough: I want no such aides as you about me," said General Stahl.

Lieutenant Forsyth touched his cap in silence, and left the room, overcome by his disgrace.

" And now, Mr. Wilmot," continued the general in a pleasanter tone, " I have great pleasure in releasing you from further annoyance. Major Phillips, our surgeon here, will see your wounds dressed; and I know your brother officers will take pleasure in seeing you equipped in the uniform of your rank. It will never do to let you go to Washington in that guise."

" Come, Wilmot," said Osborne gleefully: " I'll take you in charge for old Harding's sake, who thinks you dead and buried. Lord! won't he be surprised when he hears that you are so much alive!— May I take the captain with me, general?"

" Certainly; and I will send you a pass, captain, in time for the afternoon train;" and the general cordially grasped my hand as I withdrew.

I was once more free!

" Upon my word, Osborne," said I an hour or two afterwards, as we stood on the railroad-platform, waiting for the train, " you turn up in the most unexpected places. How came you in this out-of-the-way corner?"

" It's going to be a very important corner before long," replied Osborne, " or you wouldn't see me here. I can not tell you all I know, for the War Department holds a tight rein over us correspondents; but this I can say,— the Shenandoah is destined to be famous before the end of the summer."

" You can not mean that Lee is going to attempt another invasion?"

" Well, you are not far out in your guess; but, if Lee does attempt it, he is going to get a worse licking than ever."

" Where is the Army of the Potomac now?"

" Upon my word, Wilmot, it's positively refreshing to have

you ask such a question; though of course you can not know. Why, my boy, Grant has driven Lee all the way back to McClellan's old ground, and has carried the army across the James River, where he is besieging the Confederates in front of Petersburg."

"That seems amazing to me, for I have heard nothing except that our army had sustained defeat after defeat," said I.

"Of course: that's what all our returned prisoners say. Well, old fellow, here is the train."

"Good-by, Osborne: you are my good genius."

"There's many a general who wears the silver star can say the same," laughed the correspondent. "We newspaper men make more generals than we break."

The whistle of the impatient locomotive warned us that it was time to part: so with a warm grasp of the hand I left my friend behind me, and entered on another lease of hospital-life at Annapolis.

CHAPTER XXXIII.

BY MINE AND SAP.

"The cannons have their bowels full of wrath;
 And ready mounted are they, to spit forth."

AVING failed to break Lee's Wilderness line on opening the campaign of 1864, Grant, by a clever flank movement towards his left, gave battle at Spottsylvania; only to find the Confederate leader stubbornly confronting his new position. These tactics were repeated again and again, and a series of battles ensued until the armies met on the North Anna River; where Lee gave check, compelling Grant to cross the Pamunkey River, and traverse McClellan's scene of operations. The desperate and bloody battle at Cold Harbor resulted in the Federal army crossing the James River, and joining the forces under Butler. Holding the interior line, Lee stopped Grant at Petersburg by a strong line of intrenchments, compelling the latter to enter on a siege. Though the overland campaign had terribly crippled the Confederate army, their general had shown his military genius by holding on to Richmond, always the strategic point of attack. The loss of life on both sides had been awful; for thousands upon thousands of brave men lay, buried and unburied, amid the forests through which the contending armies had struggled and fought.

In July, Lee made his favorite move on Washington in hopes of shaking off Grant; but the latter met the Confederate col-

umn in the Shenandoah Valley by sending another under Sheridan, who crushed Early, and destroyed the wheat-crop upon
which the latter depended to feed his troops.

Meanwhile, Sherman had assumed the offensive, and, defeating Johnston by turning his flank, marched straight for the
city of Atlanta, Georgia; capturing the place despite the efforts
of Hood, who had succeeded Johnston in command of that
portion of the Confederate forces.

Such was the situation of affairs in the field when one Octo-
ber morning I again approached the confines of the Army of
the Potomac.

My wounds had been slow in healing, so I had passed the
summer months in hospital. Permission to join my regiment
was given at last, and I joyfully abandoned the quiet hospital-
life for the excitement to be found in campaigning.

Leaving Washington by steamer, I reached Fortress Monroe
the following morning, and ascending the James River, arrived
at City Point during the afternoon. All the way up the James
we found the river alive with steam and sailing craft, their
number increasing as we proceeded. At last we turned a sudden bend in the river, and I caught a glimpse of the army's
base of supplies. Above and below the line of rude wharves,
along the left bank of the muddy stream, four or five gunboats
lay at anchor; while around them river and ocean steamers
were moving to and fro, as they sought to discharge their
freights of food and ammunition, or retired for fresh cargoes.
Here and there clusters of schooners, their broad sails all
housed and furled, were being towed round the bend by tugs
puffing noisily over their tasks. Nestling under the bluffs
were long lines of railroad-cars; and the shriek of a locomotive-whistle pierced the ear as a train moved slowly from
behind the immense storehouses, and passed out of sight
through a wide cutting. The bluffs were crowned by canvas
towns, which, even at that distance, I knew to be the sutler's
domain. On the extreme end of the point, some distance above

the wharves, stood a tall pole, from the top of which floated a huge garrison-flag; and under it a cluster of huts.

"What does that flag mean?" I asked a burly sutler who was exchanging signals with a friend on the cliff we were now approaching.

"Grant's headquarters," was the laconic response. "Guess this is your first visit here, seeing you didn't know Grant's camp."

"Yes," I replied: "I've been in hospital ever since the Wilderness."

"So! why, I have lost and made a fortune since then. Had mighty bad luck at the White House: army moved too quick," said the sutler half in soliloquy. "Well, you'll find it mighty queer work here, among the ditches and bomb-proofs, I can tell you."

I nodded in silence, having no sympathy with the sutler's gains or losses. A few minutes after, the steamer touched the wharf, and I was on shore.

"Oh! your corps is away in the extreme left of the line," said an officer I had approached for information. "Just get on top of the first car you come to, and go as far as they will take you."

Before I could return thanks for this concise and lucid explanation, an officer in the uniform of my own regiment pushed through the crowd. It was my old friend Dennis.

"An' hev ye come at last? Bedad, it's mesilf that's glad to see ye," was his salutation, as he threw his arms around me.

"How is the regiment? Is the colonel well?" I asked.

"The boys are all well, those of 'em that's left; and won't the colonel be deloighted to see ye!"

"Not more so than I will. But, Dennis, when did you get your commission? Colonel Harding did not mention it in his letters."

"That was to be a surproise to ye. It was only last week that I got the sthrap on my shoulder, an' moighty quare it feels even now. But the colonel said I desarved it; so here I am wid a gould laced cap and sword, loike yersilf."

"I am delighted, Dennis. You were luckier than I in getting back to the regiment. When was it?"

"Jist afther Could Harbor, which I wasn't sorry to miss. Ah, Frank! whin you parted from me in that hot corner in the Wildherness, an' I saw ye runnin' to catch up wid the b'yes, I felt like cryin' because I wasn't wid ye. But I knew it was no use, so started back. An' whin I heard ye had been killed, me heart was broke intoirely. But whin the papers at Alexandria said that ye hadn't bin dead at all, but was aloive and kickin', why, I got well right off, and kem out for another bit of the shindy. Hev ye any baggage?"

"Only this valise," I replied, smiling at the rapidity with which Dennis jumped from one subject to another.

"Well, we mustn't sthand here talkin' all day, or we'll miss the train;" and Dennis began elbowing his way through the crowd still gathered on the landing-stage.

Following him, I clambered to the roof of a car; and we were soon moving towards that ever-receding line, "the front." At Washington I heard a passenger, bound for Fortress Monroe, remark to a friend on the dock that he was going to the front. At the Fortress, people spoke of City Point as the front; and now I was leaving the Point itself in search of the mysterious line; only to learn, on reaching my quarters, that the picket-trenches were the only front the soldiers now recognized.

The trip from City Point to Warren Station, a distance of eleven miles, was peculiarly interesting to me. Scarcely had our train emerged from the deep cut in the cliff, when Dennis pointed to a long line of fresh earth on our right about a mile away.

"Do ye see thim breastworks, Frank?" said he.

"Yes. What of them?"

"Well, that's the first trenches the b'yes dug, after crossin' the river; and now there's more than fifty miles of 'em."

"Fifty miles!" said I in surprise. "Why, you said our corps was only thirteen miles from the Point."

"An' it isn't any more. Ye forgit the approaches, and the parallels, and the forts, and the curtains, and the divil knows what all. Shure, they're loike burrows in a rabbit-warren."

The intrenchments were not the only evidence of the presence of our army, for the ground was bare. Not a rail or a post remained to mark the fields; and every tree and shrub for miles around had been swept away to supply timber for the bomb-proofs, or fuel for fires. Even shade-trees had been sacrificed, a broad expanse of blackened stumps alone indicating where woods and groves had once gladdened the landscape.

Passing over a high trestle of rough poles, we crossed a wide ravine, through which trickled a dirty-looking creek; and then we dashed on over the undulating surface of the land. Unlike most railroads I had seen, there was no attempt made here to grade the track: so the train rose and fell in its progress like a ship rolling on the billows of the sea. The jolting over the rudely laid rails was terrific, making it difficult to retain our seats as the cars rocked to and fro beneath us. Reaching Meade Station, near the center of the siege-line, we ran quite close to the fortifications, and I saw a brigade at drill in a wide hollow.

"What road is this?" said I to Dennis as we passed an old-fashioned roadway, the wide ditches and ragged hedges betraying its character.

"The Jerusalem plank," replied Dennis. "Though the planks hev gone into the breastworks long ago. That big fort down there beyant is Fort Hell. Begorra! it's well named."

Following Dennis's finger with my eye, I saw a great mound of earth rising like a gigantic ant-hill. As I looked, a puff of smoke rose above the fort, and a deafening detonation filled the air.

"Be jabers! an' they're at it agin!" exclaimed my companion. "It's not often they're quiet down there."

The puff of smoke grew larger, and the sound of other cannon came to my ears; while more distant reports showed that the Confederates were replying. The rapidly moving train, however, did not permit our seeing the result of the artillery duel.

"I wonder if we are to get a shot ourselves," said Dennis, as he peered attentively towards the line.

"Why, can they fire at the trains?"

"Troth, an' they can; and, what's more, they do — bad 'cess to them! A bit furdher on, the train runs through a ditch because of the murdhering shells."

As if to emphasize Dennis's words, a shell at that moment went shrieking over our heads.

"Hurroo! Didn't I tell ye? It's lucky we're moving, or they moight be putting a shell into the ammynition."

"Ammunition! Is there any on board this train?" I exclaimed, startled at the suggestion.

"Ye may well say that," responded Dennis coolly. "Shure, the car we're sittin' on is crammed to the muzzle wid powdher. If a shell hits it, we'll all be blown to the moon."

Laughing at Dennis's grim humor, I clung to my seat as the train rushed into a cutting; the ridge of earth thrown up being intended as a protection, the necessity therefor being shown by a shattered locomotive lying a little distance off. As we plunged into the ditch, — for it was nothing more, — with a lurch that threatened to sweep us all from the roof, both Dennis and I were suddenly sprinkled with a shower of sand.

"Arrah! an' wasn't that close quarthers?" exclaimed Lieutenant Malone, shaking himself. "How d'ye loike that?"

"Why, it was only a little dirt blown from the bank," I replied contentedly.

"Blown from the bank? You're right, me b'ye; but it was not the wind, but a shell that struck there above us. Shure, they've got the range beautifully."

"Upon my word, Dennis, this is exciting traveling!"

"Isn't it? I thought ye'd loike it," replied Dennis confidently.
"But then it is nothin' whin ye git used to it, as the eel said
whin he was bein' skinned."

So this was siege-life! How different from the long and
rapid marches, the picket-posts on river-banks and in shady

GOING TO CAMP UNDER FIRE.

woods, or the skirmishes and battles in field and forest! Compelled to burrow like moles in the ground, the troops were
exposed to shell and shot by day and night. The angry bark
of mortars, and the sullen boom of siege-cannon, were ever in
the ear; the reverberating thunder of the heavier ordnance
being only enlivened by the rattle of musketry as the pickets
were roused into sudden action. Even as I mused over the
change, the confused sounds of the never-ending conflict

deafened me ; and it was a relief to find the train leaving the
vicinity of the main line.

We were now on comparatively new ground ; for the woods
were as yet untouched, and the hedges more trim and even in
their outlines. Large bodies of troops lay here encamped,
evidently in reserve. Next we came to the camp of the
cavalry division ; and in a few minutes more the train dashed
through a sea of army-wagons, and halted at a long platform.

"This is Warren Station, and yonder is our amby-lance," said
Dennis, scrambling down from the car.

Descending from my perch on the roof, with stiffened limbs,
I was an hour afterward in our regimental camp.

My brother officers received me warmly, but there were only
five or six of those who entered the charge with me at the
Wilderness. Among the new faces, I recognized several sergeants who had earned promotions during my absence. To my
surprise, they greeted me by the title of Major !

"Ye see, Frank, I wasn't to tell ye," said Dennis in answer
to my question. "Colonel Harding intended it as a surprise."

But at what a cost had I attained my rank ! All my seniors
at the beginning of the campaign were now either dead, or
disabled for life. Such are the chances and vicissitudes of war.

CHAPTER XXXIV.

IN FORT AND FIELD.

"A scaly gauntlet now, with points of steel,
  Must glove this hand."

ERY long absence now made siege-life any thing but tedious to me, however monotonous it might be to my comrades. Though I could no longer volunteer for picket-duty, my rank gave me frequent command of our brigade-line; and I never wearied of the excitement to be found in the advanced trenches. Indeed, I often amused myself, while off duty, by visiting the center; and passed many a night in the forts, watching huge bell-mouthed mortars send ten-inch shells into the enemy's works, or listening to the fierce cross-fire of solid shot as it played across the front of our fort from neighboring redoubts, the active pickets in the trenches below adding to the din by their sharp and continuous volleys, the men lying enveloped in the smoke of our guns. The Confederate fortifications would soon be concealed by heavy banks of smoke, through which vivid flashes constantly played, as the gunners replied to our iron hail. Now and then a missile would go whizzing over our heads, or come crashing through the earthwork, scattering gravel and sand in all directions. A groan often betrayed the effect of these visitors, and two or three men would go crawling to the rear in search of a surgeon. Hour after hour would slip away, yet the tremendous roar and rattle seldom ceased until cannon and mortar grew too hot to handle. Then piece after piece would gradually slacken its fire, and finally become mute, the picket-firing being checked, and a portentous silence falling upon the scene. Then, as the white smoke lifted from parapet and trench, the outlines of the opposing lines became once more visible, and the sun's rays again shone over the marred and shattered landscape.

These bombardments, though exciting and thrilling enough in the sunshine, were exceeded in their awful grandeur when witnessed in the night. Standing by the side of a silent Parrott gun, whose huge dimensions towered above my head, I leaned with Dennis one evening over the parapet, gazing with curious eyes on the combat. The flashes of the opposing cannon were so frequent that the outlying fortifications on both sides of the struggle were clearly visible in the darkness; while narrow ribbons of fire ran fitfully up and down the advanced trenches, like oil burning on water, as the opposing pickets maintained an angry, incessant fusillade on each other. The ground beneath my feet actually trembled under the repeated concussions; until it seemed as if I were standing on the brink of a volcano, instead of watching a deadly artillery duel between two great armies.

Fascinated by the spectacle enacted before my eyes, and awed by the awful detonations of the heavy siege-guns, the sharp rattle of musketry, or the dull reverberations of bursting bombs, I forgot the danger of the moment until recalled to my senses by a monster shell tumbling into the traverse we occupied. As the blazing bomb fizzed and sputtered at my feet, Dennis seized my arm, and dragged me into the next compartment. He was not a moment too soon; for, as we gained the other side of the wall of gabions and sand-bags, the missile exploded.

"Moses in the bulrushes! but that was touch an' go," exclaimed Dennis, as we instinctively shrank from the bits of iron whistling over our heads. "Arrah, Frank! why will ye timpt Providence in this way? It's bad enough to take our turn on the line when it comes, but coming here whin we moight be lyin' shnug in the bomb-proofs isn't the thing at all."

"If you don't like it, why did you insist on coming with me?" said I.

"Why did I? Why, because ye couldn't take care o' yersilf alone, though ye *are* a major. But it's small thanks I get for comin', anyway."

"Come, come, Dennis: you know I am glad to have you by my side."

"Then why foind fault wid me?"

Touched by my comrade's devotion, I grasped his honest hand in silence, as we continued to watch the progress of the midnight engagement.

The whole of our line was now engaged; and the roar of the guns deepened as the increased torrent of shot and shell poured across the ground between us and the enemy, until we knew that fully five hundred pieces of artillery were in action. Looking up and down our line, I could see luminous clouds of smoke rising, and enveloping the land; the flashes from the guns giving an unearthly light to the scene, while bursting shells in mid-air added to the glare. For hours did this ceaseless cannonading continue, only slackening when the first faint streaks of daylight appeared in the east. Then, and then only, did the exhausted artillerists pause in their horrid work, and the thunder perceptibly lessened in volume as the sun reddened the horizon.

Rousing Dennis, — for he had been quietly sleeping at my side for over an hour, — we retraced our steps to our camp; finding on our arrival that orders had been issued for the corps to go on a reconnoissance towards the Meherrin River.

All was now bustle and excitement, for the prospect of a change from siege-duty to that of open campaigning was a delightful prospect to both officers and men. Knapsacks were speedily packed, extra ammunition served out, and ten days' rations of hard-bread, coffee, and sugar, safely stored away in the haversacks; shelter-tents were rolled up, pack-horses laden with officers' stores, and a long train of wagons stood in park, ready for the road. By ten o'clock all was in readiness; and at the sound of our bugles the corps marched to the rear, towards the Jerusalem road, a strong body of cavalry covering the advance of our column.

Amid the bustle of our preparations, I received a summons from General Fletcher to join his staff, so rode gayly forward to the head of our brigade. The day was bright and clear; the December frost being just sufficient to keep the road in good order, and lessen the fatigue of the men as they marched forward under their heavy loads of clothing and food. As we passed through the woods, and lost sight of the intrenchments before the beleaguered city of Petersburg, squirrels scampered up the trees and chattered noisily at our intrusion, while a few belated birds flitted among the branches. A march of six miles brought us to the side of a stream; and, going into bivouac under the trees, we slept as only tired soldiers can.

"General Fletcher," said an aide from the corps-staff, as we began the march at sunrise the next morning, "General Ayres requests you to send an officer down that road, to see that the stragglers get no apple-jack."

"Major Wilmot, will you please ride down, and see that the general's orders are obeyed?" said the brigadier, as he returned the aide's salute.

Lifting my cap in acknowledgment, I galloped off. About a mile down the road I came to a clearing, with an old-fashioned Virginia mansion in its midst. Around the house were several infantry soldiers, who prowled about evidently in search of something to carry off. At the sound of my horse's feet they began scattering. Riding through the gate, I perceived an elderly man and two women on the veranda.

"Come, men, get back to your regiments!" I shouted to the stragglers. "What are you doing here?"

"They are looking for apple-jack," said the planter; "an' I've bin a-telling 'em they'll not find any here."

"I am glad of it," was my reply, as I watched the men sullenly move off towards the road over which the corps was moving.

"Will you step in, sir, and have some breakfast?" said the youngest of the two women, a scarlet jacket setting off her pretty figure to great advantage; a fact she seemed to fully appreciate, judging by her coquettish glances.

"Thank you, miss. Breakfast in times like these is not to be despised or refused."

Entering the house, I was soon enjoying a bountiful meal, my entertainers being very grateful to me for driving away the stragglers. They were naturally curious as to the meaning of our movement, it being the first time so large a body of troops had passed that way; but I was almost as ignorant as themselves, so could give them very little information. As I rose from the table, we were startled by the sound of horsemen. Fearing a trap, I ran to the door, to find the lawn in possession of a troop of Federal cavalry.

"Halloa, major! What are you doing here all alone?" exclaimed the officer in command.

"Driving up stragglers," I replied. "May I ask your errand?"

"Searching for apple-jack."

"You will find none here. This old gentleman assures me he has none," said I.

"I'm not so sure of that," replied the lieutenant. "Some of you men go into the cellar and look."

Two or three obeyed, but soon returned with the information that they could find no liquor.

"Lucky for them," said the officer. "If we had found apple-jack, it would have been spilled on the grass; but we mustn't go empty-handed."

"Why, what else do you want?" I asked, wondering what he meant.

"Something to eat, to be sure. Sergeant, what is that over there?" and the officer pointed to a rude table of split logs in the rear yard.

"Them's my hogs, sir," said the old man: "we killed 'em last night."

"Pork, eh! Just the thing."

"Surely you will not rob these people of their provisions?" said I indignantly.

FORAGING ON THE ENEMY.

"You just wait and see," he replied nonchalantly, as he nodded to his men.

They were quick to take the hint, and running eagerly to the pile of hams and shoulders soon had them scattered and fastened to their saddles.

"Come, major, you had better ride with us: these woods are getting dangerous," said the lieutenant, as he gave his men the order to mount.

Disgusted at the barefaced robbery I had witnessed but could not prevent, I made my acknowledgments to my hosts, leaped into my saddle, and rode after the detachment, though I did not soon forget the indignation visible on the faces of those who had treated me so hospitably.

The movement we had undertaken occupied ten days; the infantry finding nothing to do but listen to the sharp skirmishing of the cavalry in front, until we reached the river and the line of the Weldon Railroad. After destroying a couple of bridges, we next tore up the track for a distance of twenty miles, and warped the rails by placing them on piles of blazing ties. It was hot and suffocating work though, for the smoke from the countless fires filled the woods and parched our throats.

As night fell on the second day after this work of demolition and destruction had begun, I repaired to brigade headquarters, tired and hungry by my exertions; being glad to find, on my arrival, that the general and staff were beginning supper.

"Why, there's Osborne!" exclaimed Lieutenant Jenkins as the clatter of knives and forks commenced: "I'll call him over. He'll get his supper, and we'll get the news."

"Sit down, Mr. Osborne," said General Fletcher, as the correspondent rode up in response to Jenkins's hail. "I presume you are hungry like the rest of us."

"Hunger is no word for it, general," replied Osborne. "I'm famished, for I have eaten nothing but a few biscuits since breakfast."

"What's going on down by the river?" asked one of the staff. "I heard heavy firing about noon."

"Oh! Wilson made a dash across with a few regiments, and so took the bridge," replied Osborne. "It's a whopper, and will make a mighty big blaze to-night. After that is gone, the railroad will be entirely useless to Lee. We shall probably start back some time to-morrow."

The meal over, we stretched ourselves before the great fire built by the orderlies, and smoking our pipes chatted over the events of the campaign.

"Osborne, what was that you had tied to your saddle when you rode up?" asked young Jenkins.

"Only half a dozen chickens," replied the correspondent, with a laugh.

"Foraging, eh?" remarked General Fletcher. "Don't you know foraging is strictly forbidden, except to the cavalry?"

"Oh, yes! I know," indolently responded Osborne. "That was just what General Warren asked me down the road."

"And what did you say to him?" asked the general with a smile of amusement on his face.

"Well, you see, general," said Osborne, refilling his brier-wood pipe, "I went down to the bridge where the cavalry were fighting, just to see if I couldn't find something pictur-esque to put into my dispatches, and found a lot of cavalry-men at a house near by, chasing chickens. One of the men recognized me, and offered me some of the fowls; which I of course accepted, and tied to my saddle, at the same time giving the fellow a dollar to buy tobacco with. On riding back, who should I see but General Warren, standing on a stump by the side of the road, watching the cavalry skirmish on the other side of the river! Just as I was passing him, the confounded chickens gave a flutter, and so frightened my horse that he wheeled clean round and exposed my plunder."

"You were nicely caught, Charley," said the brigade surgeon.

"Wasn't I? Well, the general of course wanted to know where I got them. Remembering the dollar, I boldly said I had bought and paid for them. General Warren shook his head as if he doubted my assertion, but waved his hand in dismissal, and continued his observations of the movement in front. So I took the hint, and rode on."

"Well, you got out of the scrape rather luckily," said Major Curtis, the adjutant-general, when we had ceased laughing over the incident. "You newspaper men have fine times of it, rid-ing all over the country just as you please. I often envy you correspondents, for the life must be an easy one."

" Not so easy as you fellows imagine," replied Osborne: "we run many a danger you do not dream of."

" Of course you go under fire now and then," said Major Curtis, " or you couldn't describe the battles as you do. But what I mean is, that you have so much freedom."

" Queer freedom," retorted the correspondent disdainfully. " I don't deny the life has its attractions and fascinations. But when a battle is over your work is done, and you can rest; while the hardest part of mine commences, for then we must write our descriptions, and frequently risk our lives in getting to the rear in order to send them off. Why, do you know, I saw the battle of Winchester under Sheridan in the Shenandoah Valley, and your fight at Peebles's farm, in front of Petersburg, in the same week."

" Oh! come, now, Osborne. Two battles in two different armies in one week," said Major Curtis incredulously, — " isn't that a little steep?"

" Not at all. But it's a pretty long story: perhaps you would not care to hear it."

" Tell it, by all means, Mr. Osborne," said the general: " I am sure it will prove interesting."

Thus encouraged, Osborne laid aside his pipe, stretched himself into a more comfortable position on his blanket, and proceeded to tell the story which will be found in my next chapter.

CHAPTER XXXV.

THE CORRESPONDENT'S STORY.

"The keen spirit
Seizes the prompt occasion, — makes the thought
Start into instant service."

T HE major over there knows that I spent several weeks last summer in the Valley of the Shenandoah. At the time of which I speak, Sheridan and Early had been for several weeks marching up and down after one another; and the two armies were facing each other near Mount Summit. Our troops had thrown up a line of breastworks just beyond Charlestown, — where old John Brown was hung, you know. Every thing was provokingly quiet and uninteresting, viewed from a correspondent's standpoint. The seat of war seemed to have drifted away from that section, and I began to think there would be no more fighting in the Valley.

Others besides myself believed that Sheridan's scope of offensive operations was at an end; for my chief, in the office, ordered me to proceed to the lines before Petersburg. I gladly obeyed, and, reaching Washington in due time, applied for a pass to City Point.

I need not remind any of you that red-tape is a staple article at the capital, so I was not surprised at being told that the pass would not be ready for a day or two. As that probably meant a week, I decided to visit some friends in Baltimore.

On Sunday morning, the memorable 18th of September, as I was sitting on the piazza of Barnum's Hotel, I was handed the following telegram : —

"HARPER'S FERRY, VA., Sept. 18, 1864.
" *To* CHARLES OSBORNE, *Correspondent.*
" Your horse is dead. Will get you another. Will need two hundred dollars. "STEVE."

This, of course, was a message in cipher. It had been sent by an old friend of mine, a staff-officer on duty at the Ferry. Translated by the code we had arranged for such emergencies, it conveyed to me the following information : —

"Every thing is in motion here and at the front. A battle is imminent. I think it will be a decisive one. Come up at once."

It was all very well for Major Post to say, "come up;" but there was no train, it being Sunday, and I knew that Sheridan would not wait an hour, let alone a day, for all the correspondents in the country. It was quite evident to my mind, as I sat there twiddling the telegram in my fingers, that the movement on foot must be an important one ; for, if my staff friend thought so, he had good solid grounds for his opinions. Besides, I remembered that Grant had visited Sheridan a few days before, and probably planned it with him.

But there I sat, over a hundred miles from the scene of operations, and no train before the morning. If Sheridan was already moving, as the dispatch indicated, he would probably fight the next day; and unless I reached the field before noon I could do nothing. It was apparently a hopeless case.

All at once I began to see daylight, and some hopes of success.

I must first tell you that in the early part of the summer, when Hunter was skedaddling towards the Ferry, after one of his brief skirmishes, I was accidentally able to render a good bit of service to the Baltimore and Ohio Railroad.

I had left Hunter's main force, and succeeded in reaching Harper's Ferry before it was known there that he was falling back. On arriving at the railroad-platform, I noticed that there were but few cars lying under the hill, and on inquiry learned that two or three freight-trains had gone up to Martinsburg a few hours before. Nobody at the Ferry seemed to be aware that Hunter's flank had been turned; but I knew that the enemy were marching direct for Martinsburg, if they had not already entered the town. I therefore decided on a bold stroke.

You see, I realized that if the Confederates burned the railroad-bridge just below Martinsburg, as they had often done before, these trains would be captured and destroyed. Entering the telegraph-office, I wrote a message to the station-master, ordering him to start down all the locomotives and cars in his hands, at the same time telling him of his danger.

The astonished operator hesitated at first to accept my dispatch, knowing very well that I had no authority on the road; but on my assuring him that there was no time to lose, the message was soon flashed to its destination.

It did not go a moment too soon. In less than ten minutes after my warning arrived, locomotive after locomotive rattled down the road towards the Ferry.

The three trains crossed the bridge in safety. It was a narrow escape, though; for as the station-master stood on the rear platform of the last train, and saw the timbers of the bridge glide under his feet, the sharp rattle of musketry broke on his ear, a few of the bullets crashing through the windows of the car at his back. The bridge was actually in flames before the trains were out of sight: so there was great glee among the railroad-officials, over the escape of their rolling-stock.

When Mr. Smith, the master of transportation, learned how the trains had been warned by me, he promised me any facility he could extend in the future, as a return for the service.

So, as I sat fumbling the provost-marshal's cipher message, I remembered this promise, and at once decided to avail myself of it.

Taking a cab, I started in search of Mr. Smith, finding him at church, where I explained the situation, and my anxiety to reach the valley that day.

"You shall have a locomotive, Osborne," said he. "Come! drive me over to the depot."

Half an hour after, I was seated in the cab of an engine, whirling over the rails for my destination. It was an exciting ride; for there were, of course, no stoppages. As we passed station after station, dashed over bridge after bridge, or went whizzing through tunnel after tunnel, I enjoyed the speed amazingly, and began believing that luck was again on my side.

The wrecked bridge below Martinsburg was reached just as the sun was dropping behind the mountains; and I gleefully leaped from the cab, bidding my friend the engineer a hearty good-by as I did so.

Soon after passing Harper's Ferry, we had heard frequent cannonading; a fact which made it evident to my mind that fighting was going on somewhere in the Valley above. As mile after mile was gained above the Ferry, these guns sounded louder and louder, their reverberations being at times so distinct, that the engineer more than once laid his hand on the lever and looked inquiringly into my face. I re-assured him by saying that the cannonading seemed near, because the guns were being fired at the foot of the mountains; consequently we were in no danger. But I noticed, that, as soon as Mr. Engineer had fairly got rid of his passenger, he lost no time in retracing his iron path to the Ferry.

I was now on foot, entirely alone, with only a navy revolver in my belt, and a small flask of brandy in one of my blouse-pockets. But I was near the battle-ground: that was quite certain, and it was better than being idle and helpless in Balti more. I might accomplish something where I was: in the city I could do nothing.

Walking quietly up the road in that delicious light that comes in the Shenandoah between the hours of sunset and darkness, I soon reached the town. The place was almost empty, some half dozen intoxicated cavalrymen being the only signs of Federal occupation.

Like humpbacked Richard in the play, I would have given at that moment whatever kingdom I possessed, for a horse: the question was, where to get the animal.

Meeting a trooper who had been making too free with apple-jack, I purchased his horse for fifty dollars, and was soon after galloping over the turnpike towards the scene of hostilities.

By the time I had got clear of the town, the rays of sunset had entirely disappeared, and the cannonading had slackened considerably; only an occasional gun uttering its sullen roar as the shades of evening grew deeper.

Forward I rode, until the night darkened my path; the silence broken only by the reverberations of my horse's hoofs on the macadamized road; through woods that seemed doubly dark in the uncertain starlight, past fields stripped of their fences, and across brooks and creeks the possession of which had been so often contested during the summer: on I rode until my eyes were at length gladdened by the sight of the cavalry watch-fires as they occupied the right of Sheridan's line.

Riding into General Custer's headquarters soon after day-break, I leaped from my horse; the poor brute being utterly broken down by the severity of his journey. Custer, the good-hearted fellow he always is, furnished me with a fresh horse from his train, and over a good breakfast gave me a clear and graphic description of the movements during the previous day. It had been a cavalry engagement entirely, and had been forced on the enemy for the purpose of turning his flank in anticipation of a more decided and complete assault along the entire line. I had arrived just in time; for already Sheridan had his three corps of infantry moving, and there was every prospect of a desperate battle being fought before the day was over.

During the whole of that day, I saw for myself the progress of the battle which, to use Sheridan's own words, " sent Early whirling through Winchester." I witnessed the several desperate charges made during the afternoon by the Sixth and Nineteenth Corps, and was within a stone's-throw of General Russell when that cannon-ball carried away his head. I was present at the headlong dash made by the cavalry, under Merritt and Custer, as they were hurled by Sheridan like an avalanche on the enemy's wings ; and I watched " Little Phil " himself as he coolly directed the movements of his troops, and won the field which gave him renown and promotion. In fact, I saw all there was to see, and was satisfied.

When the army entered Winchester, and pushed on in pursuit, it was almost nightfall. Finding that Early's forces were in rapid retreat, I knew that the next thing for me to do was to get to a telegraph-wire, and so tell my exciting and wonderful story.

The scene at the little stone bridge just outside the town of Winchester was, at that moment, a peculiarly striking and interesting one. The moon was rising over the mountains, their dark shadows lying in long stretches across the valley, while numerous camp-fires in the fields revealed the trains belonging to the Federal army. The narrow streets of the little city were thronged by heavy columns of infantry, as they followed our cavalry already far in the advance ; the rough cobble-stone pavements resounding now and then with the low rumble of artillery, as battery after battery went forward to some designated position beyond the town. It was indeed a thrilling scene of war, for my ears were still ringing with the roar of cannon and the rattle of small-arms. As I sat there on my horse, watching the ambulances moving in with the wounded, I again heard, in fancy, the cheers of the infantry as they rushed into the charge, saw the bright flash of the sabers as they kissed the sunlight, the flutter of the gay pennons as the cavalry made their remorseless descent upon Early's discomfited lines.

Hearing all these sounds in imagination, and calling to mind again the exciting episodes of the battle, my brain was still busy with plans how to return safely to the line of communication with the East.

Suddenly the sharp clatter of horses' feet reverberated in

GOING TO THE REAR WITH DISPATCHES.

the night air, and I saw a small detachment of cavalry coming over the bridge. As it passed me I inquired its destination.

"Going to the rear with dispatches," was the brief reply.

Here was my opportunity at last. Spurring forward, I soon explained my wishes to the lieutenant, when he cordially invited me to accompany him.

Hour after hour our little body of horsemen cantered over the dirt-road, on our way to Berryville; which village we reached soon after midnight. Here we found the supply-trains, securely parked, waiting for the dawn, to take the road up the Valley. The straggling little town was crammed with teamsters; and as usual, they were full of wild rumors and hidden dangers. They told us of midnight assassinations by bushwhackers, and desultory attacks on their flanks by Mosby and his men. In fact, every man we met was afraid of his own shadow.

To my disgust, the escort lieutenant became infected by these fears, and decided to remain in bivouac until daylight.

This, of course, did not suit my book at all; for I knew, that, unless I reached the Ferry in time for the regular train for Baltimore, all my previous hard work would be lost. I therefore announced my intention of riding on alone. Tightening the girth of my saddle, and carefully reloading my revolver, I set out on my lonely and somewhat dangerous ride.

The distance from Berryville to Harper's Ferry was too long and hazardous for me to attempt: so I struck out to the left at the fork of the roads below the town, in the direction of Martinsburg.

I had been fortunate, during the afternoon, in being able to exchange the animal given me by General Custer for one I caught while it was quietly grazing on the battle-field, among the corpses strewn over the plain: so I knew I could make good time.

The moon was now shining bright and clear, so the road lay distinctly defined before me. But I was naturally nervous through want of sleep, and I knew any clump of bushes by the roadside might conceal a bushwhacker. So on I cantered until daylight came, when my horse broke into a gallop, and I soon reached Martinsburg.

Walking down to the trestle bridge, I found the railroad-construction party busily at work. Being provided with an order from Mr. Smith, I presented the document to the chief of the party, and requested him to send me down the road to the Ferry. As the order was an imperative one, my demand was obeyed, and I was soon enjoying another rapid ride on a locomotive.

I caught the Baltimore train in good time; and, as I stepped on board, no one dreamed that I had come so rapidly from the battle all knew had been fought somewhere up the Valley. Sitting in the train, I collected my thoughts, and arranged the few notes I had taken. I had now been without sleep ever since Sunday morning, had passed two nights and one entire day on horseback, and here on Tuesday afternoon was on my way to Washington with full details of an important and glorious victory.

I reached Washington that evening, and for over three hours lay on a couch, dictating my description of the engagement. I was so exhausted by fatigue, it was impossible for me to write: so we employed stenographers. Page after page these nimble writers took down my words, and page after page my story was sent over the wires to our newspaper, and read by thousands over their breakfast-table the following morning.

Midnight came as the task was ended; and I was preparing for a good long sleep, when, to my surprise, a fresh demand was made upon me. The fact of my arrival so soon after the battle had been noised about, for in Washington such news flies fast; and a polite message had come from the President, requesting me to visit him before retiring. Such a request could not be ignored: so I jumped into a carriage, and was driven to the White House. On my arrival, I found Mr. Lincoln, with Secretaries Seward and Stanton, waiting for me.

"We are very sorry, sir, to put you to so much trouble," said Mr. Lincoln; "but the fact is, Mr. Correspondent, we are anxious to learn the details of General Sheridan's victory. We can not wait for your printed story. You know so much, and we so little, I thought you might be willing to tell us your news in person."

"I shall be only too happy, sir, to tell you what I have seen in the Valley," I replied. "But I supposed General Sheridan's dispatches had arrived long before this: he had the wire at Harper's Ferry, a privilege I was denied."

"Yes: we received Sheridan's report some hours ago," said Mr. Stanton; "but, though eminently satisfactory in stating the general results, his dispatch is so brief and curt, it gives us no adequate idea of the scope of the fight."

"Well, gentlemen," said I, "I will do my best. Please

order me a few sheets of paper, and some colored pencils, for rough maps of the different movements."

For two long hours I sat at a table, all alone with the three principal officers of the government, telling a simple story of a battle, fought only a few hours before, one hundred miles away. As I drew my maps, and related how the engagement had been pushed here, and given up there; how the heavy mass of infantry in the center had moved steadily forward in the face of a galling fire; how the cavalry had finally given the *coup de grâce* by swift, resistless charges on the enemy's flanks; how Russell had died, and Sheridan acted, — I felt all the enthusiasm of the fight again come over me; and my three auditors participated in my excitement.

The contrast presented by these three distinguished men, as I talked, was a striking one. Lincoln's homely but expressive features seemed to lighten up as he listened to my description of some exciting scene. He appeared to see the awful vortex of death and flame, as the Nineteenth Corps moved into it to relieve the pressure on the Sixth. His lips parted, and he straightened his tall form, when I spoke of the rapidity of the artillery fire, and the flash of the bright sabers of the cavalry drawn in the sunshine. He was, for the moment, on the ground itself; and his mind ran ahead of my words, and saw with his own eyes the entire scene of operations. Seward was fully as much interested and carried away as his chief, though he manfested it in a totally different way. His shaggy eyebrows fell lower as he leaned forward gazing at my diagrams, and he gave an audible sigh of relief or satisfaction when I came to a turning-point in the tide of battle. Stanton stood up almost behind me; and he would ask a brief question now and then, which showed how well he grasped the situation. His voice was, however, calm and collected; and his soft eyes glistened through his spectacles as he stroked his luxuriant black beard.

I lost my sense of weariness; and we all forgot the lapse of time until I had fairly finished, and rose to leave. All three of the gentlemen thanked me warmly for my courtesy.

" Can we do any thing for you in return ? " asked the President.

" Yes, sir," said I, " you can. I am under orders to join the Army of the Potomac, and made application for a pass five days ago. I am the more anxious now to get there ; for, Early having been doubled up in the valley, Grant will no doubt be stirring at Lee to prevent his sending reinforcements to the Shenandoah. I would like to have my pass in time for to-day's steamer."

" I see you have studied the art of war to some purpose," remarked Mr. Lincoln with a genial laugh. " Mr. Stanton will see that you have your pass at once."

I then went to bed, being roused at noon to find my pass ready to my hand. That afternoon I embarked for City Point, and reached the siege-works the next day, in time to see Warren extend his lines beyond the Weldon Road, when you fellows carried the earthworks so gallantly, and began the movements since kept up on Lee's right. So you see, gentlemen, that was how I came to be present at two battles in two different armies within a single week. But I shall never forget the fatigue attending the effort.

CHAPTER XXXVI.

DEATH OF A SPY.

"There's not so much danger
In a known foe, as in a suspected friend."

HAT'S an excellent story of yours, Charley," said Major Curtis as Osborne finished his narrative. "No wonder you enjoy the life of a newspaper correspondent. Why, it beats staff-duty all hollow."

"There's more excitement about it," replied Osborne, "and not half the danger."

"I don't know about that," said young Jenkins: "there's plenty of danger in those night-rides of yours. I'd think twice before risking myself as you did."

"Then, I'll recommend you for dispatch-duty," said Osborne with a sly laugh.

"Bah! that fellow had his escort, while you went it alone as one does at cards when he's got a good hand," replied the aide.

"Well," said General Fletcher, "I think that Mr. Osborne had not only a good hand, but a better head, when he rode away from Berryville.—Your story has interested me very much, sir, and I shall esteem you correspondents more highly hereafter. I had no idea that you ran such risks, or encountered such perils."

"Very few people do, general," said Osborne: "they read a newspaper, and then toss it aside without a thought of the labor and pains taken to furnish them with news."

"Your story, Osborne," said Major Curtis, "reminds me of something Custer did, while I was in the Valley, during the beginning of Sheridan's campaign. You all know I came to the Fifth Corps because of the promotion it gave me."

"Tell us all about it, major," said I: "these stories will pass away the time."

"All right: here goes." And the adjutant-general proceeded as follows: —

We had made a rapid advance from Halltown Heights, just outside of Harper's Ferry; and, after a running fight covering several days, we went quietly into camp in the deserted meadows at the foot of Cedar Mountain, where Sheridan afterwards made his famous ride.

The cavalry had done most of the skirmishing during our advance; the Confederates offering very little opposition beyond the occasional firing of a field-piece, or a sudden flurry among the pickets, in order to gain time and give their trains a chance to gain safer distance from our main body.

General Custer at that time commanded what was known as the Iron Brigade, composed mostly of Michigan regiments. He had gone on as far as Front Royal, up in the mountains somewhere, and enjoyed a sharp brush with the Confederate cavalry, which happened to be in tolerably strong force in that neighborhood. On their return, the brigade passed through a little bit of a village called Painted Post, not far from Cedar Creek. While the command was trampling through the dust that lay hoof-deep in the road, one of Custer's officers captured a tall, fine-looking man in one of the houses; and they brought him on to camp.

I had ridden over that evening to see George, my old chum at West Point; and was sitting with him and his staff, round the camp-fire, after supper, just as we are doing now, when I noticed that Custer was abstracted and thoughtful.

"What's the matter?" said I. "You seem sad."

"I have good reason to be, my dear fellow. — Yet I see no other course open to me," he added, as if speaking to himself, while he kicked a log into the fire.

"What do you mean? Is it another move, or army secret I should not know?" I asked.

"Oh! there's no secret at all," replied Custer. "You know we captured a man in the village, down the road."

"Yes. What of him?"

"Only that my adjutant-general has just recognized him as one of the Confederate guards who escorted him and the other Federals taken prisoner at the cavalry engagement we had last summer at Brandy, near Beverly Ford. He has gone, with two other officers who were captured at the same time, to see the prisoner."

"You think the fellow is a spy, I suppose."

"That's just it," exclaimed Custer, rising to his feet. "I feel that he is a spy, and a dangerous one too, judging from his looks and demeanor. We are surrounded by spies in this valley."

At that moment the three officers came up to make their report.

"Well, gentlemen," said the general, "have you seen the prisoner? What do you think of him?"

"They both recognized him at once, general, as one of our old guards," replied the adjutant-general; "and were given no previous hint from me, as you expressly desired."

"Is this so?" queried Custer in an anxious tone; and as he spoke he gazed intently into the faces of the two officers.

"I would know him among fifty," said the taller of the two, a big, broad-shouldered, gentlemanly-looking man, whose rusty shoulder-strap showed his rank to be that of lieutenant-colonel.

"So would I," remarked the other. "That blue powder-mark on his chin recalled him to my mind at the first glance."

"I *know* he was one of the guard," added the adjutant.

"Very well, gentlemen," said General Custer slowly. "The

evidence seems to be very clear. I will not detain you any longer."

The two officers withdrew; and, as they rode off to their respective commands, General Custer turned to his adjutant, and ordered the prisoner to be brought before him.

The scene in the Valley at that moment was a very beautiful one. The sun had just dropped behind the hill-tops, and the air was cool, while a delicious breeze sprang up and came to us laden with the perfume of the fields and woods. The scattered fires among the camps were beginning to burn brighter as the shades of evening grew darker, and the warlike appearance of the landscape assumed a softer beauty. The tents, the fires, the shrill neighing of the cavalry-horses, the hoarse challenges of the sentinels, and the occasional dropping shots on the distant picket-lines, gave active life to the picture. In the foreground was being enacted a stranger scene, one involving life and death.

The prisoner came to our fire between two sentries, and, on seeing the general seated on the other side, drew himself up stiffly as though resenting his arrest.

" My man, we think you are a spy," said General Custer in a quiet voice. " What have you to say to the charge? Can you prove yourself not to be one? "

" There's a woman here, from the village," replied the prisoner, ignoring the general's questions : " she will tell you I am her son. I live in the village. Does that make me a spy? "

" Where is the woman? " exclaimed Custer.

Here a woman of elderly appearance, and evidently in some terror, came forward, and stood silently looking at the general.

" Is this man your son? " was his first question.

" Yes, he is," was her reply.

" How long has he been in the village? "

" Ever since last spring."

" You are sure, quite sure, he is your son? "

" Yes."

" Does he belong to the Southern army? "

" I dunno."

" Will you swear that he is your son? "

" Yes."

At this moment an orderly came up on horseback, and, dismounting, whispered a few words in the ear of the adjutant-general, at the same time handing him a bundle.

The adjutant stepped forward, and, quietly unrolling the bundle, disclosed a Confederate uniform.

GENERAL CUSTER AND THE SPY.

" General," said he, " this uniform was found in this **woman's** house, where we captured the prisoner."

A sudden flush in the man's face, a swift look of anger, **and** a glance exchanged between him and the woman, was all **the** answer either made to the announcement.

" That will do," remarked General Custer gravely : " remove the woman."

As she turned to follow the orderly, the woman gazed **for a** moment into the face of the prisoner ; but it was evident to all that she was not his mother, — as indeed the man afterwards admitted, — for she made no effort to bid him farewell, or to embrace him.

"My man, it's a clear case," said Custer, as soon as the woman was out of hearing: "you *are* a soldier of the Confederate army, and inside our lines in disguise. You are therefore a spy according to the rules of war. It is my duty to inform you that you must die."

"Die? What! without a trial?" exclaimed the prisoner in a startled tone.

"You have been tried just now. And I, as a general in the service of the United-States Government, have condemned you as a spy. I beg of you to believe me when I say that there is no hope for you. You die at eight to-morrow morning. I will send the chaplain to you, and trust you will endeavor to prepare yourself for your fate."

"Are you in earnest?" demanded the prisoner.

"Indeed I am. Remove the prisoner. If he attempts to escape, shoot him," and the general turned to his tent.

The condemned man walked away scornfully, evidently believing that some trick was being played upon him. The chaplain, however, spent the night with him in the guard-tent, and finally succeeded in convincing his charge that the sentence of death would really be carried into effect.

Sure enough, a gallows-trap was prepared at daylight by nailing a barn-door by its hinges to the projecting limb of an apple-tree, in a hollow near brigade headquarters. At the appointed hour, the Confederate was brought out, and hanged in the presence of the entire brigade. The prisoner met his fate bravely, with scarcely a word; and, in a few minutes after, his body was buried in a grave at the foot of a tree.

After the execution, General Custer invited me to ride over with him to General Sheridan's headquarters. We met the general as he was about sallying forth on a tour of inspection along the lines.

"Ah, Custer! good-morning. Any thing new over your way?" was his salutation.

"Yes, general. I came to report that we caught a spy at Painted Post yesterday, tried him last evening, and hanged him this morning."

"The devil you did!" exclaimed General Sheridan. "That's excellent. That's the way to do it. If a little more of that sort of thing was done in this Valley, we should have fewer spies among us."

"I am glad you approve of my action," said Custer, "for"—

"There, there, never mind the spy, Custer. He's safe enough now. Are your horses fit for another reconnoissance? That's far more important," said General Sheridan in his quick, impulsive manner.

"Ready at any moment, general," replied Custer, his eye kindling at the prospect of another dash.

"All right. I may want you to cut around the mountain here. If so, I'll send you your orders this evening. Good-day."

And that was all there was about the spy.

"That was just like Sheridan," remarked Osborne as the major concluded. "He knew the danger of spies. The Valley was full of them at that time. I remember the execution very well, but knew none of the particulars. The hanging of that man probably did more to drive spies away than any thing else. Sheridan and Custer were quite right."

"I agree with you," said General Fletcher. "A single human life counts for nothing in this mighty game of war. When a man becomes a spy he takes his life in his hand."

"Well, gentlemen," said Osborne, "I think we had better get some sleep. You know reveille waits for no man, be he a general or a simple correspondent."

"That's a very sensible suggestion," remarked the general, curling himself up in his blanket. "Good-night, sir."

The example was soon followed by the rest of the party, and in a few moments we were all wrapped in slumber.

CHAPTER XXXVII.

A LAST EFFORT.

"Ah! the smoke has rolled away;
And I see the Northern rifles gleaming down the ranks of gray."

HE winter of 1864–65 had passed, and the fields were beginning to wear that first faint tinge of green which is the sure harbinger of spring. Sherman had accomplished his wonderful march to the sea. Wilmington had fallen by the capture of Fort Fisher, and the lines before Petersburg and Richmond were being drawn tighter and tighter. Lee was evidently restive, for one or two unimportant engagements had been forced by him. In the Shenandoah Valley, Sheridan was gathering up his reins for a bold raid which was to bring him into Grant's lines. The Sixth Corps had returned to our siege-works. Every thing pointed to some decisive movement on the part of the Army of the Potomac, so long tied down to parallel and trench. The busy note of preparation was everywhere visible. Reinforcements and supplies were arriving; and the army waited with impatience for the crisis which all believed would end the war, and release a million of men for the pursuits of peace.

I had ridden along our picket-lines, as field-officer, one night in March, reaching my hut long after midnight, tired and sleepy. The fire on the rude hearth was smoldering, and Dennis peacefully snored in his bunk. Kicking the few remaining embers together, and throwing on a stick or two, I mused over the events of the past few years, — the changes that had occurred, the scenes I had witnessed. How long I sat there in the genial warmth of the blazing logs, I know not; for I fell asleep in my chair. Suddenly I was awakened by a tremendous and continuous roll of musketry, closely followed by some sharp cannonading.

"Begorra! there's something up," cried Dennis, as he sat up among his blankets, and rubbed his eyes. "Major, did ye hear that firin'?"

"Hear it? Of course I heard it. There it goes again!"

"I wonder where the divil it is, anyway."

"Some distance away," I replied, "judging by the sound."

"They're hard at it, wherever it is," said Dennis, leaping to his feet, and beginning to dress. "It's all rifle-firin' now. Maybe we're attacked."

"Very likely," said I; "for, if we were attacking, our corps would be under arms."

"Major Wilmot, are you awake?" asked Colonel Harding, putting his head, at that moment, through the door.

"Yes, colonel. I have not been to bed yet."

"That was an awful volley just now," said the colonel. "By heavens, they're at it again! I wonder whereabouts it is."

"That's just what I was axing myself just now," remarked Lieutenant Malone, as he pulled on his second boot. "Have ye any ordhers, colonel?"

"Yes, Malone: as you are dressed, just run along the lines of the officers' huts, and rout them out. We must get under arms, else brigade-orders may find us napping. Wilmot, will you order the drummers to sound the long roll? Good God! listen to that musketry. Ah! the artillery are beginning to wake up. It was high time."

Leaving the colonel to finish his speech to himself, I ran to the drummers' quarters, finding the boys all outside their huts listening to the heavy firing. Several had their drums with them : so we soon had the rataplan going, thus adding to the racket, the other regiments following suit.

It was not yet daylight ; but during the half-hour that elapsed between the beginning of the fusillade, and our getting under arms, the row along the lines on the right and center had grown rapidly in volume and intensity, coming nearer and nearer as the batteries and forts along the front were involved in the action. No orders came for us beyond the word that our brigade would form at the sound of our general's bugle : so the regiment stood in line, listening to the engagement, wondering what it could all mean.

"Major Wilmot," said young Jenkins, riding up, "General Fletcher wishes you to go down and see if you can ascertain what is going on over there. — He thinks you can spare him, colonel."

"Certainly, Jenkins, if the general desires it," was Colonel Harding's response.

"All right. I'm off," said I, pleased at having something to do.

In a few minutes I reached the main road, leading to the center of our position, and galloped on, glad to notice signs of the coming day. Although I had had very little sleep, my senses were all alert, and I enjoyed the rapid pace of my horse as he plunged forward under the spur. In half an hour I reached the Jerusalem road, and found large masses of infantry hurrying towards the scene of the battle now evidently progressing somewhere inside our line.

"What has happened?" said I to a mounted officer as he passed me at a hard gallop.

"Lee has broken through our lines, and captured Fort Steadman," was the reply.

This was a surprising bit of news, and fully explained the intensity and fierceness of the musketry. The Confederates must have attacked suddenly and in heavy force, else so strong a fort could not have been taken so quickly.

Daylight had now come; and, as I rode past the camps of Hartranft's Pennsylvania troops, I saw they were empty, so the division must be already on the field. In a few moments more I was myself on the ground.

The reddening of the eastern sky clearly revealed the situation. A heavy column of the enemy was pouring through the wide gates of Fort Steadman, and hastily pushing forward to support the advance. At a glance I saw that the aim of this

THE CONFEDERATES CAPTURE FORT STEADMAN.

desperate movement was to cut off the main body of our army from its base at City Point.

Finding my horse completely blown by his long gallop, I drew rein on a knoll, and watched the Confederates as they steadily formed in the hollow. By this time a second column had found ingress to the left of the fort, and came up rapidly; the two columns forming a gigantic wedge as the heads met. At that moment General Hartranft rode up with a couple of aides. Seeing me apparently idle, he shouted, —

"Major! do you know where that battery has gone to?"

"Just behind that knoll yonder, general," I replied, pointing to a rolling bit of ground on my right where I had seen
the guns a moment before.

"Please ride over and bring them into action at once," said
the general, turning his horse, and riding to meet his troops
now forming in line.

I dashed off, and found the battery standing in the hollow
behind the hill.

"What are you doing here?" I cried.   "Get your guns up,
and open on that column."

"Our captain has just been killed by a shell," replied the
lieutenant: "I was only waiting for orders."

"Hurry up, then: you have no time to lose," said I.

"By sections to the left, wheel!" shouted the young officer;
and the guns came tearing up the slope.

"Now then, sir, give it to them," I shouted: "for God's sake,
open fire quickly!"

"We'll give them a few rounds of solid shot, and then the
grape," replied the lieutenant coolly.

The pieces were soon barking angrily; and the heads of the
united column began to feel the effect, for men were falling
at every discharge as the balls played through their huddled
ranks.

"Now, sergeants, give them shells, four-second fuse," cried
the artillery-officer, quietly leaning over his horse's neck and
patting the animal as he spoke.

I turned to see what Hartranft was doing, being just in time
to see his division go yelling down the opposite hill as it
charged on the enemy.

"Look out, sir!" said I to the battery-commander: "you
will soon be firing on our own men."

"All right, major: I'll give them a round of grape first, then
we'll shell their center."

The grape and canister went whistling through the air; and,

as the two bodies of infantry met, the guns of the battery were slung a little to the right, and a shower of iron hurled into the center of the advancing column of Confederates. Two other field-batteries had by this time come up on our right, and opened a furious fire; while there were more at work on the other side of Hartranft's column. This artillery cross-fire now grew too hot for our assailants: they wavered for a second under the combined attack, and then began a retreat.

In twenty minutes more the battle was practically over, and in less than an hour the fort was again in our hands. The victory had cost us dear, however; for the field was thickly covered with Federal dead and wounded, and the entire garrison of Fort Steadman had been captured. A few hundred Confederate prisoners had, however, been taken; and their loss in killed and wounded had also been heavy.

There being nothing more to do or see, I decided to return to my command: so rode slowly off the field, passing General Hartranft and his staff as I did so.

"Your name, sir?" said the general, as he returned my salute.

"Major Wilmot, of the —th New York," I replied.

"Why, you belong to the Fifth Corps. How came you to be here, major?"

"I galloped over, under orders, sir, to see what was going on."

"You made good time," said the general pleasantly, "and did us good service with that confounded battery. I shall not forget you in my report, depend upon it."

Gratified at the warm praise I had received, I could only mutter my thanks as I lifted my cap and gave my tired steed the spur.

On arriving at brigade headquarters I found that my news had gone before me, for the regiments had broken ranks; though my description of the engagement was eagerly listened to by General Fletcher and his staff as we sat together at breakfast.

"'Pon my soul, Wilmot, you always have luck!" exclaimed

Jenkins: "you are the only officer of our corps who has been engaged in the affair."

"You forget that Wilmot missed our summer campaign," remarked the brigadier. "He is only trying to make up for lost time. But come, gentlemen, we are to be reviewed to-day by the President."

"A review to-day!" I exclaimed in surprise. "Surely Lincoln will not think of such a thing, after the hubbub we have had."

"Oh! what does he know about it?" replied General Fletcher. "Besides, Lee will scarcely make another assault to-day, after his repulse of this morning."

The general was correct in his surmises, for during the afternoon our corps stood in line for review. A few minutes after the bugles had ceased their clamor, hoarse commands ran along the lines, and the tall figure of the President galloped past. Then came the marching salute in column; and, as I dropped the point of my sword in salute, I saw the President's wife, surrounded by a group of ladies, enjoying the pageantry of the occasion. Scarcely had our brigade passed the reviewing stand, when a tremendous crash of musketry broke out on the extreme left of our position. As it grew in fury, we were not surprised to find ourselves marching straight for the scene of the disturbance. Dropping the punctilious movement of parade, the corps went forward at a run; the men in the ranks laughing over the sudden change in the day's programme.

The battle was at an end, however, when we arrived; for after a few stubborn volleys the Confederates fell back in sullen mood, thus yielding ground they had hitherto held so tenaciously. Moving farther to the left, after some delay, our corps bivouacked *en masse* for the night.

"Well, major," said Osborne the correspondent, suddenly riding up, "this day eclipses every thing I have seen yet. Do you know, I left flags of truce flying over Fort Steadman while the Confederates were receiving their dead who had fallen inside our lines, only to find your corps on review in the center, and a sharp fight going on here! Peace, parade, and a battle, at the same moment, only a few miles apart, is almost too much even for an enterprising correspondent."

"I suppose you have been very busy to-day, Charley," said I.

"Busy! I should say so. Why, when that awful crash broke out this morning, I saddled my horse and galloped to the scene, saw most of the fight, and then rode to City Point in time to send off a hurried dispatch by the mail-steamer. I have been in the saddle since daylight, used up two horses, and must sit up the greater part of the night writing my description of this wonderful day's operations. Can you give a fellow any thing to eat?"

"To be shure we can," replied Dennis, "an' a cup of whishky to kape ye warm, too."

Osborne talked rapidly as he discussed the beefsteak provided by our cook, and predicted a general movement by the whole army within the next few days. But it needed no prophet to tell us that.

The tattoo roll-call over, Dennis and I rolled ourselves in our blankets, leaving Osborne seated before the fire, writing. With a couple of blankets wrapped round his shoulders to keep off the wind, and the lid of a cracker-box across his knees, the correspondent scratched away with his pencil by the flickering blaze. As I lay watching him at work, I realized the fascination which possessed the journalist; for he had evidently lost all sense of his surroundings, until compelled to pause and stir the dying embers into brighter flame. As each page was written, it was thrust into the leg of his big riding-boot for safety. When I awoke again at midnight, Osborne was still busy, having sacrificed his impromptu table to keep the fire going; his crouching figure showing out against the starlit sky like a silhouette, as he scribbled away in the uncertain light of the camp-fire.

CHAPTER XXXVIII.

BEGINNING OF THE END.

" Steeds neigh and trample all around,
   Steel rings, spears glimmer, trumpets sound."

Y the end of two days, no field-orders having come, the men began to build camps. It was the deceitful calm before the storm. Lee, shut up as he was in one corner of the board, had hoped, by his assault on Fort Steadman, to open a path between himself and Johnston. But the move failed; and, having lost the initiative, the Confederate leader was compelled to wait on the humor of his antagonist.

On the third morning I received orders to report at brigade headquarters, losing no time in doing so.

" Major," said General Fletcher on my entering his tent, " I know how you delight in special service: so, when I was called to furnish a field-officer, I at once thought of you."

" You were very kind, general: nothing pleases me better. What am I to do?"

" Nothing very hazardous. There is some delay about our ammunition; and, as we expect orders to move at any moment, General Warren is naturally anxious to hurry it up. I want you to go to City Point and attend to the matter."

" I understand, general, so will ride over to the train at once."

" Never mind the train," said the general: " you had better

ride straight to the Point, for there's no telling where we may be when you return."

" Is the movement so imminent, then ? " I asked.

" Yes: Humphrey's corps will probably join us here to-night."

" Indeed ! but won't that weaken the force along our old line ? "

" To some extent," replied General Fletcher. " But part of the army of the James is already crossing the river to reinforce us, and Sheridan has arrived from the Valley. But I must not detain you, Wilmot, for time is precious."

Taking the hint, I withdrew, and galloped away on my errand.

I had not ridden far before I realized how active were the preparations for the approaching campaign. Long trains of cars were rattling up and down the rude railroad, carrying supplies ; camps were being struck as whole divisions marched to some new position ; horses were being re-shod in the field-batteries, and caissons packed with fresh ammunition. Hundreds of wagons were passing to and fro between the stations and their respective commands, and an air of intense activity was visible at every turn. The army was indeed stripping for the fight.

As I rode along the fortified lines a strange, unwonted silence prevailed, for cannon and mortar were mute ; not even a musket in the picket-trenches gave note of its presence. The only sounds were the creaking of the wagon-wheels as they slowly lumbered over the corduroy roads, and the discordant bellow of some stubborn mule, or the neighing of the cavalry-horses as they listened to the musical strains of some distant bugle. Accustomed as I was to the constant roar of our batteries and the rippling fusillade of the pickets, this absence of artillery thunder was all the more startling.

" Halloa, major! what are you doing away down here ? " exclaimed the familiar voice of Correspondent Osborne as I crossed the Jerusalem plank-road.

"I am going to City Point, to see after our ammunition," I replied.

"Oho! that's another sign!" cried Osborne.

"You mean, it is a sign of a move?"

"Exactly. We shall probably start to-morrow, as I told General Meade just now," he replied.

"General Meade! he must have been vastly amused, Charley, at your volunteering information, seeing that he commands the army." And I began laughing at my friend's conceit.

"It was rather funny," said Osborne coolly; "and I don't wonder you laugh. You see, I met the general all alone, near the station; when he, in that whimsical way of his, asked me for the news. I at once told him the army would move inside of twenty-four hours, judging by the signs. He wanted to know what I meant by signs: so I alluded to the fact that the roads were being repaired, and the blacksmiths were busy in the batteries and cavalry camps. The general remarked that horses *would* cast loose shoes, and the roads needed mending; but I reminded him that army blacksmiths were proverbially lazy, and that the roads were seldom mended unless they were needed for the passage of artillery."

"And what did the general say to that?" I asked.

"It staggered him, for the old gentleman rode off saying that I had sharp eyes: as if correspondents didn't need to have sharp eyes, and use them too! But any fool can see with half an eye that we are on the eve of important events."

"You are right, Osborne," said I: "it is the beginning of the end. What do you judge the scope of operations to be?"

"Why, don't you see, Wilmot, that Grant is going to repeat his old tactics, and swing round his left like an immense sledge-hammer, and so double Lee up? He has been at it ever since we crossed the Rapidan. While the main force is pegging away at Lee's communications, these old forts will bombard the city as it has never been bombarded before. They have been carrying shot and shell to the magazines in immense quantities these three days. I suppose you know Ord is coming over to take a hand in the final scene."

" I heard somebody was coming across the river," said I ; "and Sheridan is here too, I understand."

"Pooh!" replied Osborne contemptuously at my ignorance. " Why, he's come and gone off again, — going to strike Lee's rear. He started this morning before daylight."

" Indeed! that looks like business," I remarked.

" Don't it? " said Osborne eagerly. " There will be plenty of warm work all along the line, once the ball fairly opens. But I must be off, major: good-by for the present."

Reaching City Point at noon, I found the entire place in a wonderful bustle. The ordnance-wharves were crammed with all the varied material of war, — spare caissons and guns for the field-batteries, chests of small arms for infantry, sabers for the cavalry, axes, spades, and pontoons for the engineers, boxes of ammunition, bales of blankets, — in fact, every thing that ingenuity could devise for strengthening and equipping an army. Near by were the commissariat stores. Boxes of hard-bread, bags of grain, and bales of hay, were piled up in every direction. Under the hills, trains were being crammed with all these *impedimenta* of war, and a fleet of steamboats lay in the stream with fresh cargoes to discharge. The cries of the stevedores, the puffings of locomotives, and the piercing steam-whistles on land and water, made a Babel of sounds, deafening and confusing the ear by their discordance.

Carefully picking my way through all this seeming confusion, I made known my errand to the officer in charge of the wharf.

" You have had your trip for nothing, major," was his reply. " The Fifth-Corps ammunition was sent forward three hours ago."

" I am glad to hear it," said I ; "though it is rather provoking to ride twenty miles just to ascertain the fact."

" Why didn't you come by train? You could have got here in time to go back with your own ammunition."

" Simply because I was ordered to come on horseback."

" Well, join me at dinner. You must have a good appetite after your long ride."

" Thank you. I must confess I am hungry."

While discussing the meal, I learned that the extraordinary activity at the Point was occasioned by orders to furnish General Ord's corps with supplies at the terminus of the railroad: so it was evident his command was included in the contemplated movement on the left.

" How many men does Ord bring over? " I asked.

"About ten thousand, judging by the orders for supplies. But there are other troops besides Ord's crossing the river: *they* are for the intrenchments."

" To relieve Humphrey, no doubt," said I. " I know he is under orders to join us in the advance on the left."

" Precisely," replied the ordnance-officer. " Parke, with the Ninth Corps, is to hold the old line, while you cut loose for a flank movement; and he will open a bombardment at the proper moment. If all goes well, there will be music in the air before many hours."

My horse having been fed, I bade my entertainer good-by, and rode away. Reaching Meade Station at nightfall, I stopped at a sutler's tent, hoping to obtain something to eat; a few drops of rain falling as I descended from my saddle.

" Want supper? Certainly: you are just in time," said the sutler hospitably, when I explained my wishes. " But what are you doing 'way down here?' he continued, noticing the Maltese cross on my cap.

" I've been down to the Point, and must get back to my regiment to-night," I replied.

" You'll have a precious slim chance of doing so," said the sutler. " Don't you know the Fifth started out to join Sheridan to-day, before noon?"

" How could I, when I left it soon after reveille?"

" Well, there's no use your trying to find them in the dark, major. Besides, don't you hear the rain? Just bunk in here along with us, and give that horse of yours a rest. He'll go all the better in the morning."

The advice was not to be disregarded, so I accepted the hospitable offer with thanks. Passing into the barnlike tent, I found several officers belonging to the station-guard, already at supper.

"Well, Jerry," said a tall, black-haired lieutenant, as he courteously made room for me at the rude table, "I guess our mess will soon break up now."

"I shouldn't wonder if I pulled up stakes in a day or two," responded the sutler. "Business will be uncommonly dull now that the hull army is moving."

"Lord, how it rains!" ejaculated another of the group, turning an ear towards the canvas roof, and listening to the patter of the heavy drops. "It will make the roads as soft as putty for the artillery and wagons."

"Lieutenant Marsh," said a sergeant, hurriedly entering the tent, "there's two more trains just come up, chock full of ammunition; and the major wants you to see it put into the wagons."

"Confound shot and shell, say I!" exclaimed my black-haired neighbor in a petulant tone. "I thought we were done with them for the present."

"The wagons are all ready, sir, and waiting," remarked the sergeant, seeing that his superior made no movement.

"Oh! I'm coming," grumbled the lieutenant, rising and flinging an overcoat over his shoulders. "Go and see that the lanterns are all ready, sergeant, and turn out the men."

"May I go with you?" said I.

"Certainly, major, if you don't care for the rain. You will find it precious dull work though. What they want with all this ammunition bothers me. The magazines must be overflowing;" and Lieutenant Marsh held up the flap of the tent for me to pass.

On reaching the railroad-platform, an exciting and picturesque sight presented itself. Lighted lanterns were swinging
at the door of every car, and men inside were rapidly passing
boxes of powder and shells to the wagons ranged alongside.
Now and then a solid shot would go rumbling over the car-floor
as it was kicked towards the wagon, and fall into the vehicle
with a sudden thump. The dim lights, the whistles of the
locomotives, the shouts of the drivers, and the swishing sound
of the falling rain, made the scene a weird and novel one, even
to my eyes.

"There, that job's finished," said the lieutenant as the last
wagon went groaning away in the darkness. "Come, major,
we must run, or we'll be drenched before we can reach Jerry's
tent."

I was on the road early the following morning, being naturally anxious to overtake the corps before the impending engagement. Cantering over the muddy road in the cool, balmy air,
and watching the mists as they sluggishly rose before the rays
of the sun, I saw that great changes had taken place during
my brief absence. The reserve batteries were gone; and in the
fields where I had left thirty thousand men in bivouac, nothing
was now to be seen except extinguished fires and the usual
débris of deserted camps. Both the Second and Fifth Corps
had disappeared, their places in the line being taken by Ord's
men. Every thing was strangely silent: the guns in the forts
were still mute, and the pickets gave no sign of life. Even
the railroad was deserted; for, now that the army was moving
for battle, all the trains were huddled together at City Point,
awaiting the issue. No army-wagon jolted its complaining
wheels over the exasperating corduroy roads, and neither mule
nor steed gave vocal token of his presence; the harsh cry
of a solitary crow flying over my head being the only sound
to break the ominous silence.

Passing over the dismantled embankment of the Weldon
Railroad just beyond Warren Station, I found the road deeply

scarred by wagon-wheels, so rode slowly through the mud until I reached the woods : here I discovered further traces of the passage of a column of troops,   Plodding on for a mile or two, I unexpectedly encountered General Meade, attended only by a couple of orderlies.

"I beg your pardon, general," said I, lifting my cap, "but is this the road the Fifth Corps took?"

"Yes, sir, it is," replied the general, peering at me sharply over his glasses.   "How came you to be so far in the rear?"

TAKEN PRISONER AGAIN.

"I was sent to the Point, sir, and am now trying to rejoin my command," said I, heartily annoyed at being compelled to explain.

"Duty is duty," remarked General Meade in a pleasanter tone, as if to set me at my ease.   "I'm glad we have met, Major, for you can be of service.   Do you know the road we cut when the advance was made over the Boydton plank?"

"Perfectly, general : it runs through the pines towards the Taylor house."

"Exactly.   Well, I want you to find General Humphrey,

and tell him to extend his line until he touches Warren's right. There's a dangerous gap between them, I find."

" All right, sir: I'll carry your order, and then ride along the line until I find my brigade."

" That will be your best plan; and tell General Humphrey that my headquarters are at Warren Station for the present," said the general, returning my salute and galloping away.

I lost no time in seeking the road, and, entering it, rode gayly on, rejoicing in my luck in having something to do.

But all these bright expectations were suddenly quenched; for I had gone scarcely half a mile when ten or fifteen Confederate soldiers broke through the undergrowth, and surrounded me. I was again a prisoner.

CHAPTER XXXIX.

SMASHING THE TRAP.

"They entered: 'twas a prison-room
Of stern serenity and gloom."

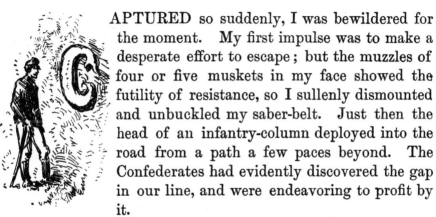

APTURED so suddenly, I was bewildered for the moment. My first impulse was to make a desperate effort to escape; but the muzzles of four or five muskets in my face showed the futility of resistance, so I sullenly dismounted and unbuckled my saber-belt. Just then the head of an infantry-column deployed into the road from a path a few paces beyond. The Confederates had evidently discovered the gap in our line, and were endeavoring to profit by it.

"Halloa! where did you get that horse?" demanded the officer in command, on catching sight of my steed.

"Hev jist gobbled him an' this 'ere Yank," replied one of the men. "He's jist what yer need, kurnel."

"Sorry to deprive you, sir, of the animal," said the Confederate colonel politely. "But the fortune of war, you know. How came you out here alone?"

"Simply rejoining my command," I replied. "I had no idea you held possession of this road."

"We can scarcely claim to hold it, sir, being merely on a reconnoissance. But come, you will be in Petersburg before you expected," and the colonel laughed good-humoredly.

"Well, I shall not be a prisoner long," I retorted, nettled by the badinage of the speaker.

"Perhaps not," he replied stiffly. "But we are not conquered quite yet. — Take your prisoner to the rear, corporal."

Returning the polite bow of the colonel, who was comfortably seated in my saddle, I dejectedly followed my guard, heartily disgusted at the untoward result of my adventure.

Passing down the path for a few hundred yards, we struck the Confederate pickets, and soon after came to their line of battle. The men eyed me curiously as the corporal and his men hurried me through the ranks; one or two officers near me courteously removing their hats in salute, — a compliment I promptly acknowledged. Though I was not permitted to linger, I saw that an important movement was in progress, for the force at that part of the field was a large one. In a few minutes, probably, the engagement would take place; and the gap between Humphrey and Warren might prove fatal. Had I not been captured, this danger might have been avoided. But there was no use complaining.

Soon after leaving the Confederate main line, we entered a wide road, which Corporal Packer informed me led to the city. Half a mile down the road we met heavy masses of infantry, evidently moving up to strengthen the force I had seen in the woods; showing that Lee was endeavoring to ward off the blow threatened him. The appearance of these men was in striking contrast to those of our own army. Their uniforms were faded and torn, their equipments battered and rusty; but the men moved with vigorous, eager step. Brave and undaunted, these soldiers in butternut and gray pressed forward, apparently as confidently and hopefully as when the chances of war were more equally divided. After all, they were Americans, consequently full of ardor and self-reliance.

It was noon before we reached the suburbs of Petersburg, and on entering the streets I was surprised to find them almost deserted. Here and there I caught glimpses of women's faces at a window, and once we met an elderly citizen who stopped and gazed inquisitively after me. On the outskirts we had encountered a few wagon-trains, but here there was nothing to betray the presence of an army besieged. Passing up one street and down another, we came at length to a sort of open square, evidently the business center of the city before the heavy hand of military occupation had put an end to all peaceful pursuits. Stopping in front of a low building which had once been occupied by a barber, I was confronted with the provost-marshal, who having taken my name, rank, and regiment, ordered the guard to lead me away.

Corporal Packer now led me towards the river, until suddenly turning a corner we halted at the door of a big brick building which I knew must be the prison. Originally a tobacco-warehouse, it had a forbidding appearance; and my heart sank at the prospect of a sojourn within its walls. In a few minutes I was in the midst of a group of Federal officers, prisoners like myself.

" Halloa ! Here's a fresh fish in the net," cried one in a merry voice. " I say, major, has there been another battle ? "

" Not yet," I replied, " but there will be one very soon."

" How came you to be gobbled, then ? " inquired another officer of my own rank.

" I ran across a reconnoitering column in the pines."

" Pines ? why, what's going on there ? " exclaimed two or three voices.

" The whole army is in motion," said I. " Ord has come over, Parke holds the old line, and all the rest are swinging round on the left with Sheridan's cavalry."

" Huzza ! " shouted the captain who had announced my arrival. " The siege will soon be over, then good-by to this infernal prison ! "

" Stop that noise in there ! " said the sentry angrily, putting his head in at the door.

"How long have you fellows been here?" I asked when the guard had retired.

"Only a few days," replied the major. "We were captured when Lee made that desperate dash of his on Fort Steadman. Do you think this last move of Grant's will be successful?"

"It looks like it," I replied: "I can not see how it can prove otherwise."

"Let us hope so. It's a good sign, at all events, their keeping us here. If all were going well with them, we should have been packed off to Richmond long before this."

My fellow-prisoners continued questioning me and discussing the situation until nightfall, when, a scanty supper having been served out, we lay on our blankets in the dark, speculating in whispers on the chances of our being soon released or exchanged. One by one they fell asleep, until at length I found myself surrounded by sleepers; so followed their example.

At daybreak we were awakened by our guards, who seemed strangely excited, though they refused to explain what was the matter. While we were wondering at their queer conduct, the sound of distant cannonading could be heard.

"They're fighting," whispered some one near me. "I wonder if they are going to take us away."

What the orders were, we never ascertained, for beyond calling the roll our guards left us undisturbed until breakfast-time; the cannonading growing in volume and vigor as the day advanced. Clustering near the narrow windows, we listened to the booming of the guns in feverish impatience. At length the sounds of the battle died away; and we learned from the sentry that the engagement had occurred at a place called Five Forks, afterwards to be historical as the scene of the last pitched battle of the war.

The next two days passed without incident, for we heard no cannonading. At midnight of the third day, however, we were startled from our slumbers by a tremendous outburst of

artillery, the concussions of which fairly shook the floor under
our feet.

" It's a general bombardment along the lines, you may depend
upon it," said Major Rathbone.

We could see nothing from our windows, except the reflection of the light from the guns in action. Yet we lingered,
content to watch even this imperfect evidence of a determined
effort to capture the beleaguered city. As the first faint streaks
of daylight appeared, fierce volleys of musketry could be distinguished amidst the thunder of contending cannon, sounds
which told us that an assault was being made. Now the noise
of the conflict grew louder and louder until it seemed that
even the streets of the city were invaded.

" I say, gentlemen, do you know it's Sunday?" remarked
some one at the window next mine.

" So it is, Woodbury," replied Major Rathbone. " Halloa!
what's this?" he exclaimed the next instant in an eager voice.
" Yes, it's an infantry-column, and going like the very devil."

A glance into the street showed us that the major was right;
for the narrow pavement was full of men, who were moving as
fast as their legs could carry them. What the movement was,
we could not imagine, unless it was reinforcements going to
some threatened point.

All day long we stood and listened to the awful music of
artillery, intensified and strengthened in its monotone by frequent volleys of well-sustained musketry. It seemed to me
terrible to be shut up like rats in a trap, while our comrades
were so bravely fighting. When night came, some one remembered that we had been given no dinner, a fact we had entirely
forgotten in the fierce excitement experienced while listening
to the bombardment. Though it was now the hour for supper,
our guards neglected to bring that also. What could it mean?

" It's my opinion they're going to evacuate the city," said
Major Rathbone, " and have something else to think of besides
feeding us."

Whatever the cause, we received no food; nor could we get any response from the sentry at the door of our loft, beyond the pointing of his bayonet at any one who questioned him. Hungry, yet elated by hope, we were unable to sleep, so chatted in groups by the windows. A painful silence had by this time succeeded the cannonading and musketry, but we were certain it would be renewed at dawn. About three o'clock in the morning, a young lieutenant discovered that the sentry was no longer at the door.

"Steady, gentlemen," cried Major Rathbone, as a rush was made for the landing. "Let us go cautiously to work."

"But the guards have been withdrawn," exclaimed Captain Woodbury.

"All the more reason for caution," replied Major Rathbone. "If the guards are gone, there's no harm in reconnoitering. But let us do it regularly. Major Wilmot, you and Woodbury will please explore the passage-way. Meanwhile, the rest of the gentlemen must remain quiet."

Captain Woodbury and I moved cautiously to the door, and found it unfastened. Pushing it open, we listened a moment or two, but there were no sounds.

"Have you a match, major?" whispered Woodbury in my ear.

Without replying, I opened my match-safe, and struck a light. Holding it over my head, I could see nobody.

"By Jove! they *are* gone!" exclaimed my companion, as the flame of the match expired and left us in darkness.

"It seems like it," I replied. "Let us go a little farther before we report."

Creeping down the stairs, we soon reached the lower landing, and, by the aid of another match, ascertained that no guard was on duty.

"Do you go back, Woodbury," said I, "and tell Major Rathbone we think the coast is clear. I will wait here until you return."

The captain ascended the stairs, and left me alone in the darkness. Excited as I was by the novelty of the situation, I felt strangely stirred at my position; and my heart throbbed tumultuously, for there was no knowing what danger we might encounter.

In a few minutes Woodbury returned, followed by Major Rathbone and the rest. Whispering for them to move quietly, I led the way down the last flight of stairs. On reaching the street-door, we again found no sentry; but the door was locked. Here was a dilemma!

"By the by," said Captain Woodbury, "the day they brought us here, I noticed a door in the side wall. Have you any more matches, Wilmot?"

Striking a light, we saw that the captain's memory was not at fault. There *was* another door, and it proved to be unfastened.

"Hold on a bit!" exclaimed the lieutenant who had first discovered the absence of the sentries. "I've a piece of candle in my pocket. Let us explore with it."

Pushing the door open, and following our leader, we soon came to the end of a passage, and in another moment were in the open air.

"Isn't this funny!" cried Woodbury. "Where can our guards have gone to?"

"Followed the army evidently," replied Major Rathbone. "But come, let us push on."

The major led us across a sort of court-yard, but his progress was soon checked by a high wall: we had simply gained access to the warehouse-yard, not the street.

"Well, what are we to do now?" said Captain Woodbury impatiently.

"Why, return to the passage, of course," replied the major. "Look around, and see if any of you can find something — a bit of iron — to break the lock on the front door."

"Here's something heavy I've stumbled over," said one of the other officers.

"The very thing," said Major Rathbone, examining the object with his candle. "It's one of those bars formerly used in the tobacco-presses. — Come, Woodbury, you take the lead now, and batter off the lock for us."

We all hurried after our new standard-bearer, who, on reaching the door, succeeded, by a few well-directed blows with his crowbar, in forcing the cumbrous lock from its fastenings. As the heavy door swung open, we poured eagerly into the street like a parcel of schoolboys. We were free!

It had now grown quite light, yet the city seemed deserted and silent. Remembering the route I had come, I led the way to the open square, which was also entirely empty. While we stood there, wondering what was best to be done, Major Rathbone caught sight of an advancing column of troops approaching. A second glance showed them to be Federals.

"Why, how did you get in?" demanded the officer in command. "I thought we were the first to enter the place."

"We didn't get in," replied Captain Woodbury in a whimsical way: "we've only just got out."

"I don't understand," said the picket-officer, evidently mystified. "What do you mean by that?"

"He means that we were prisoners," replied the major, "and have only just discovered that we were unguarded."

"Prisoners, eh? Well, I congratulate you. You had better remain with me until our corps comes in. I expect General Parke will soon be here."

"When did you discover the enemy had evacuated?" I asked.

"At daybreak. A darky came in and told us: so I sent word to the rear, and marched in."

Here a few citizens made their appearance at the corner of the square. They seemed in doubt, and conversed among themselves. The picket-officer beckoned to them, a summons they obeyed with evident reluctance.

"You have nothing to fear, gentlemen," said the lieutenant-colonel. "The city having fallen into our hands, the inhabitants will be protected by us."

"Has General Lee and his army gone clar away?" asked one of the men incredulously.

"It looks like it. Don't you see we are in possession?"

As the colonel spoke, we heard the sound of horses' hoofs on the stone pavement; and, a moment after, General Parke and his staff rode up, closely followed by several infantry regiments, coming along at a swinging trot.

Major Rathbone approached the general, and explained our presence, at the same time introducing me as belonging to the Fifth Corps.

"Indeed!" replied the general. "I'm just sending an escort with my dispatches to General Meade. If you would like to join your command, I'll give you a horse."

"Thank you, general," said I. "I *would* like to reach my regiment very much. I may be in time for another brush."

"Well, I can not promise you that," said the general, smiling. "I guess the fighting is pretty well over by this time."

Learning that we were all very hungry, General Parke gave orders that we be properly cared for; then rode away to make proper disposition of his troops. An hour after, I was in the saddle, riding towards the main body of the army, which was now racing after Lee and his men. Before we entered the belt of woods where I had been captured, deafening explosions occurred on the river; and a black cloud of smoke in the sky told me that the city of Richmond was in flames.

CHAPTER XL.

LAYING DOWN THE SWORD.

"Peace, thy olive wand extend,
　And bid wild War his ravage end."

THE position of the Army of Northern Virginia had now become an exceedingly critical one. Compelled by Grant's tremendous swoop on his line of communications to abandon both Richmond and Petersburg, Lee gathered his forces for a leap, which, if successful, would enable him to join Johnston, and give battle with more equal numbers. But the brave army proved unequal to the effort, yet struggled hopelessly on, until, being brought to bay at last, it surrendered with honor.

When I rode out from our old lines with the dispatch-escort, the Sixth Corps was on the march endeavoring to overtake the advance columns, whose artillery gave evidence of the severity and persistence of the pursuit. Ord was farther ahead, having had nearly a day's start over Wright. All day long we could hear heavy cannonading, with now and then a brisk roll of musketry. Every road was occupied by the troops and trains, haste being evidently the order of the day. So crammed were the roads, that our party, at times, found it difficult to push forward; and for hours we struggled past long lines of wagons and ambulances, or cantered by the side of the infantry. The men were, of course, greatly elated by the sudden change of affairs in the field, and trudged merrily over the dusty roads, singing camp-songs, and cheering on the slightest occasion. They seemed to appreciate the fact that the end was near, and forgot fatigue in their eagerness to witness the closing scenes.

By nightfall we had reached the vicinity of Burke's Station, finding it to be the temporary center of our operations. As is always the case where large bodies of troops are massed, the scene was a busy and confused one. Thousands of little fires were scattered over the plain, and dark patches showed where

CAVALRY IN PURSUIT.

whole divisions were moving into bivouac. All the familiar sounds were afloat in the air: hoarse commands were uttered by mounted officers; teamsters yelled and cursed at their exhausted animals; cattle bellowed mournfully, as if they knew they were going to slaughter; artillery rumbled along the road; timber fell with crashing sound before the blows of the ax-men; and the pickets kept up an incessant racket on the outposts. Now a glitter of steel would flash across my eyes, as the bayonets of some moving brigade glanced in the reflections of the blazing fires; and I caught glimpses of fluttering colors as they waved like shadows in the uncertain light.

Amid this confusion I found it impossible to gain definite intelligence of my corps. Some had seen it march into yonder woods, others knew that Warren's men were encamped just beyond the station. Disappointed at every turn, I was blindly riding past the railroad-platform, when a man suddenly rose from the ground under my horse's feet.

" An' where the divil be ye a-goin'?" he exclaimed. "Why don't ye put specs on yer horse's nose to kape him from tramplin' honest men to death?"

" Is that you, Dennis?" said I, for the voice sounded familiar.

"Yis, that's one of me names," he replied; "though how the divil ye guessed it bothers me."

"Don't you know me, Malone? or have you lost your own eyesight?"

"It's the major, be all that's holy! An' where hev ye bin, Frank, all this while? Troth, ye tuk yer own time in gittin' back."

"I was captured while coming up, and only escaped when Petersburg and Richmond were abandoned," said I.

"Taken prisoner an' escaped!" exclaimed Dennis. "Did ye say Richmond is 'vacuated?"

"Yes. But where's the regiment?"

"I dunno. They detailed me here for guard-dooty furninst the station, and then marched off in a jiffy. Arrah, Frank, me darlin'! but I'm glad to see ye wanst more, safe and sound, like a new-made whishky-barrel wid both heads in."

"Well, Dennis, as I can not find the regiment, I'll stop here with you. Can you give me any thing to eat?"

"Troth, an' I can. There's a shank of a ham, plinty of coffee, and a sup of whishky. Sit down, me boy, and make yerself comfortable."

While eating my supper, I gave Dennis an account of my

adventures; the recital greatly interesting him. In return, he told me that my brother officers had heard I had been killed, and predicted that my arrival would be the source of rejoicing in the regiment. During the battle of Five Forks the command had not suffered greatly; though one of our officers, Captain Seymour, had been fatally wounded by a round shot, death ensuing soon after his reaching the surgeon.

Dennis and I chatted for over an hour; when, feeling the need of sleep after my long ride, I wrapped myself in a blanket, and did not awake until the bugles and drums began their noisy reveille. Seeing the corps-flag flying up the road, I mounted my horse, and was soon among my comrades, enjoying their hearty welcome very much.

During the next five days we made long and rapid marches, diversified at times by sudden halts and sharp skirmishes. We knew that General Ord was now following the cavalry in its endeavor to cut off Lee's advance on the Lynchburg Railroad. If Sheridan was successful in this, the Confederates would be caught on both flanks.

On the afternoon of the fifth day our corps entered the village of Appomattox, finding the Confederates in line-of-battle on the slopes beyond the picturesque little town. Though we also formed in regular order, our general made no aggressive movement, despite the fact that considerable cannonading was in progress towards the left.

"An' why don't we make a dive at 'em, and settle the business at wanst?" exclaimed Lieutenant Malone, as he stood leaning against my horse's shoulder.

"Do be patient, Dennis," I replied. "We will get the word when the proper time comes."

As I spoke, a confused murmur ran along the ranks, and the men on our right seemed strangely agitated.

"What's up now?" cried Dennis.

"A truce! a truce!" shouted a hundred voices.

Shading my eyes from the rays of the sun, I saw two or

three small white flags waving in front of the Confederate line. As I looked, a horseman galloped across the hollow from our side, carrying a handkerchief on a ramrod.

It was quite true: the Confederates had called for a parley.

"Begorra! an' that's the purtiest thing I've seen since we marched down Broadway in '61, biddin' good-by to the gurls!" exclaimed Dennis.

THE FLAG OF TRUCE.

"Well, Wilmot," said Colonel Harding, coming towards me, "this ends our campaigning: General Lee has signified his acceptance of General Grant's terms, and will surrender."

Cheers now ran along the lines like waves beating on the seashore. The army was intoxicated with joy.

"This ends the war," said the colonel musingly, as he listened to the cheers.

"You forget that Johnston is still in the field," said I.

"He will be compelled to follow Lee's example, now that two armies face him."

"True: I had forgotten that."

At that moment Osborne the correspondent rode up.

"Well, gentlemen," said he, "I've come to say good-by."

"Why, where are you going?" I exclaimed, noticing that he had his blankets strapped to his saddle. "You seem in regular marching order."

"I have need to be, for I must reach City Point in time for the steamer to-morrow."

"City Point!" said Colonel Harding in surprise. "Why, man, it's fully ninety miles from here. You'll never do it on one horse."

"Never you fear, colonel," replied Osborne with a smile on his lips: "I looked out for that long ago. I've got a horse at Burke Station, and General Parke has another at his head-quarters for me."

"You will have to ride all night," said I.

"Of course. It isn't the first time, you know. But I must not stay any longer. Good-by: I shall probably not see this army again."

"Why not?" said Colonel Harding. "Surely your usefulness is not over."

"Oh! somebody will look after you for us," replied Osborne. "I am going to Mexico."

"Mexico!" I exclaimed.

"Yes, Mexico. It was all arranged when last I was in the office."

"I see," said Colonel Harding. "This war being in reality at an end, you are looking for more exciting scenes for your note-book?"

"Exactly," replied the correspondent. "Now that Lee has capitulated, I can easily be spared. While the steamer is plowing her way to Washington, I shall write the story of this surrender, and, after seeing it put on a wire, start for New York. Within twenty-four hours after my arrival I shall be on my way to the Rio Grande."

"What will you do there?" asked the colonel.

"Make the best way I can to Juarez' army, to be sure, and watch the course of events."

"Upon my word, Osborne, yours is an exciting sort of life," said I.

"You are right. There is nothing like it. Despite the danger and hardship attending the life of a war-correspondent, there is a fascination about it I can not resist. But, really, Wilmot, I must be off. Time is precious with such a ride as I have before me. Good-by, old fellow. Good-by, colonel."

He waved his hand, put spurs to his steed; and then the brave, good-hearted fellow was gone.

When evening came, the entire country seemed to be in a blaze, for our army was enjoying its old-time luxury of huge fires. On the other side of the little valley, where the Confederate army lay shattered and despairing, but little light was to be seen. As I lay before the blazing logs, in company with Colonel Harding and Dennis, my thoughts again reverted to Tom Marshall; and I wondered if he were still alive.

The fact that the enemy had given up the struggle naturally relaxed the severity of campaign-duty. The picket-line was a mere formality, and the night air was not disturbed by musketry; the unwonted silence being all the more remarkable for its novelty. Neither the colonel nor Dennis spoke; and we were silently gazing into the fire when young Jenkins rode into the circle of light, and dismounted.

"Well, colonel," said he, "the campaign is over. Lee has surrendered unconditionally."

"Are those the terms?" asked Colonel Harding.

"Not exactly. General Fletcher says that when Grant and Lee met, terms were not discussed. But it is understood that the rebels are to lay down their arms, and accept a parole. In a few days the Army of Northern Virginia will be dispersed for ever."

"It will live in history," said I.

"Indeed it will," said Colonel Harding. "No army deserves it more."

"Begorra! it's quare to think we are to hev no more scrimmages," exclaimed Dennis. "What will we all do, now that foightin' is over?"

"Do? Why, go back to citizen-life, to be sure," said the colonel.

"Aisy to say that, colonel dear. But it'll be hard for some of us."

"At first, perhaps."

"For my part," said Jenkins, "I shall try and get into the Regulars. Of course we shall need an army."

"For a time, no doubt," responded the colonel; "though I think it will be but a small one. There is no necessity for a large force."

"Well, I am glad the war is over," said I, "though it seems odd that our swords will no more be drawn in battle."

"When is the formal surrender to take place, Jenkins?" asked Colonel Harding.

"The day after to-morrow. We must first supply the Confederates with food. I hear they are positively starving."

"Faix, an' ye moight hev known that," said Dennis. "Thim divils wud niver hev given up else."

"You are right, Dennis," said the colonel. "So much the more glorious for us."

"Well, good-night, gentlemen," said Jenkins as he remounted and rode away.

Early the next morning I rode across the line in search of Tom. Scarcely had I crossed the creek when I saw proofs of the destitution of Lee's troops. In an orchard, near the roadside, stood a park of artillery. Nearly all of the horses seemed to be dying of hunger and fatigue. All along the road similar sad scenes were presented, and I soon realized the sore straits to which the Southern army had been reduced before it had consented to abandon the struggle. Brave to the last, these Confederate soldiers had reason to be proud of their record, and the fame history would accord them.

After riding for nearly a mile, I halted and looked about me.

"Where's the Third Virginia?" said I to a man lying moodily on the tender grass by the roadside.

"Right here," he replied without moving; "that is, what's left of 'em."

"Have you an officer named Marshall?"

"Yes, he's our colonel. There he is, sitting under that tree," said the man, getting up and pointing across the road.

I turned my horse, and approached my friend.

LEE'S SHATTERED ARMY.

"Tom, don't you know me?"

"Frank!"

We clasped hands in silence; then Tom burst into tears.

"This is a sad meeting, Frank," said he in a broken voice.

"I feel it so," I replied; "though I am one of the victors, and should be rejoiced."

"Oh! it's all right. We were bound to be beaten in the end, though the reality is hard to bear."

"Well, Tom, you have the consolation of knowing that the South deserved to win, for the bravery shown by her sons."

"Your words are generous, Frank; but I am sick of war and all its horrors."

"So am I. Let us pray that peace may now rest upon the land for ever."

"I echo your prayer, Frank, with all my heart," said Tom thoughtfully.

"Yes," I exclaimed, "in future, let there be no North, no South; only one common country, one kindred."

"That's it," said Tom reverently, "one country, one flag. And let our swords hang on the wall until a foreign foe compels us to take them down together."

"Amen!"

AT THE HOMESTEAD,
JULY 20, 1872.

MY DEAR HUSBAND, — Baby is asleep in her crib, and Frankie is swinging in the hammock with Grandpa under the walnuts: so I find time to write. I am sitting by the window where you rushed in that dreadful night that Charlton had me in his power, and I can see the valley spread out before me. (By the way, Tom heard the other day Charlton had been killed in a brawl somewhere in Texas.) You don't know how much the dear old Shenandoah has improved during the years we have been away. The great gaps made in the fences by the artillery are now covered by the vines, while those horrid earthworks down by the river are green and picturesque in their present ruined state. The fields are golden with ripening wheat, the river murmurs as softly as ever, the mountains bask in the sunshine; and I almost forget that there ever was a war in this fair land.

Tom is getting along splendidly with the plantation, though he finds some difficulty in getting hands for the reaping; but Pomp is his right-hand man now, and, as he has a share in the crop this year, he works hard. I know you will laugh when you see Pomp, he is so awfully wise and dignified, and talks of " dem boys," as though he had never been an idle scamp himself. Both Tom and Grandpa want you to come soon, and Frankie says you may have his hammock : so come, dear, as soon as you can ; for, though I am glad to be once more in the valley where I was born, I miss you so ! Ah, Frank dear ! people may still talk about the North and South as much as they please ; but, for me, I love my husband best of all, before all. Write soon, there's a dear, and let us know when you are coming ; and bring Mr. Malone with you too. With kisses from Frankie, baby, and me,

Your loving wife,

KATE.

THE END.